THE THRESHOLD

**50 Days of Prophetic Keys and Biblical Insights
for Crossing Over**

Even though the author resides in the UK, he has taken the decision to use Americanized English throughout this book as most of the readers are in the United States. He apologizes to all Anglophiles out there for whom this will be deeply distressing.

CONTENTS

INTRODUCTION

At the beginning of 2024, I decided to write 100 daily devotionals to help God's people start the new year strong. It was intended that these would include a selected passage of scripture, a few hundred words of insights and thoughts, and some prophetic encouragement.

It very quickly became clear that this was a bigger project than I had originally intended. Perhaps it was my inability to write with brevity. Or maybe it was divine inspiration. Who knows? But these small and simple devotionals turned into complete book chapters. One hundred of them.

Every morning at 6.00 am I would sit before a blank screen and type until I was finished. Usually, it took a few hours. Sometimes I was still sitting there at lunchtime. But I kept going, Monday to Friday, for five months.

And each day, I would receive emails and messages telling me how that specific chapter had spoken directly to people's lives and personal situations. I was encouraged, but also growing weary. However, when I commit to doing something, I follow through. I'm stubborn like that.

More than 272,000 words later, THE THRESHOLD was finished.

I already knew this was more than one book. It was at least two, if not three.

There seem to be a natural difference in emphasis between some chapters and others.

Approximately half the book was more about transition and stepping into the next season from a personal perspective.

Others were much more focused around what was happening in the wider world and how we as believers can stand firm on God's character and His Word.

This first volume, THE THRESHOLD, focuses more on internal transition, personal change, navigating uncertainty, relationships, letting go of the old, and embracing the new.

The next volume, called THE SHAKING, will be available soon.

I pray that God uses His Word and my meandering ramblings and thoughts to guide you through what, I believe, is one of the most pivotal and significant seasons you will ever experience.

He is faithful. May you cross over the threshold into His good promises and purposes.

Every blessing in Christ,

Craig

DAY 1

GOD IS SOVEREIGN AND YOU ARE RESPONSIBLE

BIBLE READING

"In the year that King Uzziah died, I saw the Lord, high and exalted, seated on a throne; and the train of his robe filled the temple.

Above him were seraphim, each with six wings: With two wings they covered their faces, with two they covered their feet, and with two they were flying.

And they were calling to one another:

"Holy, holy, holy is the Lord Almighty; the whole earth is full of his glory."

(Isaiah 6:1-3)

"At once I was in the Spirit, and there before me was a throne in heaven with someone sitting on it...

...In the center, around the throne, were four living creatures, and they were covered with eyes, in front and in back. The first living creature was like a lion, the second was like an ox, the third had a face like a man, the fourth was like a flying eagle. Each of the four living creatures had six wings and was covered with eyes all around, even under its wings. Day and night they never stop saying: "'Holy, holy, holy is the Lord God Almighty,' who was, and is, and is to come."

(Revelation 4: 2; 6-8)

DEVOTIONAL

We are living in a pivotal moment in history.

It is a defining time for the nations - and for you personally.

I believe that in one year from now, our world will look very different.

And your life will be different.

But much of what that "different" looks like isn't set in stone.

It is TBD - To Be Determined.

You get to partner with God and shape the future.

Perhaps not about the major social, economic, and geopolitical issues.

But you get to choose how you will live.

What your life will look like.

And how you will respond to what's going on around you.

You see, we live in a tension – between God's sovereignty and our responsibility.

And it's vital that we understand God's part and our part.

So please, stick with me for a few moments as we explore this tension between what God controls - and what He has given you and me responsibility for.

Getting clear on this will have a huge influence and impact on how you approach the life God has granted you as a gift to steward.

GOD IS SOVEREIGN

Let me be clear: I absolutely believe our God is sovereign. He rules as Lord and King over all things.

There has only ever been one throne in Heaven, occupied by Yahweh, the one true God.

He is the uncreated One, the eternal Source and originator of everything that exists.

He is matchless in splendor, majesty, and authority.

He is perfect in every way.

He is the essence of truth, beauty, justice, righteousness, and love.

Another way to say this is that our God is *holy*.

Holy simply means different, set, apart, distinct, not like anything or anyone else.

Not only is God holy. The Bible tells us He is *holy, holy, holy*.

In our two Bible readings today, written over 700 years apart, the prophet Isaiah and the apostle John have separate visions of what is presently happening in heaven during their day. The similarities are stunning.

They both see God securely seated upon His throne. Around that throne, angelic beings constantly sing the same song, over and over:

"Holy, holy, holy is the Lord God Almighty."

Right now, 2000 years later, if you could peel back the veil and see into the third heaven, you would discover that the angelic anthem would be the same:

"Holy, holy, holy is the LORD God Almighty."

As you walk through this next turbulent season, you can be fully confident of this:

5

The One seated on the throne is in charge.

No one can ever doubt or dispute that.

He is the sovereign king of Heaven and Earth.

He has no contenders or rivals.

Over the next 50 days, we're going to explore many subjects together: transition, relationships, alignments, the prophetic, current events, the church, and much more.

But above all, I want you to know that your God is sovereign.

This is the foundation of everything.

No matter how chaotic or confusing things become, never forget that your God has not abdicated or vacated His throne.

He rules with absolute authority and complete supremacy.

God has a sovereign plan that He is working out.

And everything is moving in a predetermined direction - towards the feet of Jesus and the renewal of all things:

"The kingdom of the world has become the kingdom of our Lord and of his Messiah, and he will reign for ever and ever." (Revelation 11: 15)

One day, Jesus is going to return in glory, and all things will be made new.

You can stake your life on that.

It's where we find our confidence, security, peace, assurance, and direction.

So, I hope we have established that God is sovereign.

But...

And this is a BIG BUT...

In God's sovereignty, He has chosen to give you and me a huge amount of responsibility and authority.

6

YOU ARE RESPONSIBLE

God's complete sovereignty and total supremacy do not absolve you of taking responsibility for your life.

God does not control your life.

You do that.

That's the way He made you.

You are not a puppet on a string. You are not a robot.

You are a spirit, with a soul, in a body, made in the image and likeness of your wonderful Creator.

God has given you autonomy and authority.

You can make choices. Good choices or bad choices.

But you make them. And your decisions matter!

Many Christians don't like to hear that. It makes them responsible for their choices.

But it's true. It always has been. That's why there were two trees in the garden (Genesis 2:9).

God does not control what you do today, tomorrow, or any other day.

You control you. You get to choose. That's why a fruit of the Spirit is 'self-control' (Galatians 5: 22).

The sooner you accept this, the more chance you have of stepping into the fullness of all the amazing potential that God has placed inside you.

Your choices really matter. In so many ways, you get to determine what happens in your life during this significant time in history.

Of course, God will throw in some surprises and unexpected turns.

And the behavior of others and external events out there in the world will have some impact on you.

And when you do mess up, He works all things together for good (Romans 8:28). I'm so thankful for that!

But overall, what your life looks like will be determined by how you walk daily in faith and obedience.

That begins today.

Not tomorrow.

Today. Here. Now.

By your decisions today, you choose a direction for your life this year.

And that direction ultimately leads you to a destination. Or we could call it a *destiny*.

I recently heard Evangelist Jonathan Shuttlesworth put it like this:

"Decisions dictate seasons."

As Christians, we talk a lot about what 'season' we are in. And usually, it feels as if we have zero control over our current season any more than we can control the weather outside.

However, often our 'season' is the direct result of our decisions. **Different choices in your life would have brought about a different season.**

Think about it.

Even if you really don't like the weather outside, you can choose to move to a different state or country, and there you'll experience a completely different 'season'.

Or you can stay where you are and complain every winter because it's too cold. (That's what I do. Ireland is way too cold for me!)

This isn't some weird theology I'm making up. It's always been this way. This is found in Genesis 1:

"So God created mankind in his own image, in the image of God he created them; male and female he created them. God blessed them and

said to them, "Be fruitful and increase in number; fill the earth and subdue it. Rule over the fish in the sea and the birds in the sky and over every living creature that moves on the ground." (Genesis 1:27-28)

God made you to be fruitful and fill, to rule and steward His creation.

Even when humans sinned and messed things up, He never revoked that 'dominion mandate'.

So never underestimate the choices you are making today.

And tomorrow.

And the next day.

They may seem small and insignificant, but they set your life on a trajectory that leads somewhere.

In fact, **when you look at your life today, it is, in large part, the sum of the decisions you have made up until this point.**

A single different decision at some stage in your past may have led you to a different place than you are right now.

That's why we have regrets at times.

Because we know we could have made a better decision at some point in the past.

We know that things didn't have to be the way they turned out.

We can't change what has already happened. But we can choose today to minimize our future regrets.

The future lies before you. Each day is pregnant with possibility and potential.

And you get to choose what each one looks like as you partner with God in the decisions you make.

Throughout history, God has often challenged his people to make the right choices:

"This day I call the heavens and the earth as witnesses against you that I have set before you life and death, blessings and curses. Now choose life, so that you and your children may live and that you may love the Lord your God, listen to his voice, and hold fast to him." (Deuteronomy 30:19-20)

Choose life!

I recently heard about a Christian man who lost several million dollars in a bad investment. He is well into his seventies, and this was his retirement money, so this was a big blow.

How did this happen?

He took some bad financial advice and put his money where he shouldn't have.

But this man doesn't see it like that.

He said, *"God is in control. I guess he didn't want me to have all that money."*

In other words, God is to blame for his loss.

Really? Did God want him to lose all his money?

I don't really believe that. Do you?

It might be easier than admitting his own faults. But in the long run, it doesn't help him at all.

The sooner we understand that God has given us authority and responsibility for our daily decisions, the better our choices will be. And our lives can begin to change.

We are not passive puppets at the mercy of some pre-ordained plan.

We are partners and co-laborers, working alongside the Sovereign King of Heaven and Earth.

What an honor and privilege He has bestowed upon you!

You matter.

10

Your decisions today matter.

What your life looks like one month, one year, and five years from now, is in large part, down to you.

Of course, God wants to lead, guide, and direct you.

I absolutely believe that.

But even then, you can choose to listen to God's voice and respond in obedience.

Or you can choose to go your own way.

He will not force you to do anything.

But your life will look different if you obey Him.

It will be better. I promise you.

So, let's land this plane today.

Ultimately, God is sovereign. He rules over everything.

He has decreed the end from the beginning.

He is the creator, sustainer, and Lord of heaven and earth.

He can do anything He chooses.

But for now, He has chosen to partner with you.

That's why you need to hear His voice.

That's why you study His Word.

That's why you pray and intercede.

That's why you share the Gospel.

That's why you feed the hungry and clothe the naked.

That's why you live a Godly, courageous, passionate, faith-filled life.

11

In doing all these things, you are partnering with God, and bringing His Kingdom into our world.

This is a pivotal and significant season.

But you are not a passive observer.

You are God's son or daughter, and you matter.

Your daily decisions matter.

Your relationships matter.

Your work matters.

Your thought life matters.

Your generosity matters.

Your kindness matters.

Your holiness matters.

Your daily time in the Word and prayer matters.

Don't underestimate any of it.

God has wonderful plans for your life.

He has places that He longs to take you beyond anything you can even imagine.

He has people He wants to bring into your life and things He desires for you to experience.

There are doors He will open and incredible opportunities He will place before you.

There are new ministries and spiritual gifts He will entrust to you.

But you get to choose what to do with each of these.

Choose well.

Choose life.

Choose obedience.

Choose joy.

Choose faithfulness.

Choose Him.

Thank you for starting this 50-day journey with me. Each day will be different. We will explore so much together. And I will give you wisdom, prophetic insight, and practical tools to flourish in these days.

But what you do with them…well that's your choice.

PROPHETIC ENCOURAGEMENT

HE BROUGHT YOU THROUGH.

In this past season, you experienced shaking and shifting, confusion and change, hurt and heartache, weariness, and loss - but God has brought you through.

You have deeper roots and greater resilience than you realize.

After all of the turbulence and turmoil, you're still standing firm.

I know that you're a little battered and bruised, tattered and torn - but you're here.

Celebrate that. Give thanks. Pour out your worship and gratitude.

The LORD has been so incredibly faithful to you.

He has kept you, protected you, preserved you, and provided for you.

Your progress this year has seemed slow. There has been delay and disappointment.

At times you didn't know if you could take any more, but He strengthened and sustained you.

In the loneliness and isolation, He came close to you.

His presence surrounded you.

His peace calmed you.

His Spirit settled you.

You're stronger than you were a year ago.

Yes, I know you're tired. Warfare and wilderness will do that. But you have been developed, deepened, equipped, and prepared for this next important season.

The Father wastes nothing. Even those things you would rather avoid. He has used them to shape and refine you.

There are things that He has ahead for you that you're now ready for - assignments and alignments, opportunities and openings, relationships and connections, enlargement and impact.

Don't stop or get stuck here.

Pause, rest, reflect, and refocus on your vision.

14

But don't stay here too long.

The Father has so much more for you than you have seen, experienced, or even imagined.

Let go of limitations or mindsets that are holding you back or keeping you contained.

Drop the baggage and burdens that have been weighing you down.

Relinquish everything that isn't aligned with the future that God is showing you.

The next season will have sharp turns and more shaking.

But it will also be full of 'suddenlies' and surprises.

God is about to advance and accelerate some things you've been waiting on for a long time.

Blockages will be removed.

Barriers will be lifted.

Confusion will clear.

The extent of the changes may shock you at times.

You will step into places and spaces you feel totally unprepared and unqualified for.

But don't be afraid. You're more ready than you realize.

You're bigger on the inside than what can be seen.

You have everything you need.

Christ is in you - the hope of glory.

Get ready. Face forward with expectancy, courage, and confidence.

It's time to stretch beyond old boundaries.

Move beyond the comfortable, safe, and familiar.

The Father has so much more prepared for you in this next season.

HE BROUGHT YOU THROUGH.

DAY 2

STANDING AT A THRESHOLD

BIBLE READING

The Lord had said to Abram,

"Go from your country, your people and your father's household to the land I will show you.

"I will make you into a great nation,
 and I will bless you;
I will make your name great,
and you will be a blessing.
I will bless those who bless you,
and whoever curses you I will curse;
and all peoples on earth
will be blessed through you."

So Abram went, as the Lord had told him; and Lot went with him. Abram was seventy-five years old when he set out from Harran. He took his wife Sarai, his nephew Lot, all the possessions they had accumulated and the people they had acquired in Harran, and they set out for the land of Canaan, and they arrived there.

(Genesis 12: 1-5)

DEVOTIONAL

Have you ever noticed that God usually doesn't give you a lot of details up front?

You don't get a roadmap or a 20-point list of directions: *"To fulfill your destiny do this, then this, and then this."*

Most often, He gives you the next step.

Just one step of obedience.

And it's usually risky or costly or doesn't make sense.

"I need more information, God. What will I tell my family and my friends when they ask where I'm going?"

"Just take the next step," He replies.

"What if it doesn't work out?"

"Take the next step."

"But I'm scared."

"Take the next step."

There comes a point where you must make a choice – obey with the limited information you have. Or disobey.

I know that sounds too blunt. Too black and white.

But it's true. God isn't changing His mind.

He says, *"Go - then I will show."*

I'd prefer He would show – then I would (probably) go.

In one of our own major transitions that I share in the opening chapter of my book *The Tension of Transition*, God gave me an open vision of being released from a prison cell.

I was free to go.

However, as I walked towards the exit of the prison, I had only one question on my mind: *"Will there be anyone waiting for me on the other side?"*

I didn't know the answer. I simply had to keep on walking into freedom.

Looking back, when we eventually did take that scary step of faith, it was months before we discovered that God had gone ahead of us and prepared the way.

But first, I had to leave.

That's just how it goes.

There has to be an exit before you can enter.

There is an ending before a new beginning.

You leave the old so you can enter the new.

In Genesis 12, God told Abram to leave his family, his community, and his culture. Basically, leave behind everything he had ever known and get moving.

But where?

God keeps that a secret, for now.

He wants to see if Abram will obey based on the little that He has been told.

Because, if He won't take that initial step, the story ends here.

If he won't obey the first thing God told him to do, why would God assume He'll obey the next thing?

It makes me wonder:

How many stories never make it past this first instruction?

How many destinies have been forfeited because of our need for more information?

More security?

More certainty?

Abram (or Abraham, as he became known) is called *the father of our faith* for a reason.

He was willing to believe God and obey, even when he didn't know where it would lead him.

He courageously crossed the threshold, even when he had no idea what was on the other side.

A threshold is defined in the dictionary as:

"The level or point at which you start to experience something, or at which something starts to happen or change."

Today, you are standing at a threshold.

Personally – in your life, work, relationships, ministry.

On a wider scale – globally – you're positioned at a pivot point in history.

You don't know what lies ahead.

Yes, you might have ideas and plans. Perhaps even goals, hopes, and dreams.

That's good. There's nothing wrong with any of that.

But truthfully, everything right now is uncertain, blurry, and a little fuzzy.

You don't know where this is all leading.

You have no idea what twists and turns await you in the next 12 months.

None of us do.

Five years ago, did you expect to be where you are today? Probably not.

So, what do you do when there's so much uncertainty, confusion, shaking, and shifting?

You take the next step – in obedience and faith.

It might only be one step.

One call.

One move.

One conversation.

One email.

One application.

One decision.

You go with the little that you have, trusting that God will give you what you still lack, along the way.

You begin to really live a life of faith, believing that God has called you to a greater adventure than a life of predictability and certainty.

Or…and you do have a choice…

You can stay where you are because you don't have all the details up front.

It's up to you.

But ask yourself this: *In 20 years, if my life was made into a movie, which journey would be worth watching?*

Me - if I stay?

Me - if I go?

I'll be honest, there's risk if you go.

Things might not work out.

There will probably be sacrifice - people, places, things you will have to leave behind.

But there's also a cost if you stay. Your life will look much the same as it does right now.

Which is fine if you're walking in complete fulfillment and living the life of your dreams.

But you're probably not. Because, let's be honest, we could all do with shaking some things up a little. (Or a lot.)

Abraham was willing to risk leaving his father's household and everything familiar and set out on a journey to a new land.

We read the story without realizing just how radical his move was.

People just didn't do that back then. They had a cyclical view of history in which everything that has happened will happen again. They believed that you're born into a cycle of events, and you'll die somewhere in that same cycle of events as the cycle endlessly repeats itself.

In other words, there's nothing new. What happened to your ancestors will eventually happen to you, and then it will happen to your children as your family goes round and round the cycle.

But then Abraham leaves.

He steps out of the cycle.

He breaks the pattern.

He walks into a new future, one that hasn't happened before.

No one had ever done that before because no one had ever conceived of the world and life and the future like that before.

This was a new idea in human history - that you weren't stuck, that you didn't have to repeat everything that had already happened.

Today, God wants you to know – you don't have to be stuck in the same old cycle any longer.

Your future does not have to look like your past.

You don't have to accept that this is just how life is going to be.

You don't have to stay stuck in a cycle of failure or addiction.

You don't have to settle for less than you know God has placed inside you.

You don't have to be just like your parents.

You don't have to live out someone else's plan for your life.

Whatever you have been through - divorce, heartache, sickness, loss, rejection, pain - It doesn't need to have the final word.

Whatever labels have been placed on you, or even those that you have placed on yourself – they don't have to define you.

Your history does not determine your destiny.

You can begin again.

With God, you get to write a brand new script… a better story… one worth watching if it were made into a movie.

And it all starts with one step of obedience and faith, usually into the unknown or uncomfortable.

Give Him your unconditional 'yes'.

Cross the threshold.

PROPHETIC ENCOURAGEMENT

STEP ACROSS THE THRESHOLD.

This is a threshold moment. You are standing at a demarcation line – between old and new – what was and what is to come.

You're sensing something shifting and stirring. Change is pressing in on you.

You want it, but you don't want to get your hopes up. There has been too much delay, too many false starts, disappointment after disappointment.

Yet, you feel it in your gut. Something is different.

You're seeing glimpses of the future. Snapshots of where the Father is taking you.

Your conversations are different. There is more expectation, even excitement than there has been for a long time.

It's subtle but significant.

It's spiritual, but there are signs of evidence of it appearing around you.

Pay attention to what you see, sense, hear, and feel.

God is communicating with your whole being. Don't limit how you hear His voice or discern His leading.

You will begin to feel an urgency on things you have been putting off.

A strong desire to contact people or visit places.

An inexplicable yearning for particular things, connections, locations.

Notice what you're noticing.

Pay attention to your thoughts and desires.

Something is rising up inside you.

The tide is turning. The dam is breaking.

Take a bold, brave move out of comfortable boredom. Break out of predictable safety.

Get out of the boat.

Build the ark.

Put your foot in the Jordan.

Pick a fight with a giant.

Pray that the sun would stand still.

Stretch out your staff over the sea.

Give away your last few coins.

Ask for a double portion.

Heaven is waiting to come in behind you. Angels are watching to see if you'll go all in.

Don't hold back. Stop second-guessing yourself.

Start that business.

Write that book.

Seize that opportunity.

Launch that ministry.

Leave that toxic environment.

Take that class.

Propose to the one you love.

Stop waiting for perfect conditions and a guarantee of success.

He has promised you Himself - His presence, His provision, His power.

That's enough.

Stop telling yourself that it's not your time.

That you need more… money, education, information, confidence, experience, resources.

God will supply all you need as you move.

You are ready for the new.

And the new is ready for you.

STEP ACROSS THE THRESHOLD.

DAY 3

BECAUSE YOU SAY SO

BIBLE READING

One day as Jesus was standing by the Lake of Gennesaret, the people were crowding around him and listening to the word of God. He saw at the water's edge two boats, left there by the fishermen, who were washing their nets. He got into one of the boats, the one belonging to Simon, and asked him to put out a little from shore. Then he sat down and taught the people from the boat.

When he had finished speaking, he said to Simon, "Put out into deep water, and let down the nets for a catch."

Simon answered, "Master, we've worked hard all night and haven't caught anything. But because you say so, I will let down the nets."

When they had done so, they caught such a large number of fish that their nets began to break. So they signaled their partners in the other boat to come and help them, and they came and filled both boats so full that they began to sink.

(Luke 5: 1-7)

Early in the morning, Jesus stood on the shore, but the disciples did not realize that it was Jesus.

He called out to them, "Friends, haven't you any fish?"

"No," they answered.

He said, "Throw your net on the right side of the boat and you will find some." When they did, they were unable to haul the net in because of the large number of fish.

(John 21: 4-6)

DEVOTIONAL

What does Jesus know about fishing?

Just about as much as He knows about every other area of life.

Everything.

Here we have a picture of frustration. Simon Peter is doing what he's supposed to be good at - catching fish - but it's not working.

I don't mind being a poor soccer player. I don't like the game. But if I preach badly, that's a different matter. It's what I'm called to do.

In both cases (in Luke 5, and later in John 21), Peter has been working on the water all night but has nothing to show for his labor. He's come up empty. And nets without fish mean no money for his family that day.

Sometimes God will frustrate the things we're supposed to be good at.

Things others praise us for.

Work that used to come easy to us.

Areas where we are naturally skilled.

We've begun to rely on our natural gifts and experience instead of fully depending on Him.

And that works for a while. Until it doesn't.

We're drawn back to the humble realization that, *"Apart from me, you can do nothing"* (John 15: 5).

This is one of the ways that God leads us into transition and points us in a new direction.

Things that used to work, stop working.

The work we used to find easy, now feels exhausting.

The habits that were once fulfilling are now draining.

We come to the end of ourselves, or a career, or a relationship.

And we long for more. We desire different.

We're no longer satisfied to keep doing what we've always done.

Something has to shift.

Jesus uses that frustration to point us to a deeper change that must take place in our lives.

Peter is ready to pack up the nets and go home, empty-handed. But this night of failure isn't final. Jesus enters into his place of discouragement and disappointment. The One who created the sea and the fish doesn't do lack.

I want you to see the variation in Jesus' instructions to Simon Peter in the two separate Bible passages.

Look at them together:

"Put out into deep water, and let down the nets for a catch." (Luke 5: 4)

"Throw your net on the right side of the boat and you will find some." (John 21: 6)

GO DEEPER

At the beginning of Simon's ministry, Jesus tells him to 'go deeper'.

There are times when the answer to our frustration is to go deeper and further in the same direction.

We've been in shallow water for too long.

Paddling around no longer satisfies.

It's time to push out and explore the depths of our walk with God: deeper truths, deeper intimacy, deeper relationships, deeper communion, deeper encounters and experiences.

That's where we'll find the good stuff - in the depths.

In the places beyond where we have already been.

Outside the spaces that have become comfortable and familiar.

Sadly, most Christians never move beyond the shallows. They paddle and splash around in ankle-deep water for decades and then wonder why their walk with God never really brought the satisfaction and fulfillment they were promised.

The truly abundant life promised by Jesus (John 10: 10) is only found by going deeper:

"When they had done so, they caught such a large number of fish that their nets began to break." (Luke 5: 6)

In these pivotal days of shaking, shifting, and sifting, God is done with shallow, superficial Christianity.

He's calling His church to go deeper.

To push out into uncharted waters.

To leave behind the safety of the shore and explore the fullness of the ocean.

He won't allow us to settle for less when He has made so much more available.

However, I also want you to see the subtle difference in the later account in John 21:

"Throw your net on the right side of the boat and you will find some." (John 21: 6)

REPOSITION YOURSELF

Jesus doesn't call Peter deeper. He calls him to reposition himself.

To go to the 'other side'.

To try his labors in a new place.

To cast his nets in a different location.

Sometimes we don't need to abandon what we're doing. We just need to try it in a new place.

That may mean moving to a new location. Perhaps changing jobs or roles.

It could be leaning into a different area of ministry.

Or adopting a new method or strategy.

More effort in the same place just won't work. You can fish there for months and you'll still catch nothing.

However, even a small change of position can yield incredible results:

"When they did, they were unable to haul the net in because of the large number of fish." (John 21: 6)

A minor adjustment in positioning brought Peter a massive change in productiveness.

In both cases, the nets *almost break*. They don't tear apart. But they almost do.

Because blessing brings its own pressure.

Abundance and enlargement bring tensions.

With Jesus, they can be managed. But it's worth being aware of.

Success, just as much as failure, can stretch you to the point where you feel as if you're at breaking point. But Jesus won't let you snap.

THE SECRET TO 'SUCCESS'

So, how do you know what to do?

Should you push out deeper in the same direction?

Or should you try somewhere else?

The answer is given in Luke 5: 5:

"Simon answered, "Master, we've worked hard all night and haven't caught anything. But because you say so, I will…"

"But because you say so, I will…"

That is the key to everything.

It might not make sense, *"But because you say so, I will…"*

It may not be popular in this culture, *"But because you say so, I will…"*

It could upset some people, *"But because you say so, I will…"*

It may mean earning less money, *"But because you say so, I will…"*

It might be scary to walk away, "But because you say so, I will…"

Obedience to the word of God is ALWAYS the key to experiencing His blessing.

Even reluctant obedience is better than disobedience.

Frustrated, frightened, or confused obedience is better than disobedience.

Yes, occasionally God will bless you despite your disobedience or stupidity.

His grace is greater. My life is a testimony to that.

But I'd rather count on Him blessing my obedience than covering my mess.

I want to live a fruitful life of abundance and enlargement.

I don't want to waste my days fishing in the wrong place, frustrated that nothing seems to be working.

I don't want to pour out my best energy and still always feel empty.

I don't want to keep doing the same thing, day in, day out, and never find true fulfillment.

Therefore, I must be continually attentive to the voice of God as I go about my daily life.

Just as small keys can open huge doors, so too, minor adjustments can make a massive difference in your life.

Is there any area in your life right now where things just aren't working?

You know there has to be more than you're experiencing right now.

You're doing what you've always done but it's become less and less fulfilling.

You're faithful but not fruitful. Or not as fruitful as you'd like to be.

Have you brought it to God in prayer?

What is He telling you to do?

Push out deeper?

Or try somewhere or something new?

Take time in His presence. Ask Him.

He longs to lead, guide, and direct you into a life of fruitfulness, fulfilment, enlargement, and abundance.

PROPHETIC ENCOURAGEMENT

YOU HAVE NOT LOST YOUR WAY.

I'm just taking you on a different route.

A new trajectory, an unmapped journey.

You had everything all planned out.

But I have My own blueprint for your future.

Where our plans deviate, I have reoriented you towards My greater purpose.

The road is unfamiliar.

The territory is rugged.

The turns are unpredictable.

But the destination is stunning.

I know you've been praying for breakthrough.

I understand that you're weary.

I've seen your disappointment and confusion.

I've heard your sighs, your frustration, your longing for clarity.

If you could only see what I see, your perspective would shift;

Your countenance would lift;

Your expectation would rise;

Your heart would be full again.

Some journeys take longer than you anticipated - not because you've done anything wrong - but because the next place is so completely different and new.

You had become so bored with 'same old'.

That's why I'm taking you on this unpredictable path.

At times it feels as if you're travelling alone.

But others are on their way - from different regions and places.

You all look different on the outside - but your spirits are the same - passionate, pure, wild, free, fearless, faith-filled, longing for more.

This process that you have been in has been hard to make sense of. It's been difficult to discern the way through. It seems never-ending.

That's because there are processes within the process, steps in every stage, wheels within wheels.

Everything is intentional.

None of it is wasted or pointless.

You may not see it, but you are advancing.

Even though life often feels stationary, you're still pressing forward, taking ground, moving beyond old boundary lines and borders.

Pause, if you need to. Rest for a moment, but don't give up.

Recognize just how far you've come.

You're not where you were.

You're not who you were.

You have deeper devotion, stronger foundations, a broader vision, a bigger heart.

There will be more twists and turns, uphill slogs and uneven surfaces.

But step by step, you will climb with steadiness and sureness.

The narrow road will open up into a broader space.

The finish line will come into view.

The way will be clear.

Lift up your head. Look at me.

It will all soon make sense.

The pieces will fall into place.

You'll be amazed at what I have done. By how far you've come.

I know you're not sure how much more you can give.

But keep going. With every step…

…I will restore your joy.

…I will renew your strength.

…I will replenish your energy.

…I will refuel your fire.

You may not be sure where you are right now, but I want you to know…

YOU HAVE NOT LOST YOUR WAY.

DAY 4

A SEASON OF ACCELERATION

BIBLE READING

"Nearby stood six stone water jars, the kind used by the Jews for ceremonial washing, each holding from twenty to thirty gallons.
Jesus said to the servants, "Fill the jars with water"; so they filled them to the brim.
Then he told them, "Now draw some out and take it to the master of the banquet."
They did so, and the master of the banquet tasted the water that had been turned into wine. He did not realize where it had come from, though the servants who had drawn the water knew. Then he called the bridegroom aside and said, "Everyone brings out the choice wine first and then the cheaper wine after the guests have had too much to drink; but you have saved the best till now."

(John 1: 6-10)

"The days are coming," declares the Lord,
"when the reaper will be overtaken by the plowman
and the planter by the one treading grapes."

(Amos 9: 13)

DEVOTIONAL

"There are decades where nothing happens, and there are weeks where decades happen."

When I heard the above quote recently (which has been attributed to Russian revolutionary Vladimir Lenin), the Holy Spirit stopped me in my tracks. I sensed Him say:

"That's the seismic shift that you're currently living through. You are going to witness decades of change in a very short space of time. This is a season of great acceleration."

When I was a kid, my dad went through a phase of winemaking.

Not with grapes from a vineyard. That might have been cool.

No, it was with a wine-making kit he purchased from our local pharmacy.

I distinctly recall a huge glass jar of pale liquid 'fermenting' in our airing cupboard for months. It looked disgusting and I'm convinced it didn't taste much better.

In Jesus' day, the process was much slower.

The seeds were sown, the shoots tended until they became vines, and the grapes were grown.

Once they were ripe and ready for harvest, they were crushed in a stone press or by foot, and the juice was extracted.

Natural yeasts present on the grape skins would then aid the fermentation process before the matured wine was filtered and clarified to remove sediment and impurities.

The entire process, from sowing to being ready for consumption would take several years.

At the wedding in Cana, Jesus accelerated this entire arduous process into an instant.

He instructed the servants to fill the large ceremonial stone jars with water.
Why water? Was it not wine that they needed?

Because God always starts with what we have.

He takes our ordinary and makes it extraordinary.
He takes our natural and infuses it with His supernatural.
He takes our two loaves and five fish and feeds thousands of people.
He takes our little jar of remaining oil and fills every vessel until there is nothing left to fill.

If we will surrender what we have, even though it never looks like enough, He will multiply it and transform it into more than enough.

THE AGE OF 'FAST'

In John 2, when the six stone water jars were full *"to the brim"*, Jesus instructed the servants to take a sample to the Master of Ceremonies at the wedding. He was stunned by the amazing quality and vast quantity of the wine.

The point is, **Jesus accelerated a process that should have taken several years into a millisecond.**

The natural time frame for wine production was circumvented. An instant transformation took place.

In these days, everything is becoming faster.

Advances in technology have sped up communication, travel, financial transactions, shopping, and even dating. Experts say that the speed of computing doubles every 18 months. With the growing use of Artificial Intelligence and other technological 'advancements', it's difficult to conceive what our society will look like by 2030.

There's also been an acceleration of the work of the enemy with the extreme liberal ideologies being widely pushed and promoted, especially on children.

Who could even have imagined 10 years ago that we would see 'drag queen story hour' for young kids or that governments would fund confused teenagers who want to permanently mutilate their own bodies?

Satan is having a field day in destroying the identity of a generation.

It appears that division, hostility, and conflict around the world are accelerating. Wars and rumors of wars abound, between nations and within nations. With the most contentious US election in our lifetime happening in 2024, we can expect the flames of division to be stoked further.

But – and this is important - I believe we are also going to see an acceleration in the work of the Holy Spirit.

God is going to move quickly.

The miraculous will become more commonplace.
Advancement will be hastened.
Progress will be quickened.

What should take years will happen in months.
What should take months will occur within days.
What should take days will come about in moments.

Normally, God takes us through a long process of preparation. There is a period of waiting, patience, and perseverance.

However, there are seasons when God accelerates the process.

An addict who should spend six months in recovery or rehab is instantly delivered of any desire for drugs.

Someone with cancer who would normally spend months going through treatment will be instantly healed.

A promotion at work that should take several years will be fast-tracked into a few months.

A long financial process of raising funds or clearing debt will happen overnight as the resources are supernaturally supplied.

Someone in their late 30s or 40s who has been single for years will fall in love and get married within six months.

TIME IS SHORT

As we look at events unfolding in the world around us, it is becoming clear that the time is short. We don't know exactly when Jesus is returning, but we know it's closer than ever before. The signs are there. The birth pains are getting closer and more intense. Therefore, we should expect an acceleration in the Spirit as we approach the Day of the LORD.

Think about natural pregnancy.

For nine months, this little person is slowly developing, hidden inside the womb. Then within minutes, they emerge into the world and turn their parent's lives upside down.

It all seems incredibly sudden. But it's simply the revealing of what has been taking place underneath the surface.

That's the times we're living through.

Much has been going on behind the scenes. There have been hidden agendas, plans, and deals happening behind closed doors for decades.

The LORD has also been at work - sifting, pruning, and preparing His Church for a last days awakening. Jesus expressed it like this:

"There is nothing hidden that will not be disclosed, and nothing concealed that will not be made known and brought to light." (Luke 8: 17)

In the coming months, expect to see a sudden revealing and exposure of what has previously been concealed. The plans of the enemy and the purposes of God will come into full view.

In Amos 9, we read this prophecy:

"Things are going to happen so fast your head will swim, one thing fast on the heels of the other. You won't be able to keep up. Everything will be happening at once - and everywhere you look, blessings!" (Amos 9: 13 MSG)

Another translation says:

"...the plowman shall overtake the reaper and the treader of grapes him who sows the seed..." (ESV)

Normally, the plowman (who tills the ground in preparation to sow seed) and the reaper (who collects the harvest) never meet because the time of plowing and reaping are months apart. Similarly, the treader of grapes never meets the sower.

However, this prophetic promise of the plowman overtaking the reaper and the treader of grapes overtaking the sower is a picture of an accelerated and abundant harvest.

Growth and increase are taking place so quickly that even as the plowman is plowing the ground, the harvest comes.

It is also a picture of abundance - that the harvest goes on and on until it is sowing time again. The supply never stops!

I believe we are going to walk in the fulfillment of this prophetic decree. Things are going to happen much quicker than we are used to. God is telling His people:

"I will exceed all you expect."
"I will increase all you invest."
"I will accelerate time to accomplish My Kingdom purpose through your life."

I know it's daunting to think that *"things are going to happen so fast your head will swim."* But if we fully trust that our Sovereign King is accelerating His plans and purposes, we can have confidence that we will see His goodness and experience His power in ways previously unimaginable.

So, get ready.

Where you have experienced setbacks and delay, something is going to supernaturally shift.

God is going to make up for lost time.

Divine acceleration will bring His plans to pass at a much faster rate than is humanly possible.

PROPHETIC ENCOURAGEMENT

THERE IS A SUPERNATURAL GRACE FOR BIRTHING AND BUILDING.

Now is the time for dreams and visions, blueprints and plans to come to fruition and fulfillment.

Birthing and building for your future.
Birthing and building a business.
Birthing and building a ministry.
Birthing and building a family.
Birthing and building new relationships.
Birthing a movement and building His Kingdom.

Even things God spoke to you long ago - this is the time to step into these promises and prophecies.

This is not a time for passivity or procrastination.

It is a time to initiate and put into action what the Lord is showing you.

It is a time to:
Build and rebuild;
Create and re-create;
Invent and reinvent;
Initiate and implement;
Reposition and relocate.

Don't keep waiting for perfect conditions.
Stop holding off until you have everything you think you need.
You don't need more 'confirmations'.
Unless the Spirit gives a clear "no" or "not yet" - there is no better time than now.

You've supported other's dreams.
You've helped birth other's visions.
Now, what's inside you must come out.
What's in your heart must begin to take a tangible shape.
That which has been conceived and gestating inside you must be delivered.

It will take hard work and effort.
But like Nehemiah, the hand of the LORD is upon you to build.

The right people will come alongside you.
The required resources will be made available.
The Spirit will give you the strength and stamina you need to labor.

Don't be swayed by the naysayers.
Don't be deterred by negative voices.
Don't be stopped by small setbacks.

The enemy will make noise and bluster... But he cannot stop you.
The favor resting upon you is greater than the opposition against you.

Once you step out and start, things will advance much quicker than you expect.
Advantage and acceleration will accompany your obedience.

Great faith will bring great favor.

Great boldness will bring much blessing.
Now is the time. No more delay.
Begin to build. Bring it to birth.

THERE IS A SUPERNATURAL GRACE FOR BIRTHING AND BUILDING.

DAY 5

CLARITY IS COMING

BIBLE READING

They came to Bethsaida, and some people brought a blind man and begged
Jesus to touch him. He took the blind man by the hand and led him outside
the village. When he had spit on the man's eyes and put his hands on him,
Jesus asked, "Do you see anything?"
He looked up and said, "I see people; they look like trees walking
around."

Once more Jesus put his hands on the man's eyes. Then his eyes were
opened, his sight was restored, and he saw everything clearly.
Jesus sent him home, saying, "Don't even go into the village."

(Mark 8: 22-26)

And Elisha prayed, "Open his eyes, Lord, so that he may see." Then the
Lord opened the servant's eyes, and he looked and saw the hills full of
horses and chariots of fire all around Elisha.

(2 Kings 6: 17)

DEVOTIONAL

I'm nearsighted. I wear glasses when I'm driving or looking at anything in the distance.

Several years ago, quite suddenly, I realized that, even when wearing my glasses, everything still appeared blurry and out of focus.

Fearing that my sight was deteriorating rapidly, I immediately made an appointment with an optometrist.

He tested my eyes and the results showed that my prescription hadn't changed at all.

That was strange. How then could he explain the blurry vision when I was driving?

The optometrist asked to see my glasses. As he inspected them, a smile crossed his face.

"Where do you keep your glasses when you're not wearing them?" he questioned.

"I just place them on the dashboard of my car," I replied.

"That explains it," he said. *"The lenses have become warped. The sun shining through the car window has distorted the lens of the glass and therefore everything you look at through the lens is blurry and out of focus."*

The good news was that I wasn't going blind.

The bad news was I had to spend a lot of money on new lenses.

WHEN LIFE FEELS BLURRY

Often life feels out of focus.

Our vision is blurry and distorted.

We struggle to get clarity for where we're going.

Especially in the past 3-4 years. Many things that used to feel so clear now seem hazy and difficult to define.

My thinking often feels fuzzy and foggy. And I don't think it's because of 'long COVID'.

There's an unusual intensity in the spiritual realm.

A swirl of invisible conflict all around us.

It's mirrored in the chaos and confusion in our world. And it can affect our own ability so see clearly and perceive a way forward into the future.

We know that God speaks. We're a prophetic people.

However, if we're honest, at times it's so difficult to discern what the Spirit is saying.

We long to do the Father's will. We just don't know what His will is.

It's hard to see where we're going.

It's difficult to make solid plans – at least long-term plans – without a vision of our future.

It's hard to know who to trust. There was a time when if something was reported by the mainstream media or the government - we believed it. Many of us no longer trust either establishment because we've been fed a mixture of truth and lies.

Things aren't as clear as they used to be.

I often feel like the man who encountered Jesus in Mark 8. The Savior has touched my life and removed my spiritual blindness. But I'm still struggling to see clearly. Look at verses 23-24:

"Jesus asked, "Do you see anything?"

He looked up and said, "I see people; they look like trees walking around."

The man essentially tells Jesus:

"I'm not blind any longer. The colour has returned. My sight is partially back. But everything is blurry. I see people but they look like trees. I see things moving but they're not clear. I can see vague outlines and shapes. Yet everything is still hazy and fuzzy."

Maybe you can identify with this man.

You're not blind. Jesus has touched you. He has restored your spiritual sight.

But things aren't as clear and sharp as you would like them to be.

You have some sense of where He's leading you.

You discern a change is coming.

You have been feeling it for some time.

But nothing is clear. Everything still seems foggy and distorted.

It's like you're stuck between two stages.

You're not where you once were.

But you're not where you want to be.

BETTER, BUT STILL BROKEN

Does this sound familiar? Can you relate?

What do you do in this situation? How do you move forward?
Firstly, simply admit that things aren't as clear you we would like.

Then stay close to Jesus and wait for Him to make things clear.

49

That's what I love about this story.

The man was completely honest with Jesus.

Jesus asked him: *"What do you see?"*

The man didn't pretend his sight was perfect and run off home.

No. He was honest enough to admit that things were better – but he wasn't completely healed. His vision was still distorted.

I think that's where many of us are in different areas of life.

Things are better than they once were.

But they're not where they could or should be.

I'm not blind. But things aren't bright. Life still feels blurry.

That destructive habit that I used to really struggle with. It had such a hold over me. Now, I've got some victory over it. But sometimes I still give into it.

That anger issue, that lust problem, that tendency to gossip – thank God I'm not where I was a year ago. But I'm not completely free of it.

The illness, the issue with my physical health, the depression or anxiety – it's better than it was – but it's still a part of my life. And I don't want to live with it any longer.

It's important to acknowledge that things are better than they were. Be grateful and thankful for all that God has done.

But it's also okay to admit that things aren't as good as you would like them to be.

CONTENT BUT CONTENDING

I think this is where we struggle sometimes. We don't want to appear ungrateful.

However, it's possible to be thankful for what you have, while still asking God for more in any area of your life.

You can be truly grateful for all that God has given you and done for you – yet be honest enough to say:

"God, I want to see more, I want to experience complete healing, I want to be totally free from this."

You can be content – and still contend.

You can praise God for all He's done in your past – and still press in for more in your present.

The Bible says that our God is able to do abundantly above all that we can ask or imagine (Ephesians 3: 20).

We are told that our God will bring to completion the work He has started (Philippians 1:6).

The Word makes it clear that Jesus is the Alpha and the Omega, the beginning and the end (Revelation 22: 13).

He's the author and the finisher of our faith (Hebrews 12: 2).

Jesus doesn't do half jobs. He completes what He begins.

God is never offended when we ask for more. However, He is aggrieved when we settle for less than His Word and Jesus' blood have made available for us.

Press in for everything that God has for you.
Contend for greater clarity.
Hold out for complete healing.

51

That's what this man does in Mark 8.

And I've some good news for you. Jesus doesn't leave the man in this condition:

"Once more Jesus put his hands on the man's eyes. Then his eyes were opened, his sight was restored, and he saw everything clearly." (v. 25)

A SECOND TOUCH

The man gets a second touch from Jesus. And his sight is completely restored.

When his eyes are opened, the first face that he sees is Jesus. Full of tenderness, kindness, love, grace, and compassion.

I believe you're going to receive a fresh touch from Jesus today.

The LORD is going to bring a new clarity and sharpness of spiritual sight.
You may be starting to experience it already.

Where there has been fogginess, things will begin to come into focus.

Where there has been a lack of direction, the Spirit is dispelling darkness and bringing definition.

He will impart fresh revelation for the next stage of your journey.

Divine strategies and blueprints for the year ahead will be downloaded.

The future is coming into focus.

You will discern the direction you need to take and know what decisions you need to make.

Press in for more. Jesus is going to give you a fresh touch.

PROPHETIC ENCOURAGEMENT

YOUR JOY WILL BE RESTORED.

For months, there has been a slow seeping of joy from your life.

Pressures, weariness, difficult relationships, disappointment, and pain have all drained your sense of fun, passion, zeal, and fulfillment.

It's as if your life has been on pause.

At times it has felt as if you had flatlined emotionally and spiritually. You're struggling to see where you're going or any purpose in what you're doing.

You want 'more' but you're not even sure at this stage what 'more' looks like.

Yet, deep inside, you know this isn't all there is. You sense the Spirit brooding over the darkness.

The Lord is coming to restore your joy.

He is breathing new life into you.

He is lifting off the heaviness and weariness.

He is opening your eyes to new possibilities and opportunities.

He is resurrecting dormant dreams and reminding you of His past promises.

He is imparting fresh vision for the future and and a renewed sense of calling.

The LORD is going to restart your heart.

You will experience a lift and shift. An infusion of new life and fresh fire.

A clarity of direction and destiny.

A sense of purpose and passion.

You will not be empty - but full.

You will not be barren - but blessed.

Even in winter, springtime will come.

You will laugh again. The joy will return.

Press into His presence. There you will find fullness of joy and abundant life.

Breathe in His Spirit.

Receive all that He wants to pour into you.

THE LORD IS GOING TO RESTORE YOUR JOY.

DAY 6

WHEN THE BROOK DRIES UP

BIBLE READING

Now Elijah the Tishbite, from Tishbe in Gilead, said to Ahab, "As the Lord, the God of Israel, lives, whom I serve, there will be neither dew nor rain in the next few years except at my word."

Then the word of the Lord came to Elijah: "Leave here, turn eastward and hide in the Kerith Ravine, east of the Jordan. You will drink from the brook, and I have directed the ravens to supply you with food there."

So he did what the Lord had told him. He went to the Kerith Ravine, east of the Jordan, and stayed there. The ravens brought him bread and meat in the morning and bread and meat in the evening, and he drank from the brook.

Some time later the brook dried up because there had been no rain in the land. Then the word of the Lord came to him: "Go at once to Zarephath in the region of Sidon and stay there. I have directed a widow there to supply you with food."

(1 Kings 17: 1-9)

DEVOTIONAL

Should I Stay or Should I Go? was a song by English punk rock band The Clash.

It's also a question we ask ourselves at different stages throughout life.

Should I remain where I am...

...in this job?
...in this relationship?
...in this ministry?
...in this community?

Or

...is it time to move on?
...go somewhere new?
...relocate?
...try something different?

It can often be a difficult decision. Especially when we have an emotional attachment to our current place or there's a lot to lose from making a change.

We want to be sure we are doing the right thing.
We seek assurance and direction upfront.

As believers, another way we express this question is:

"What is God calling me to do?"

After much thought, I've concluded that **our primary calling doesn't change all that much throughout our lifetimes.** It might be wider or more expansive than we originally thought. But our calling is hardwired into us from conception. It's part of the Divine DNA that is expressed in Psalm 139:

"For you created my inmost being;
you knit me together in my mother's womb.
I praise you because I am
fearfully and wonderfully made;
your works are wonderful,
I know that full well."

(Psalm 139: 13-14)

God created you on purpose and with intention. You were crafted with a calling in mind.

However, while your primary calling remains the same, God will give you new assignments to fulfil that calling.

And those assignments have a set time attached to them.

Some will be long, and others will be short.

But it is really important to recognize when an assignment has come to an end.

We need to know when (and how) to move on when our assignment is complete.

Because if we don't release the old, we can't take hold of the new thing - the next assignment - that God is opening before us.

How do you recognize when it time to move on?

The story of Elijah in 1 Kings 17 gives us some clues.

1. **YOU MOVE WHEN GOD HAS CLEARLY SPOKEN.**

We read twice in our Bible passage:

"Then the word of the Lord came to Elijah: "Leave here..." (vv. 2-3)
"Then the word of the Lord came to him: "Go at once..." (vv. 8-9)

God might communicate through a prophetic word, maybe a dream, perhaps a vivid vision. Usually, the bigger and more costly the move, the greater will be the direction and confirmation.

In my book *The Tension of Transition*, I share about an open vision I had in which I was released from a prison cell. In the vision, I knew I had to keep on walking, even if I didn't know what was waiting on the other side.

At the time, I had been praying for God to 'open a door' into a new ministry. This vision confirmed that the 'door was open' for me to leave without knowing where exactly He was leading me.

When God speaks like this, He will usually confirm it through other people and situations.

You might start getting different prophetic words about moving, relocating, a new position, a different ministry.

Often your circumstances will confirm it as well. Something starts to change. Relationships shift. Your heart begins to detach from the place/role/position.

It's important not to make a major life decision based on one dream or prophetic word. As I said yesterday, **if you seek Him, He will bring clarity.**

And then there usually comes a point when He releases you from that place or position. You sense it in the Spirit. It's time to go.

2. **YOU MOVE WHEN YOUR 'BROOK' DRIES UP.**

When God wants us to move, He will sometimes allow us to experience an **unexpected depletion of resources** in an area where there was previously sufficient provision.

Elijah had originally been instructed to camp by the Kerith Ravine. Here the LORD supplied all his needs and sustained him during a severe famine. Then we are told:

"Some time later the brook dried up because there had been no rain in the land." (v. 7)

When the source of his supply dried up, God moved Elijah on to his next assignment. The depletion of resources preceded the shift in seasons.

Has your brook dried up?

Is there any area where previous provision is running low?

Maybe in your work, orders aren't coming in. Or your services just aren't in demand like they were before.

Or it could be that the passion you once had for a place or position has dried up. You used to love it. Now it drains you.
In a friendship, you were once excited to see the person regularly. They energized you. Now, it feels as if you have nothing in common. Conversation is strained. Every time you hang out, you leave feeling weary and depleted.

In a church or ministry, it increasingly feels as if you are no longer aligned. Being in this place used to feed your spirit and ignite your zeal for Christ. Now, it seems stale and as if they are simply going through the religious motions. You've changed - but they're doing what they've always done.

Sometimes unexpectedly, things just shift. There's no obvious reason for it. But it almost fails as if someone has turned off a faucet. There's no longer any flow. Everything increasingly feels dry and barren.

It could well be a sign that God is reorienting and repositioning you for the next assignment.

3. **YOU MOVE ON WHEN GOD MAKES NEW PROVISION OF RESOURCES AND RELATIONSHIPS.**

I often say that 'when the 'grace lifts in one area of your life, God relocates it somewhere else'.

New doors open, new opportunities are presented, new resources are made available, new connections form.

When the brook dries up for Elijah, God doesn't leave him without provision. He instructs Elijah:

"Go at once to Zarephath in the region of Sidon and stay there. I have directed a widow there to supply you with food." (v. 9)

In our own journey, when God called us to make a major move, we were reluctant to leave as it seemed that we had nowhere else to go. However, as we eventually stepped out in obedience, we discovered that He had already made provision in a new place. First, a home was made available to us. Then, once we relocated, new ministry positions soon opened in a church that we loved.

Sometimes it happens the other way around. God unexpectedly places a new door, opening, or opportunity in front of you. You didn't see it coming. You were quite happy in your current role.

Your first instinct might be to turn it down or to ignore it. However, you begin to recognize that God is drawing you into something new. And to step into it, you will have to leave where you currently are.

Notice that God tells Elijah to leave "at once".

In other words, **once an assignment is finished, don't hang around. There's no reason to linger or keep looking back.**

60

The truth is that most people stay too long in an assignment that has reached its expiration date. We struggle to let go of the old. We become comfortable. We love the familiar. We develop connections and relationships. We get settled. And we don't like the unknown, unpredictable, and unfamiliar.

Often you are leaving more than a job or a role. Your identity might be attached to it. You're maybe walking away from status, security, relationships, emotional support, and community.

In these days of shaking and disruption, God is calling many of His people into new roles, places, positions, and alignments.

This is a 'leveling up' season. He is placing something new into your hand.

But to fulfill his purposes and plans, we may have to make a move.

Ask yourself:

What is God speaking to me right now about my current assignment?
- *Is it complete?*
- *Is there still more to be done in this area/role/position?*
- *Am I sensing a shift in some part of my life?*

Has my brook dried up?
- *Is there still a 'flow' in this area?*
- *Or have things started to go stagnant?*
- *Is my heart fully engaged?*
- *Or have I started to flatline and lose passion?*

What is God placing before me?
- *Are there new opportunities or open doors?*
- *Is He aligning me with new connections or relationships?*
- *Are new resources becoming available?*

Don't rush on from these questions.
Pray into them.
Write down what you're experiencing.

Ask God for the next steps.

Even if you can't see what lies ahead, if one assignment is coming to an end, trust that the Father has already prepared the next thing for you.

PROPHETIC ENCOURAGEMENT

THE LORD IS 'RECONFIGURING' YOUR CALLING

As you go through this season of 're-mantling' you will begin to express different and diverse aspects of your character, personality, gifts, uniqueness, ministry, and calling that you could never have imagined just 6-12 months ago.

The gifts deposited in you are going to be expressed in new ways and in different places than they have previously been, or than you have so far seen.

There are other skills and abilities that are lying dormant inside you. They will begin to surface and come to the fore.

At the same time, you are shedding parts of your old identity that are no longer helpful or needed for where the LORD is taking you.

Here's where you're maybe feeling confusion - you're becoming increasingly clear about what you no longer have passion, vision, or a grace for - but you're not sure where you're being redirected.

In this 'messy middle' – you are in a process of discovering who you are becoming.

You will feel vulnerable and naked for a time.

You will want to run back to the familiar.

Don't retreat. Be patient. Clarity will come.

The new will emerge.

In some cases, you will need to begin a separation from the old before you take possession of the new.

You will need to break from some old alignments to embrace new partnerships.

You may have to lay down some positions or relinquish some roles.

These may even include good things and Godly people in areas where you have seen blessing and fruitfulness.

Yet, these too will have to be pruned.

The right God-ordained alignments are so pivotal in this transitional season.

Describing what you do was once simple and straightforward.

In the coming days, it will feel more multi-faceted and 'outside the lines'.

It doesn't fit neatly into a job description or career path.

It may even sound like a ridiculous move or backward step to some people.

There will be a pressure to conform. To do what's 'sensible'.

Yet, the favor and joy you experience will confirm you are moving in the right direction.

Don't be swayed. Do not hold back!

The LORD is opening up new domains, fields, sectors, and spheres.

You will be stretched and feel some strain.

Yet, you are more ready than you realize.

Don't get stuck in the previous iteration of who you are.

Stop defining yourself only by what you have done up until this point.

Don't be confined or constricted to the labels others have placed on you.

You are so much more than any of that.

You are multi-talented, multi-faceted, and multi-dimensional.

This is a good time to reinvent!

Remove the boundaries and borders around your life and explore new territory.

Seeds faithfully sown in previous seasons will begin to bear fruit.

Watch for the little shoots beginning to emerge.

They will appear in interactions and conversations, dreams and visions, opportunities and openings, articles you read, and things you hear.

As you begin to glimpse what the Father has in store, your heart will be stirred.

You will begin to imagine new possibilities and potential.

It will take steps of risk and bold faith. But the rewards will be great.

THE LORD IS 'RECONFIGURING' YOUR CALLING.

DAY 7

THERE'S MORE OIL

BIBLE READING

The LORD said to Samuel, "How long will you mourn for Saul, since I have rejected him as king over Israel? Fill your horn with oil and be on your way; I am sending you to Jesse of Bethlehem. I have chosen one of his sons to be king."

But Samuel said, "How can I go? If Saul hears about it, he will kill me."

The LORD said, "Take a heifer with you and say, 'I have come to sacrifice to the LORD.' Invite Jesse to the sacrifice, and I will show you what to do. You are to anoint for me the one I indicate."

…So Samuel took the horn of oil and anointed him in the presence of his brothers, and from that day on the Spirit of the LORD came powerfully upon David. Samuel then went to Ramah.

(1 Samuel 16: 1-3; 13)

DEVOTIONAL

There are times when you will choose to leave things behind or let people go. As painful as that can be, at least it's your decision.

However, there are other situations where God will instruct you to walk away from people, places, and assignments. They may have been a valuable part of your history - but they are no longer aligned with your destiny.

You might try to hold onto them. You've become attached to them. You want to give things another chance. You have too many shared memories together to simply move on.

Yet, God speaks clearly and tells you: *"Let them go. Move on."*

That's what happens with the prophet Samuel in 1 Samuel 16: 1:

"The Lord said to Samuel, "How long will you mourn for Saul, since I have rejected him as king over Israel? Fill your horn with oil and be on your way…"

Israel had wanted a King. God Himself was their ruler, but they wanted a monarch they could see, just like the nations around them.

The best man available at the time was Saul. He was tall, looked impressive, and was from a wealthy family. Plus, he was able to lead the troops into battle and win.

So, Saul was anointed as Israel's first king by the prophet Samuel.

Things were good for a while. But then they went downhill quickly. Because sadly, not everything that starts well, finishes well.

The biggest problem was that Saul was a people pleaser. He cared more about what other people wanted than he desired to obey God.

Popularity was his priority. And so, he made some terrible decisions. Until it reached the point where God had enough. He instructed the prophet: *"Samuel, tell Saul that I have rejected him as king."*

Saul is reluctant to relinquish his power. It's where he finds identity, status, and value. He continues to cling to kingship for many more years.

He might still have a title and occupy the throne – but the anointing and blessing of God have lifted off from his life. (Side note: Don't mistake position, title, or status for God's anointing or approval.)

That's the backdrop to where we find ourselves in today's Bible reading.

CHANGE BRINGS LOSS. LOSS BRINGS PAIN.

The prophet Samuel is really struggling with the fallout from Saul's spiritual downfall and God's rejection of his kingship. Look again at verse 1:

"How long will you mourn for Saul?"

Samuel was grieved. He was mourning. And judging by the question it appears that he has been this way for some time:

"How long will you mourn…?"

He's clearly taken the situation quite personally. He feels the loss deep in his soul. It's affecting him emotionally. He's become somewhat stuck by what has happened.

Every significant change in our lives brings some loss. And loss causes us pain.

But we will feel some losses more than others.

Ecclesiastes 3: 4 tells us that there is *"a time to mourn."*

We believe that all things work for the good of those who love God (Romans 8: 28). But we can still grieve and mourn. It's a human response to loss, pain, and separation.

However, we shouldn't get stuck in mourning. There always comes a point when we need to start moving again.

IT'S TIME TO MOVE ON

It appears that time has come for Samuel. So, God interrupts his grief and tells him:

"Samuel, it's time to let this go.
You might not want to. But it's time to move on.
You can't change what has happened in the past. But you can choose how you face the future.
I have so much more for you."

And today, I believe that the word of the LORD for you might be:

"I've seen your losses. I watched you grieve. I've seen what you've walked through.
I've seen the hurt, pain, betrayal, rejection, mistreatment, injustice. I've witnessed it all.
And it was right to mourn for a season.
It was painful. It was messy. There was so much hurt.
But I don't want you to stay in this place of mourning.
You walk through the valley of the shadow of death. You don't stay there forever. Don't camp there. Don't build a house there.
It's time to take off your funeral clothes.
Wash your face and get back on your feet.
Even if you don't feel like it. It's time to move on. I have more for you."

Sometimes you will continue to mourn as you start to move.
You will weep for a while as you walk.
You will grieve as you go.

That's okay. Just don't get stuck at the place of loss.
That season of your life might be finished.
That relationship might be over.
That role or position or place might not be there any longer.
But God isn't finished. And neither are you.

It's time to move on.

A FRESH FILLING

Finally, I believe the LORD would say: *"There's more oil."*

Again, look at verse 1:

"Fill your horn with oil and be on your way". I am sending you to Jesse of Bethlehem. I have chosen one of his sons to be king." (v. 1)

The horn was a ram's horn that the prophet filled with anointing oil to pour on the head of the king.

Oil in the Bible represents the Holy Spirit.

It also represents joy.

If God is telling Samuel to *fill his horn with oil* – what does that indicate?

That his horn was empty.

Why was it empty?

Because he had poured out all his oil upon Saul.

He had poured out his joy, poured out His energy, poured out his strength, poured out his gifting - on something, on someone – and it hadn't worked out. It had failed miserably.

It wasn't even Samuel's fault. But he'd given his all. And now he's empty.
He has nothing else to pour out.
What a waste of his oil.

That's how we can feel when something doesn't work out.

Empty. Used. Wasted. Barren. Spent.

We gave so much only to get so little in return.

We loved so deeply only to be rejected when someone else came along.

We served so faithfully only to be discarded when we were no longer deemed useful.

We poured ourselves out. And now we have nothing left to offer.

I've been there.

Several years ago, I found myself at my lowest point of burnout and depression. I honestly wondered if God would ever use me again.

I had given all that I had. And now, I was completely empty.
I had nothing left to give.
I really thought that God might be finished with me.

But here's what I discovered in my emptiness:

God has more oil.
He has complete restoration.
He has fresh mercy.
He has stronger relationships.
He has deep healing.
And He has a new empowerment of His Holy Spirit for my next assignment.

It's the same for you. **No matter how empty you find yourself today - God has more oil.**

That previous relationship might be over.
That last assignment might be complete.

Maybe it didn't work out how you had hoped or planned.
Perhaps you're disappointed and discouraged.
You've been mourning your losses.

Now, it's time to get moving again. God has a new beginning for you.
He has a fresh anointing of His Spirit.
He isn't finished with you.
Not even close.

Receive a fresh touch of His Spirit.

Allow Him to revive your soul.
Invite Him to restore your joy.
Open your heart to new relationships and connections.
Step into this next season with fresh vision and expectation.

Fill your horn with oil and be on your way.

PROPHETIC ENCOURAGEMENT

I HAVE BEEN DIGGING DEEP.

Unearthing roots that keep you tethered to places that no longer nourish you.

Removing debris from an old season that can't be part of your future.

Untangling alignments that can't go where you are going.

Pruning habits and reshaping mindsets that have hindered and held you for much too long.

I have been digging deep.

That's why some painful memories have been resurfacing.

Old wounds that were covered over but never healed.

I've placed you in uncomfortable situations to reveal the places that still need My attention.

I am restoring what you lost.

I am bringing wholeness.

I will remove the sting of the past but leave you with the wisdom of that season.

I have been digging deep.

That's why you haven't seen many visible signs of My activity.

I'm working slowly, beneath the surface. Performing spiritual surgery. In silence.

I will not settle for shallow or superficial.

No more spectators, cheerleaders, or fans.

I'm looking for warriors, lovers, holy ones.

Consecrated vessels who can carry My goodness, favor, power, and glory.

I have been digging deep.

Storm-proofing you for the severe shaking that is still to come.

Making you wholly devoted and durable, firmly established and strong.

Men will tremble in terror as the nations are shifted, sifted, shocked, and squeezed.

But my faithful ones will see My Sovereign hand at work.

You will trust. You will be confident. You will not be moved.

I have been digging deep.

Making you battle-ready.

I've been building a resilient, radical remnant of worshipping warriors. They will win spiritual conflicts in the darkest places.

You will not be unsettled by the enemy's noise and bluster.

You will not pull back when the warfare becomes intense.

You will take your place.

You will stand your ground.

You will prevail.

I have been digging deep.

I am birthing something new. Never before seen on the earth.

I am raising up a company of the humble-bold and gentle-brave.

Refined revolutionaries. Anointed ambassadors.

Fiercely loyal to Jesus.

Empty of any desire for man's praise.

Fully aware of *who* they are and *Whose* they are.

Unconventional. Unashamed. Undaunted. Untamed.

That's why I HAVE BEEN DIGGING DEEP.

DAY 8

KNOW YOUR SEASON

BIBLE READING

"There is a time for everything,
and a season for every activity under the heavens:
a time to be born and a time to die,
a time to plant and a time to uproot,
a time to kill and a time to heal,
a time to tear down and a time to build,
a time to weep and a time to laugh,
a time to mourn and a time to dance,
a time to scatter stones and a time to gather them,
a time to embrace and a time to refrain from embracing,
a time to search and a time to give up,
a time to keep and a time to throw away,
a time to tear and a time to mend,
a time to be silent and a time to speak,
a time to love and a time to hate,
a time for war and a time for peace."

(Ecclesiastes 3: 1-8)

"These are the numbers of the men…from Issachar, men who understood the times and knew what Israel should do…"

(1 Chronicles 12: 23; 32)

DEVOTIONAL

In Ireland, where I live, we sometimes joke that we have only two seasons in the year: the rain is warm, or the rain is cold. That's fairly accurate!

Life happens in seasons. Not just the seasons in the physical realm with distinct weather conditions and hours of daylight.

We also walk through seasons in our spiritual life, relationships, marriage, parenting, emotions, health, career, etc.

Ecclesiastes 3 lists no less than 28 seasons "for every activity under the heavens".

Each season has unique characteristics and a distinct feel.

It's important to examine your life and think about what season you're in because **knowing the season determines your response to it.**

You can do the right thing in the wrong season and wonder why you're not getting the results you want. You end up frustrated and confused.

In 1 Chronicles 12: 32, we read about the sons of Issachar, *"men who understood the times and knew what Israel should do..."*

These men understood the season they were in and were able to take advantage of it. They made the most of their season.

When you know what season you are in, you can respond in the right way to get the most out of it.

Knowing your season gives you certain expectations. It enables you to make better decisions and it also prevents disappointments. It helps you to enjoy it or to buckle up and endure it.

WHAT SEASON ARE YOU IN TODAY?

Generally, in any area of your life, you will be experiencing one of four main seasons:

(i)   A Growing Season (Spring)

You may be stretched to do things you've never done or go places you've never gone.

God is enlarging your capacity to handle what He has prepared for the next stage of your journey.

You will probably experience the discomfort of 'growing pains'.

Don't shrink back. Try new things, take risks, and don't be afraid to fail.

You may stumble as you navigate unfamiliar territory. But God will not let you fall.

(ii)   A Pruning Season (Fall)

In a pruning season, God may allow you to experience tests and trials.

He is stripping you back, removing anything that would hinder you from fully stepping into the next season.

He knows there are some attitudes, behaviors, and even people that you need to let go of before you enter your next season.

This pruning will feel difficult and uncomfortable but allow it to complete its work in you. There is abundant fruitfulness ahead (John 15: 1-3).

(iii)   A Wilderness Season (Winter)

Wilderness seasons are times of lack, waiting, and weariness.

Seasons like this can be very lonely, especially if God appears to be silent. You're not sure if you have enough spiritual strength and resources to make it through.

As you endure this season, fight the urge to shut down, get angry, or run away.

Resist any lies that the enemy tells you. Cling to the truth of God's Word and His character.

(iv)   A Harvest Season (Summer)

In a harvest season, you reap the benefits from the seeds you've planted in previous seasons.

It can also be a very busy season that demands much of your time, energy, and strength.

If you feel overwhelmed, it's important to remember that God has given you much because He trusts you with much.

Can you identify any of the above seasons in your life right now?

You might even experience different seasons in various parts of life.

For example, you could be struggling through a season of spiritual wilderness while experiencing a season of promotion in your job.

Or you could be enduring a season of financial challenges while your personal relationships are flourishing.

Often, we are better at recognizing a season once it's ending.

Perhaps for the first time in months, you feel happy and expectant. You look back and think, *'That was a tough season I've just been through. But I feel like something is shifting and I'm entering into a new season.'*

I like how author Kristin Armstrong expresses this:

"When the seasons shift, even the subtle beginning, the scent of a promised change, I feel something stir inside me. Hopefulness? Gratitude? Openness? Whatever it is, it's welcome."

77

SEASONS CHANGE

Daniel 2: 20-21 tells us:

"Praise be to the name of God for ever and ever; wisdom and power are his. He changes times and seasons...."

This is important to remember, especially if you're walking through a difficult season right now.

In January it can feel as though the winter will never end. Similarly, if you're going through a difficult time - maybe loss or loneliness or deep discouragement - it can seem like it will never come to an end. Life feels like one long, dark, cold winter.

Seasons do vary in length and intensity – but they do come to an end.

Your current season could last for weeks or months. But at some stage, this season will shift, things will change. Winter will become spring. Spring will turn to summer.

Some of you need to hear that today: this season you are in will pass.

Others might love the season you're currently walking through. You don't want it to change!

That's wonderful, but I'm sorry to tell you that it won't last forever. So, enjoy it and make the most of it because, like all seasons, it will change. As revivalist Leonard Ravenhill once said: *"The opportunity of a lifetime needs to be seized during the lifetime of the opportunity."*

WISDOM AND REVELATION

Frequently, I find myself praying these words that Paul wrote to the Christians in Ephesus:

*"I keep asking that the God of our Lord Jesus Christ, the glorious Father, **may give you the Spirit of wisdom and revelation**, so that you may know him better."* (Ephesians 1:17)

In these turbulent and tumultuous days, you will need both wisdom and revelation.

Revelation enables you to discern what is happening and to hear God's voice.

Wisdom enables you to interpret it and respond properly in this new season.

It is vital that we not only know what season we are in, but that we also apply God's wisdom and insights so that we align our lives to receive all that He has for us.

Whenever we sense God leading us into a new season, we must be diligent to ask Him: *'What do I need to do to align with this season?"*

It takes spiritual discernment to see the new. But it also requires wisdom to identify the old we must relinquish to embrace the change that God is bringing.

Whatever you're currently experiencing, remember this: **In every season God is present and God is faithful.**

In Ecclesiastes 3: 11, after the author lists the different seasons we walk through, he says this about God:

"He has made everything beautiful in its time."

Seasons change but God doesn't change.

In every single season of your life - even in a harsh winter - God is at work creating something beautiful.

You might not see it right now, but your God is with you.

And your God is faithful.

He is doing a deep work in you today - in this season - to prepare you for all that He has purposed for you.

PROPHETIC ENCOURAGEMENT

YOU WILL BEAR FRUIT IN THIS NEXT SEASON.

I know you look at your life and don't see much growth.

You feel barren, bare, fruitless.

You've been cut back and pruned.

So much has been stripped away.

Yet, there are so few signs of fresh life or newness.

You feel stagnant, stale, even stuck.

You wonder if something is wrong – if you've done something wrong.

I want you to know – you will bear fruit in this next season.

A deep work has been happening beneath the soil of your life.

A hidden transformation is occurring under the surface.

I have been hands-on, carefully planting, nurturing, and nourishing new seeds.

These are now starting to take root and grow.

You will see tiny, tender shoots begin to emerge.

New life will slowly push through.

Increase and enlargement are coming.

Remain in Me. Stay deeply rooted in My life.

You will begin to experience the MORE you have so longed to see.

MORE wisdom and revelation.

MORE salvations and answered prayer.

MORE healings and miracles.

MORE impact and influence.

MORE purity and holiness.

MORE confidence and spiritual authority.

MORE resources and finances.

MORE key relationships and Kingdom connections.

Where you thought things were barren, you will see breakthrough and birth.

Where there has been frustration, you will experience fruitfulness and fulfillment.

Where there has been no clear direction, you will receive an impartation of fresh vision and purpose.

Where there has been disappointment and hope deferred, you will begin to walk in the fullness of joy and fulfillment of My promises.

YOU WILL BEAR FRUIT IN THIS NEXT SEASON.

DAY 9

THE PRESSURE HAS A PURPOSE

BIBLE READING

"But you will receive power when the Holy Spirit comes on you; and you will be my witnesses in Jerusalem, and in all Judea and Samaria, and to the ends of the earth."

(Acts 1: 8)

"On that day a great persecution broke out against the church in Jerusalem, and all except the apostles were scattered throughout Judea and Samaria... ...Those who had been scattered preached the word wherever they went. Philip went down to a city in Samaria and proclaimed the Messiah there."

(Acts 8: 1; 4-5)

"But Jonah ran away from the Lord and headed for Tarshish. He went down to Joppa, where he found a ship bound for that port. After paying the fare, he went aboard and sailed for Tarshish to flee from the Lord. Then the Lord sent a great wind on the sea, and such a violent storm arose that the ship threatened to break up."

(Jonah 1: 3-4)

DEVOTIONAL

Several years ago, God spoke very clearly that our family was to move on from leading the inner-city church where we had poured out our lives for five years.

We had sensed a shift for some time. We knew our time there was coming to a close.

Then I had an open vision where God clearly directed me to leave. Also, additional prophetic words and events confirmed what we were feeling.

God had spoken.

However, we stayed.

Why?

Mostly because of fear. We had nowhere else to move on to.

Probably like you, I crave security and stability. As a responsible husband and father, it's my duty to provide for my family. I don't believe in making reckless moves. It felt like being asked to jump from a plane without a parachute.

Also, having watched other people in similar situations make careless decisions, I concluded that there is a difference between faith and foolishness.

I really thought I was doing the right thing.

And it would absolutely have been right to stay - if God hadn't spoken so clearly about moving on without knowing what was waiting on the other side.

Within the space of a few weeks, things began to fall apart.

I'll not go into details, but without any real reason, several of our closest relationships in the church became so fractured that we couldn't stay there.

We had enjoyed unusual favor and blessing there for five years. Now, it felt as if something had suddenly lifted.

A place that had become our home now seemed like hostile territory.

I knew that I had to resign – for the well-being of my family and to prevent the behind-the-scenes division spilling over into the church community.

So, as honorably as we were able, given the difficult circumstances, we promptly exited and entered the unknown.

When God speaks clearly and gives you direction, you always have a choice. You can obey or disobey.

Sometimes you won't notice the results of your disobedience. Life goes on as normal. At least for a while anyway.

Maybe God finds someone else to do the assignment He wanted to give to you. You never enter or experience what He had prepared for you.

Years ago, in the UK where I live, there was a huge evangelization project called 'Minus to Plus'.

Every home in the nation received a booklet giving a clear explanation of the Gospel. This was followed up by teams visiting houses and inviting people to events where the Gospel would be clearly communicated.

The entire project was headed up by the late evangelist Reinhard Bonnke. I recall watching an interview with Bonnke where he was asked:

"Why do you think God chose you to lead this mission?"

I'll never forget his answer:

"God didn't initially choose me. He told me He'd already asked two other people, but they hadn't obeyed. So, I was His third choice. I just happened to say 'yes'."

Wow. A statement like that puts the fear of God in me!

There are times when God gives us an opportunity to do something great for the Kingdom. **If we consistently refuse, He might simply move on and ask somebody else.** And we probably end up stuck or frustrated, wondering why we're not experiencing the abundant life promised by Jesus.

I CAN'T STAY HERE

Other times, however, when we are slow in obeying, God simply turns up the pressure.

He gradually increases your discomfort in a place that has been comfortable for too long.

Please know, **this is not to harm you but to move you into the next stage of His calling upon your life.**

Maybe you have become too settled and stagnant, and you need to be uprooted to be replanted for future growth.

Or perhaps you have become confined or complacent, unwilling to stretch or take new territory.

You once had God-sized dreams and audacious vision in your heart, but now you have settled for a life more ordinary.

You have allowed yourself to live well below your capacity. God has placed so much more within you, but it's currently lying dormant and untapped.

Or you have allowed fear or past failure to cause you to shrink back and hide.

In Acts 1: 8, Jesus instructed his disciples:

"You will be my witnesses in Jerusalem, throughout Judea, in Samaria, and to the ends of the earth."

By the time we get to Acts 8, which is approximately five years later, they haven't moved outside of Jerusalem. No one has attempted to reach Judea or Samaria.

Jerusalem was the religious capital of the nation. It was familiar territory associated with positive memories of Jesus. Judea was physically a distance away, and Samaria was a complete cultural change from what they were used to.

However, in Acts 8, verses 1 and 4 we read:

"...all the believers....were scattered through the regions of Judea and Samaria...the believers who were scattered preached the Good News about Jesus wherever they went."

What was it that pushed them out of Jerusalem?

"A great wave of persecution began that day, sweeping over the church in Jerusalem..." (Acts 8: 1)

It was the external pressure exerted on them from persecution. The level of discomfort significantly increased in the place that was once comfortable.

The discomfort and pressure you're feeling at this time could well be a sign that it's time to move or make a shift in some area of your life.

You aren't willing to jump. So God is squeezing and pressing you out of your comfort zone.

The pressure isn't punishment. It's a sign that you're now prepared for a wider influence, greater responsibility, or new opportunity.

Of course, not all pressure is good. And not all pressure comes from God.

That's where discernment and the Godly wisdom of others is helpful. Don't immediately jump just because life gets hard or relationships are difficult.

However, in our case (and perhaps in yours), God had already spoken clearly. He wasn't going to allow us to settle and stay in a place that was no longer right for us.

In the seven years since we (finally) left that church, we have experienced His provision, grace, and goodness in powerful ways.

On reflection, I am so thankful for the pressure He exerted on us. It was so painful at the time. Some of those broken relationships have never been restored. That saddens me.

However, without that pressure, we would have remained stuck, stagnant, and increasingly frustrated. Also, this ministry of *Daily Prophetic* was birthed out of that difficult transition season.

God has deposited within you gifts, abilities, talents, character, wisdom, compassion, insight, creativity, leadership, spiritual authority, entrepreneurialism, and the ability to influence and effect change.

Until you are squeezed, they might not come out. And they must come out.

If you are feeling the pressure today – ask yourself - does it have a purpose?

Is God calling you to more? If so, please obey. Don't settle for less.

PROPHETIC ENCOURAGEMENT

YOU MUST MOVE ON.

Don't let your past disappointments prevent you from entering your destiny.

You will have losses.

Some things won't work out.

It could be your fault.

It might be through the failure of others.

Not everyone who starts the journey with you will complete it. Some of them will break your heart and pierce your soul.

YOU MUST MOVE ON.

You cannot allow past pain, hurts, disappointments, or regrets from the past to prevent you from entering into the full inheritance the Lord has promised and prepared for you.

There is a time for grieving when you have lost someone or something precious to you. It is normal, natural, right, and appropriate to take some time to mourn.

But you cannot stay stuck there.

YOU MUST MOVE ON.

There comes a point when you must take off your funeral clothes and dress for your future.

Anyone who leaves your life is someone God didn't intend for you to have in your future.

They may have played a significant part in your journey up until now, but they aren't necessary for you to enter the new season God is bringing you into.

There will also be people and places you will walk away from because you simply don't belong there anymore. You have outgrown a realm and to stay there will be detrimental to your future enlargement.

YOU MUST MOVE ON.

Your past disappointments have no bearing on your present destiny. A lot of things might look the same. But it will be different this time.

The situation or circumstances may not have changed much. But you have.

You are ready.

You've been forged in adversity and prepared in the wilderness.

All of your experiences, good and bad, have brought you to where you are today.

Get your hopes up. Get ready. It's time to go.

Face forward. Don't look back. Cross over.

YOU MUST MOVE ON.

DAY 10

PREPARED AND POSITIONED

BIBLE READING

So Samuel took the horn of oil and anointed him in the presence of his brothers, and from that day on the Spirit of the Lord came powerfully upon David. Samuel then went to Ramah.
Now the Spirit of the Lord had departed from Saul, and an evil spirit from the Lord tormented him.
Saul's attendants said to him, "See, an evil spirit from God is tormenting you. Let our lord command his servants here to search for someone who can play the lyre. He will play when the evil spirit from God comes on you, and you will feel better."
So Saul said to his attendants, "Find someone who plays well and bring him to me."
One of the servants answered, "I have seen a son of Jesse of Bethlehem who knows how to play the lyre. He is a brave man and a warrior. He speaks well and is a fine-looking man. And the Lord is with him."
Then Saul sent messengers to Jesse and said, "Send me your son David, who is with the sheep." So Jesse took a donkey loaded with bread, a skin of wine and a young goat and sent them with his son David to Saul.

(1 Samuel 16: 13-20)

DEVOTIONAL

As a young believer, in my teenage years, I received many significant prophetic words about leadership and ministry. I was excited and expectant to see what God would do in the coming years. I pictured myself ministering across the globe, conducting miracle crusades.

Ten years later, I was working as a sales rep for a company that made little plastic pump dispensers for bottles of liquid soap. It wasn't exactly how I had envisioned my life!

There seemed to be a huge disconnect between my prophetic calling and my current reality. My dream and destiny looked as if it had been placed on the shelf.

We see something similar in the life of David.

One day, he's anointed by Samuel as the next king of Israel.

Where do we next find him?

Not occupying the throne, but back looking after his dad's smelly sheep:

"Saul sent messengers to Jesse and said, "Send me your son David, who is with the sheep." (v. 19)

What about the oil?

What about the word of the LORD?

PROMISE AND PROCESS

David's daily experience looked nothing like the promise spoken over his future.

David and me (and you) needed to understand something: **Between the promise and the promotion, there is always a process.**

This is where God gets us ready for what we're going to receive.

It's where He prepares us for what He has prepared for us.

It usually involves patience, perseverance, molding, shaping, opposition, obstacles, tests, trials, obscurity, and anonymity.

None of those sound pleasant! We wouldn't choose them.

Yet, **without this process of preparation, we would arrive at our destination prematurely, unable to sustain or steward all that God longs to give us.**

EVEN WHEN YOU CAN'T SEE IT, HE'S WORKING

Back to David.

Once again, he's out in the field, in obscurity and isolation, watching over his dad's sheep. Leading them to fresh grassy pastures. Fighting off the occasional lion or bear. Playing his lyre. Singing worship songs to Yahweh. There's nothing new about any of that.

Occasionally he recalled the incident with Samuel. He thought back to that day when he was urgently called to come back to the house. The look in the old prophet's eyes. The pouring of the oil on his head in front of his dad and brothers. The expression on their faces. What was that all about?

He knew that something had happened. He'd felt…it was difficult to describe. Almost like an invisible robe or cloak descending upon him. It only lasted for a moment. But it had marked him.

He snapped out of his daydream. Now he was back to the monotony of the field. One day faded into the next. His current reality looked nothing like the promise. But what else could he do?

Meanwhile, back at the palace, King Saul is experiencing bouts of intense anguish and deep torment. His servants are worried and fearful. Saul's sudden mood swings are becoming more frequent. One of them gently suggests music might bring some relief. Saul agrees. He'll try anything at this stage.

But who could fill such a role?

Incredibly, someone overhears the conversation and knows just the right candidate:

"One of the servants answered, "I have seen a son of Jesse of Bethlehem who knows how to play the lyre. He is a brave man and a warrior. He speaks well and is a fine-looking man. And the Lord is with him."
(1 Samuel 16: 18)

What are the chances? Seriously!

David has been hidden out in the field, seemingly in obscurity, surrounded only by sheep and wild animals. Yet, a servant of Saul just happens to know that the young shepherd was also gifted in playing music.

"A man's heart plans his way, But the LORD directs his steps."
(Proverbs 16: 9).

It's the same in your life.

There are people who have noticed you, but you don't realize it yet.

It might seem as if you're a nobody, forgotten, isolated, and hidden. But God has already brought you to the attention of individuals who will play a significant role in your future.

There are conversations happening that you know nothing about. People are talking about you behind your back - in a good way.

There are things He has planned that are beyond your current abilities, relationships, or resources.

Only God can orchestrate these things. Only He can take the credit. No amount of planning, scheming, effort, self-promotion, or advertising can accomplish what the Father can do. **Most of His work is behind the scenes, completely unknown to us.**

Or as Pastor John Piper says:

"God is always doing 10,000 things in your life, and you may be aware of three of them."

HE WASTES NOTHING

Back to the sheepfold.

David is once again unexpectedly summoned from the field. His dad urges him to go to the king.

I wonder, in his mind, did he think that his big moment had arrived? Would Saul hand David his crown? By the close of the day would he be sitting on the royal throne?

Not exactly.

David is ordered to play the lyre. To serve next to the throne that he was anointed to occupy.

This wasn't the fulfillment of the prophetic promise.

But it was a step closer.

At the time, I doubt that David made the connection between this musical job in the palace and his calling to be king. He probably didn't stand strumming before the king secretly thinking: "Don't get too comfortable there Saul. I'm going to sit on your throne very soon."

He was simply using one of his gifts. On the surface, the two things - kingship and music - didn't seem to be related.

It's the same with you. **There are stages in our lives when God puts us in places or circumstances that may not seem to make sense for accomplishing our calling.**

Yet these places are important because they are part of God's plan for developing us and making us ready for the time when we do step into our purpose. As Paul Manwaring says:

"God wastes nothing, and He gets us ready."

David might have been called into the palace because of his musical ability. However, as an insider, he now had first-hand exposure to royalty. As he played, he was able to observe the palace protocol. He observed the duties of the king. He gradually developed a friendship with the King's son, Jonathan.

"God wastes nothing, and He gets us ready."

God also used this season of exposure to show David the potential pitfalls to avoid. In the palace, David was able to see up close how terrible and tragic it is when a king turns away from God and stubbornly pursues his own path. Observing Saul in his torment would cause him later to cry out:

"Do not cast me from your presence or take your Holy Spirit from me." (Psalm 51:11)

The thought of what a stubborn heart and unrepented sin could do was unbearable to David. He determined that he would never end up in the same spiritual position as Saul.

In your own life, God will expose you to people who have callings similar to your own. These connections, places, and experiences are a crucial part of your education and preparation.

I have been blessed to know men and women who have served faithfully in ministry for more than 50 years. I often turn to them for wisdom and counsel. When they speak, I listen.

On the flip side, throughout the years, I have also watched many gifted leaders experience various degrees of failure. When this happens, I ask questions. Not to gossip or be nosy. But to learn. Like Saul, they have become cautionary tales used by God to help me avoid the same mistakes.

With David, God's school of preparation began in the wilderness and was now continuing in the palace. Soon it would move to the battlefield. Each place was molding and shaping David's character, training and developing his skills, strengthening and deepening his devotion.

All the stages of the process were necessary because advancement in God's Kingdom happens in steps. **There is no elevator or escalator or fast track. God will take as long as it requires to get you ready.**

GOD KNOWS WHERE YOU ARE

In these days, God is strategically positioning you. You have been prepared in the wilderness and developed in obscurity. You will emerge and take your place when the time is right.

Don't be discouraged if your current reality looks nothing like the prophetic promises that have been spoken over your life.

Twenty-something years later, I look back at that season of selling plastic pump dispensers and I see God's fingerprints all over it. There were key lessons that God taught me in that role that I couldn't have learned anywhere else. He was forming my character, developing maturity, testing my endurance, and teaching me how to communicate and interact with all sorts of people. And when the time was right, doors effortlessly opened into the next stage of my calling.

Today, God knows where you are. He sees what you're doing.

This might not be what you had envisioned or planned for your life. But He is so intentional and purposeful in how He is working, shaping, and forming you for what is coming.

There will come a moment when something will shift - a phone call, an open door, an unforeseen opportunity, an unexpected opening, a need to be filled, a service required, a demand for your skills, an unplanned conversation, an unusual connection, an invitation to move, a surprising promotion.

You won't have to force it or manipulate it.
You couldn't make it happen if you tried.
Only God…
Until then, be faithful where you are.
Grow in your gift.
Expand your skills.
Develop Godly character.
Seek His face.

And don't miss the moments of preparation and exposure to your future.

Your current day to day might appear to bear little resemblance to your dream or destiny. But don't forget:

"God wastes nothing, and He gets us ready."

PROPHETIC ENCOURAGEMENT

THIS IS A TIME OF POSITIONING.

The Lord is strategically moving His people into new paths, assignments, roles, jobs, relationships, ministries, even physical locations.
He is resetting the board in preparation for what He's about to do next.

In this last season, it has often seemed as if life has been on pause.
There has been activity but without direction or a clear sense of purpose.
It has felt as if you're treading water just trying to stay afloat.

As a result, you feel stuck. You're not sure where to go or what to do.
Some of the spark, joy, and passion have leaked out of your life. You need change!

You are now entering a time of movement and increasing momentum.
There will be a sudden shift that will get you unstuck.
Or a shaking that begins to reawaken you.

Doors and opportunities are opening up.

Some of them may not initially appear all that attractive or appealing, but you'll find your interest piqued.
Take a second look. Don't immediately rule it out.

Listen to the whisper of the Spirit.
Pay attention to the signs.
There will be an increase of visions, dreams, pictures, and other prophetic direction.
They will bring confirmation, clarity, and peace.

You're going to come alive again.
Fresh breath will enter your weary soul.
You will rise with new vigor, passion, and intention.
Where vision has been blurry, you will see things with increased clarity.
You will find renewed strength to overcome cycles and patterns that have been keeping you contained and stuck.

Press into His presence. He is your source and your life.
There is more. So much more.
But it will only be found as you seek Him first.

You are moving from dislocation to relocation, wandering to occupying, the wilderness to the promise.

THE LORD IS POSITIONING YOU FOR PURPOSE.

DAY 11

THE LONG WAY AROUND

BIBLE READING

When Pharaoh let the people go, God did not lead them on the road through the Philistine country, though that was shorter. For God said, "If they face war, they might change their minds and return to Egypt." So God led the people around by the desert road toward the Red Sea. The Israelites went up out of Egypt ready for battle.

...After leaving Sukkoth they camped at Etham on the edge of the desert. By day the LORD went ahead of them in a pillar of cloud to guide them on their way and by night in a pillar of fire to give them light, so that they could travel by day or night. Neither the pillar of cloud by day nor the pillar of fire by night left its place in front of the people.

(Exodus 13: 17-18; 20-22)

DEVOTIONAL

Several years ago, I had the same vivid dream three times.

In each dream, I entered a large exam hall and sat down behind a desk to take an important test. However, as I read the questions on the page before me, I immediately became very aware that I didn't know any of the answers. I hadn't adequately prepared for this exam. Feeling flustered and stressed, I stared blankly at the paper. I couldn't pass the test because I wasn't ready.

I knew the dream was prophetic. (They usually are when you have the same dream repeatedly.)

At that time, I had been feeling stuck and frustrated in some areas of my life. Church and ministry had become stagnant. On the surface, everything appeared fine. But I was growing increasingly bored and longed for a change. I knew God had more for me. Yet, nothing was shifting.

Through these dreams, God was revealing that He wanted to advance or promote me to the next level, but I wasn't ready.

In school, we can't move on to the next grade until we pass some tests at our current level. Similarly, there were areas of my life that needed some attention before God would allow me to advance.

The problem wasn't with God's willingness; it was my readiness.

I became intentional and proactive in attending to some areas of my life. I dealt with hidden issues of emotional immaturity and deep-rooted offense. I also found a great online mentor and confronted some character and leadership weaknesses that had kept tripping me up.

Over time, as I took my personal growth and development seriously, doors opened, new opportunities arose, and a freshness came into my life and ministry.

I was prepared for the next stage. I had passed the test.

THE DELAY IS FOR YOUR PROTECTION

When Hebrews exited Egypt after 430 years of slavery, it would be natural to assume that God would want to move them to the Promised Land as quickly as possible. Yet, look at what we read:

"When Pharaoh let the people go, God did not lead them on the road through the Philistine country, though that was shorter." (Exodus 13: 17)

God chose to take them the long way around. There was a shorter route, but He deliberately didn't lead them that way.

Why would He do that?

"For God said, "If they face war, they might change their minds and return to Egypt." So God led the people around by the desert road toward the Red Sea. The Israelites went up out of Egypt ready for battle." (v. 18)

God knew that the people were not ready yet the face an enemy. Which is strange when we look again at the end of verse 18:

"The Israelites went up out of Egypt ready for battle."

They were dressed for battle. They wore all the gear. They looked like they were ready to fight. They thought they were prepared to advance.

But God saw beyond the surface.

God knew that, although they were dressed like warriors, in their minds and hearts they were still powerless slaves.

They saw themselves as victims, not victors.

If they were to confront major opposition right now, it would be too much for them. They would be overwhelmed. The battle would destroy them.

So, God took them the long way around.

Can you relate?

Have you ever walked through a season where you thought you were prepared for the next level or stage of your life, career, relationship, ministry, or calling?

But nothing happens.

There's little or no progress.

You're growing increasingly frustrated. You need something to change.

You double down on your efforts. But no matter how hard you try, nothing shifts.

Or maybe you are moving, but you're not advancing.

There's activity, but it's not leading anywhere.

It feels like you're walking in circles.

In your mind, there appears to be an obvious and short route from A to B.

But instead, God seems to be taking you from A to K to D to T to M to B.

You're wandering around, asking: "God, what is going on? Why are things moving so slowly? Why is this taking so long? I'm ready. Have you forgotten about me?"

Have you ever been there?

By faith, you're clinging to every promise and prophetic word God has ever given you. But you're growing increasingly frustrated. You're struggling to make sense of it all.

It's not how you planned it. It's not how you thought your life would look at this stage.

I always assumed I'd be married by 27. I'm not sure why I chose that number. In my head, it just made sense. Go to college. Get established in a career. Meet my wife. Get married. Have a family. Live happily ever after. That was the plan. It sounded like a good one.

My 27th birthday came and went. I was still single.

So did my 28th, 29th, and 30th.

I'm not sure why, but there's a psychological significance about turning 30. Maybe it's because you're entering a new decade of life. But it's like you're crossing a momentous threshold. Other single people have told me the same thing. If you're not married by 30, it feels like your odds of living happily ever after have just dropped by 50% overnight.

Throughout these years, I did date several girls. Some of them were long relationships. Although they were all wonderful in their own ways, things never moved forward towards marriage.

Something major did happen when I turned 30. I was ordained into full-time ministry. But being a pastor only made my singleness issue more difficult. Not only did I have to attend the weddings of all my friends, now I also had to officiate 5-10 marriage ceremonies each year. And endure the receptions where they never quite knew where to seat the single minister. The bride and groom often strategically positioned me beside their unmarried friend in the hope that there would be a romantic spark. There wasn't. I began to dread weddings. This wasn't how I had imagined my life would be.

GOD WON'T BE RUSHED

We live high-speed world of instant gratification. Things are only getting faster. We increasingly expect everything immediately.

I subscribe to Amazon Prime because I don't like waiting more than one day for a delivery.

I pay for Netflix because I don't want to wait a week for the next episode of my favorite show. I can binge-watch an entire season over a few days.

If Amazon and Netflix can be so efficient, why can't God?

Why is God sometimes so slow?

That's what I was asking.

And I'm sure that's what His people were wondering as God took them the long way around following their exodus from Egypt.

God, in His infinite wisdom, knew something that the Israelites didn't. They might have thought they were ready to advance. But God knew that they weren't prepared. If they faced a formidable enemy now, they would be wiped out.

So, instead, He led them through the desert. He took them the long way around, through the wilderness.

Isn't that what waiting feels like at times?

A barren wilderness. A lonely, empty, desolate place.

That's how I began to feel as I entered my 30s. Most parts of my life were flourishing. My ministry was going great. I had solid friendships. The church provided me with a home and a stable salary. I prioritized my health and was in good shape. By all appearances, it looked like I had it all together.

But all of that was overshadowed by the one area of my life where I seemed to be failing. When it came to finding a life partner, nothing was progressing.

As my frustration grew, increasingly I was making some unwise choices in relationships. I was dating the wrong people and causing unnecessary hurt. Maybe, subconsciously, I thought I could force God's hand. If He saw what the mess I was creating, He would expedite the process. He would intervene and send me 'the one'. I was wrong. Most likely, I only delayed things further.

I needed to grasp the same lessons that God was trying to teach His children when they exited Egypt:

The waiting and the wilderness weren't punishment. They were preparation.

God wasn't keeping them from something good. He was saving them from something bad.

He wasn't preventing them. He was protecting them.

His plan wasn't to stop them. He was slowing them down to save them.

There was much more at stake than they realized. They couldn't see it, but this delay in their journey wasn't just about winning the battle immediately before them. It was about safeguarding their entire future.

Even if they had quickly advanced and achieved short-term success, they could never sustain it without more preparation, growth, and a change of mindset. And God could only do that as they were willing to submit to His process in the wilderness.

They were in a hurry. God wasn't. He would take as much time to get them ready as it required.

HE'S READY WHEN YOU ARE

Sadly, the process of preparation took much longer than it should have. The people constantly rebelled against God and resisted His preparation. They kept failing the test and having to re-take it. They never progressed beyond the wilderness.

But 40 years later, when they finally crossed over into Canaan, they were ready.

Everything happened very quickly. In one day, they moved from the desert into the promise.

There were battles to fight. There was territory to occupy. There was a nation to establish. The was a future to build.

But they were prepared.

Looking back, I hope it all made sense. That's why God had taken them the long way around. **He was getting them ready to receive His very best. And He wouldn't allow them to settle for less.**

That's also my own story.

At the age of 33, I had my first date with a beautiful curly-haired blond girl named Becky Fletcher. Four months and two days later, I asked her to marry me. Fifteen years later, I love her more than ever.

We often joke that if we'd met just a few years earlier, our relationship would never have lasted. We both needed to mature in some areas. But, when it did happen, we were ready. And things moved very quickly.

The 'in-between' - the wilderness - is the place where God tests our hearts, our trust, our motives, our character, our obedience, and our capacity to carry the blessings that He wants to lavish upon us.

Like Israel 3500 years ago, until we have learned the required lessons and passed the set tests, God will often keep us from advancing. It's frustrating and often painful, but His desire isn't to punish us – it's to protect us.

Today, if you're taking the long way around, please know this - the process has a purpose. I know it's hard. But God is preparing you for all that He has prepared for you.

PROPHETIC ENCOURAGEMENT

HE HAS BEEN DEFLECTING THE ARROWS OF THE ENEMY.

There has been much spiritual warfare going on around you in the invisible realm.
However, a lot of it has not directly impacted you because the LORD has been deflecting the fiery arrows that have been hurled towards you.

Yes, you might feel unusually weary and physically weak.

These past few weeks have been especially tough.
That's because of the unrelenting spiritual swirl around you.

However, you have been protected from the fiercest of the demonic attacks and assaults.
His angels are active on assignment, surrounding and shielding you.
They have been preserving and protecting you as you press through this pivotal juncture.

Don't be deterred. You are about to experience a spiritual shift.
In the coming weeks, your future will begin to take shape.
Uncertainty and confusion will give way to clarity and direction.
You will know which way to go.
You will discern the next steps you need to take. You will see the path ahead.

Finally, things are going to get moving in your life again.
The stagnancy of this long last season will give way to suddenlies, momentum, and acceleration.
Connections, calls, and conversations will come from unexpected places and people.

Regret will turn to rejoicing. Loss to laughter. Disappointment to praise.
A door that had been closed will open again. You will have a second chance to say 'yes' to an opportunity that you missed.
Dormant dreams will come alive.
A fresh sense of anticipation and expectation will begin to rise.

Yes, plans will change. Schedules will shift.
In some cases, you will be re-routed onto a completely new trajectory. You may be taken into new territory.

But it won't be a time of frustration, fear, or anxiety.
Instead, different pieces and aspects of your life will begin to fall into place.
There will be a deep sense of alignment. Amid all the changes, you'll just know that this is right.
It's what you've been waiting for. It's what you've been preparing for.

Some final hurdles, obstacles, and barriers may appear. But they're not formidable enough to hinder your advancement.
Press on through.
Watch them fall aside.

You've been through a long, barren season of waiting, praying, longing, hoping.

This battle is almost over. The warfare is waning. Reprieve is coming.

It's time to step into this new season of greater fruitfulness and fulfillment.

HE HAS BEEN DEFLECTING THE ARROWS OF THE ENEMY.

DAY 12

WHEN THE GRACE LIFTS

BIBLE READING

Once again there was a battle between the Philistines and Israel. David went down with his men to fight against the Philistines, and he became exhausted. And Ishbi-Benob, one of the descendants of Rapha, whose bronze spearhead weighed three hundred shekels and who was armed with a new sword, said he would kill David. But Abishai son of Zeruiah came to David's rescue; he struck the Philistine down and killed him. Then David's men swore to him, saying, "Never again will you go out with us to battle, so that the lamp of Israel will not be extinguished."

In the course of time, there was another battle with the Philistines, at Gob. At that time Sibbekai the Hushathite killed Saph, one of the descendants of Rapha.
In another battle with the Philistines at Gob, Elhanan son of Jair the Bethlehemite killed the brother of Goliath the Gittite, who had a spear with a shaft like a weaver's rod.

In still another battle, which took place at Gath, there was a huge man with six fingers on each hand and six toes on each foot - twenty-four in all. He also was descended from Rapha. When he taunted Israel, Jonathan son of Shimeah, David's brother, killed him.

(2 Samuel 21: 15-21)

DEVOTIONAL

When you're good at something or you've experienced success in a particular area, it's hard to let it go. It can become part of your identity. You're not sure who you are if you're not doing *that*. Perhaps others relate to you according to that role or ability. So, you keep doing it, even when its expiration date has passed.

In today's Bible reading, David has been the king for around 30 years. Yet, look at what he is doing – fighting Philistine giants. The same thing that had made him famous all those years before when he had struck down Goliath. It was the battle that had propelled him to prominence. Saved a nation. Made him a hero. They had even composed a song about his superior fighting skills.

However, this time it's different. He simply can't get any traction in this battle. We're told "he became exhausted" and was almost killed. One of his troops must step in and save him.

It could simply be that David is now older and not as strong as he once was.

Or perhaps the grace has lifted in this area of his life, but he has refused to recognize it.

I mean, he was hardly a match for Goliath all those years before. Yet, God supernaturally enabled him to discard of the giant with relative ease. Now, however, no matter what he does, or how hard he tries, it's not enough.

His troops observe what has happened. They resolutely determine that David will never go to battle with them again:

"Then David's men swore to him, saying, "Never again will you go out with us to battle, so that the lamp of Israel will not be extinguished." (v. 17)

His role and position are too important to expend his life in tasks that others can perform. He should focus on the areas of his life where the grace still rests.

What do I mean by 'the grace lifting'?

I'm not talking about the grace of God by which we're saved (Ephesians 2: 8).

I'm talking about God's empowering grace. His enabling strength.

God gives us a certain grace for particular assignments. There's an ease, a flow, a divine enablement.

It doesn't mean that everything will be easy, or life will be problem-free.

But there is a certain sense that the blessing of the Lord is upon it, the wind of God is behind you. He's giving you the strength to do hard things.

I once walked through an intense season of ministry where I was working an average of 14 hours a day, seven days a week. It was challenging, even exhausting at times. But there was a grace upon it. There was a divine enablement.

I look back now, and I don't know how I did it. But I also recognize that there was a supernatural strength that sustained me through that season and empowered me to flourish.

So, when I talk about 'the grace lifting', I don't mean that something has become difficult. God often calls us to difficult assignments.

When 'the grace lifts', you sense a shift in that area of your life. It's almost like something breaks inside you.

Maybe you can still do the job. You could have the ability and competence. But you just don't have the heart for it any longer. Something has changed inside you and it's difficult to describe or define.

Here are **five signs that the grace is lifted in an area of your life.**

Individually, none of them should be taken as irrefutable evidence that you shouldn't be there anymore. But taken together, if you can say 'yes' to many of these points, it could well be a sign that the grace has lifted.

1. **YOU NO LONGER HAVE THE CAPACITY TO GIVE ANYTHING IN THAT CONTEXT.**

It feels like you're empty, almost numb, when it comes to that job, role, or relationship.

You can do it. But you just don't care about it any longer.

You're still showing up, you're going through the motions, but you're counting the minutes until it's over. You're living for the weekend. You're living for your next vacation.

Nothing about it excites or enthuses you. You might even begin to dread it. it only feels like a burden.

2. **THINGS THAT ONCE EASY OR TOOK LITTLE EFFORT OR ENERGY, NOW BECOME INCREASINGLY DIFFICULT.**

You're feeling constantly exhausted and burdened by what used to energize you.

It takes more time and effort to get less done. Small things that you once did without much thought now feel overwhelming.

There's no joy in the job or role. It is sustained only by your effort and not by the Spirit.

3. **SOMETHING THAT USED TO FEEL LIKE A GOOD FIT FOR YOU NOW FEELS TIGHT, RESTRICTIVE, AND CONTAINING.**

You almost feel like you're suffocating. It's like a plant that had outgrown its pot and is now withering and wilting. It needed to be replanted into a larger pot so that it can flourish and grow.

4. YOU INCREASINGLY HAVE A DESIRE OR A BURDEN TO BE SOMEWHERE ELSE.

Your heart is drawn to other places, roles, or people.

You're only staying out of a sense of obligation, guilt, false loyalty, fear, or for the financial benefits.

In a sense your heart has already moved on, but your physical body hasn't caught up yet.

5. YOUR INNER BEING GETS IRRITATED BY THE PEOPLE IN THAT SPACE.

You just don't want to be around them. Maybe they were never your best friends. But you liked them, you got along with them, you tolerated them. But now you don't want to be anywhere near them.

There's no chemistry whatsoever. Everything they do gets on your nerves. You don't want to feel like this, but it's how things are.

Do any of the above sound familiar to you?

If you could relate to more than three of them, it could well be a sign that the grace has lifted on whatever you're doing. **In fact, if you think the grace has started to lift, it probably has.**

The truth is - most people overstay - and if you overstay, you often lose the ability to leave well.

The Irritation grows.

Relationships start to break down.

You begin to resent the people and the place. You overreact to minor annoyances.

When that happens, it can destroy relationships and shut doors that might have been open to you.

Does that mean that you leave tomorrow? Probably not.

But perhaps you need to begin planning a change.

You can begin to look around for another role or position.

You can start to have honoring conversations.

You can prepare to leave well.

Finally, remember this:

When the grace lifts in one area of your life, God relocates it to a different area.

Find and follow His favor.

PROPHETIC ENCOURAGEMENT

THERE IS A BLESSING FOR BUILDING

I see the LORD handing out scrolls to His people. They are 'BLUEPRINTS FOR BUILDING'.

Building for your future.
Building your business.
Building your ministry.
Building your family.
Building your relationships.
Building His Kingdom.

Some people were taking the scrolls, opening them, and studying them closely as they immediately put them into action.

Others were simply walking around with the scrolls in their hand, but doing nothing with them. They were aimless and purposeless.

The Lord is giving specific instructions, detailed directions, precise plans, strategies for success, blueprints for blessing.

But your future will depend on how closely you follow His revelation.

This is not a time for passivity or procrastination.
It is a time to put into action what the Lord is telling you to do.

It is a time to build, create, initiate, implement, shift, relocate, reorient, and reinvent.

Lean into the Spirit.
Listen and write.
Then move and make.

The timid and fearful will say…
But what about the darkness?
But what about the wars?
But what about the reaction of others?
But what about the finances?
But what about the obstacles?

But the Lord would say - this is an opportune time, a *kairos* moment.
Take hold of it.

Make bold moves.
Go all in.
Do not hold back any longer.
Ignore the doubters.
Silence the inner critic.

Great faith will bring great favor.

Know that your God is with you. He is for you.

Follow His blueprints for building - they will bring great blessing.

DAY 13

TRANSITION REALIGNS RELATIONSHIPS

BIBLE READING

David asked the men standing near him, "What will be done for the man who kills this Philistine and removes this disgrace from Israel? Who is this uncircumcised Philistine that he should defy the armies of the living God?"

They repeated to him what they had been saying and told him, "This is what will be done for the man who kills him."

When Eliab, David's oldest brother, heard him speaking with the men, he burned with anger at him and asked, "Why have you come down here? And with whom did you leave those few sheep in the wilderness? I know how conceited you are and how wicked your heart is; you came down only to watch the battle."

"Now what have I done?" said David. "Can't I even speak?" He then turned away to someone else and brought up the same matter, and the men answered him as before.

What David said was overheard and reported to Saul, and Saul sent for him.

(1 Samuel 17: 26-31)

DEVOTIONAL

Transition doesn't happen in isolation. A significant transition in one part of your life will often lead to transitions in other areas. One shift has a knock-on effect that leads to another shift.

This is especially true with relationships. Probably because our relationships are so integral to who we are as humans.

You have probably found that some of your significant relationships have changed in this past season. In all the shaking and upheaval that we have experienced since 2020, it would be surprising if this important area of your life wasn't impacted.

People you were previously close to, now seem more distant.

Perhaps, you used to meet up each week for a coffee and chat. You looked forward to it. It refreshed you. Now, increasingly you're finding that it drains you.

You once had so much to talk about. Now the conversation is strained.

You had everything in common. Now you struggle to see their point of view.

You make excuses not to meet up so often and wonder if they realize that things aren't the way they used to be.

Sometimes transition doesn't change your relationship. It simply reveals what was already there, hiding beneath the surface.

As God repositions you, promotes you, reassigns you, and reveals your true purpose, those closest to you may find it difficult to accept.

This can come as quite a shock.

You thought they would be thrilled for you and celebrate the change in your circumstances.
Instead, you are met with criticism, negativity, and even anger.

You may be misunderstood as they question your motives.

They might label you as arrogant, self-promoting, and overly ambitious.

They preferred the old version of you. For some reason, version 2.0 makes them deeply uncomfortable.

The truth is that some people want to stay at the same forever - and they want their relationships to stay the same.

This most often happens with those who are closest to you. They have always related to you as a certain person, in a particular context.

But you're changing, growing, longing for more out of life, trying new things. And now you have less in common than before. You don't connect as naturally as you once did. It might become difficult just being around that person for any length of time.

Parents sometimes do this with their children. Even when you've grown up and have responsibilities, your parent still treats you like you're a child.

Or it could be some longstanding friends. They have a 'frozen' version of you that they keep relating to - a person who doesn't exist any longer - except in their own minds.

And so, when you're in between who you were and who you are becoming, don't be blindsided or shaken if you experience some tension or strain with those who have been part of your past.

FAMILY DRAMA

We see this played out in the life of David.

He arrived at the battlefield as the little, insignificant brother, who was running errands for his dad. That was until Goliath stepped out and David stepped up to fight.

He immediately caught the attention of King Saul. But he also caught the wrath of his older brother.

In this pivotal point of transition, the whole dynamic of their relationship changed.

The eldest brother Eliab had always been the leader, the impressive one, the man in charge.

Now his little brother has caught the limelight, showing more courage than any of his superiors.

It was never David's intention, but this shift in roles makes Eliab deeply uncomfortable and angry. He lashes out, attacking David's job, his motives, and his character:

"When Eliab, David's oldest brother, heard him speaking with the men, he burned with anger at him and asked, "Why have you come down here? And with whom did you leave those few sheep in the wilderness? I know how conceited you are and how wicked your heart is; you came down only to watch the battle." (v. 28)

When God walks you through transition, your relationships will often change. Not everyone who has been part of your life will continue to be, at least not to the same degree.

Your vision, capacity, calling, and role have changed while they have likely stayed the same.

They were able to journey with you this far. But they don't have what it takes to journey the rest of the way.

It can be deeply painful and disorientating. But it's simply part of the process of growth.

Don't spend your life trying to change people who are determined to stay the same.

I love David's response. When attacked, he didn't become defensive, angry, or strike back. Nor did he doubt himself or his calling and shrink back. We read:

"He then turned away to someone else and brought up the same matter…" (v. 30)

He simply turned away from the negative voice and remained focused on the mission and cause that God had set before him.

You might need to do the same.

There doesn't have to be some big drama or falling out.

But as God transitions and realigns you, some people who were close will need to be distanced. Some gentle boundaries may need to be put in place.

As we move into the next chapter of David's life, we don't hear much from his brother. But he does form a new strong relational alignment with Jonathan, the son of the King. This deep friendship would bring protection, resources, and mutual affection that empowered David to step into his regal calling.

You too can be assured - as you leave behind some connections and relationships from the past season, God is going to bring you into new, strategic alignments that will bring life, growth, companionship, and that will resource your future.

PROPHETIC ENCOURAGEMENT

I AM PREPARING A TABLE FOR YOU.

The LORD is preparing a table before you in the presence of those who have opposed and undermined you.

They will only be able to look on as you joyfully feast on the lavish banquet that He is placing before you.

They will be confused by your total disregard for their negativity, gossiping, criticism, and backbiting.

Where you have experienced deep weariness from attacks, opposition, lies, false accusations, loneliness, and loss - a complete turnaround is coming.

What was robbed and stolen will be returned.

Restitution is yours.

Recompense is yours.

Restoration is yours.

You will wear a crown of victory.

You will walk with divine authority.

You will carry yourself with honor and dignity.

A supernatural strength is coming to rest upon you.

The LORD is placing within you a holy defiance.

An unyielding boldness. A relentless determination. A stubborn faith.

You will not bend.

You will not blend in with the world.

You will not compromise your convictions.

You will display contagious courage that will draw others out of hiding.

You are shaking off the confusion and containment of this past season.

Your voice is coming back. Your confidence is returning.

You are discovering that you are more than the labels and lids that others have placed upon you.

Release what He gives you.

Speak what He says.

Don't edit it or water it down.

Your message will resound and resonate with those who need to hear it.

Don't be preoccupied with what others think or say about you.

Don't use your best energy defending yourself or your reputation.

Your Father knows your heart. He sees your motives.

Allow Him to defend and vindicate you.

The table is set. Come and feast.

Be filled with His provision.

Be satisfied with His supply.

Be enfolded in His love.

Be surrounded by His protection.

Be confident of His care.

Surely the goodness and favor of the LORD rest upon your life.

You will lack nothing as you closely follow the leading of your Shepherd, Savior, Strength, and Shield.

I AM PREPARING A TABLE FOR YOU.

DAY 14

HIS FAVOR IS UPON YOU

BIBLE READING

Now Lot, who was moving about with Abram, also had flocks and herds and tents. But the land could not support them while they stayed together, for their possessions were so great that they were not able to stay together. And quarreling arose between Abram's herders and Lot's. The Canaanites and Perizzites were also living in the land at that time.

So Abram said to Lot, "Let's not have any quarreling between you and me, or between your herders and mine, for we are close relatives. Is not the whole land before you? Let's part company. If you go to the left, I'll go to the right; if you go to the right, I'll go to the left."

Lot looked around and saw that the whole plain of the Jordan toward Zoar was well watered, like the garden of the Lord, like the land of Egypt. (This was before the Lord destroyed Sodom and Gomorrah.) So Lot chose for himself the whole plain of the Jordan and set out toward the east. The two men parted company...

The Lord said to Abram after Lot had parted from him, "Look around from where you are, to the north and south, to the east and west. All the land that you see I will give to you and your offspring forever. I will make your offspring like the dust of the earth, so that if anyone could count the dust, then your offspring could be counted. Go, walk through the length and breadth of the land, for I am giving it to you."

(Genesis 13: 5-17)

DEVOTIONAL

Amid the fear and uncertainty in the early months of 2020, one worship song spread more rapidly than the virus in many nations. *The Blessing* by Cody Carnes, Kari Jobe, and Elevation Worship was sung as a prayer and benediction over communities across the globe.

Taken directly from Numbers chapter 6, sometimes described as 'the only prayer written by God', *The Blessing* expressed the heart of the Father for His children at a time of great apprehension. Many were especially moved by these words:

"May His favor be upon you
And a thousand generations
And your family and your children
And their children, and their children..."

To declare the favor of God over your family and their future generations is powerful.

But it's even more life-transforming when you understand that the favor of God rests upon your life and you begin to live as someone confident that they are highly favored.

What exactly do I mean by 'God's favor'?

It's a term that Christians throw around a lot, yet many aren't clear on how to define it.

God's favor is His empowering grace. In fact, in the original Greek language, the word for *grace* and *favor* are identical – they are both the word *charis*.

The favor of God is His 'demonstrated delight'.

It can be described as *"tangible evidence that a person has the approval of the Lord."*

When we favor someone, we want to be with him or her. We delight in him. We connect with her in a way we don't connect with everyone.

We usually favor people who also favor us. In the same way, God shows favor to the ones who delight in, connect with, and give honor to Him. Isaiah 66:2 says:

"These are the ones I look on with favor: those who are humble and contrite in spirit, and who tremble at my word."

Here are some other definitions that will help you understand God's favor:

• *God doing something for you that you can't do for yourself* • *Power for purpose*
• *Divine enablement*
• *Unusual or uncommon blessing*
• *Supernatural advantage*

Like grace, favor is not earned, it's not deserved. It is simply an overflow of His amazing goodness, abundant generosity, and overwhelming kindness.

I love what author and teacher Joyce Meyer says about favor:

"His favor...is a gift of His grace and cannot be earned. God doesn't want us to waste our time and energy trying to earn favor; He wants us to trust Him for it. When God gives us His favor, amazing things begin to happen. Doors of opportunity will open for you. You will end up with benefits and blessings that you haven't earned or deserved."

Often, we can identify God's tangible favor on others more than we recognize it on ourselves. We see them enjoy the material blessings, the promotion, the good health, the way things always work out - and we wonder – *why can't I have that?*

Or we see God's favor as being located in particular places. It seems that certain ministries and churches are especially favored by God. Favor doesn't always seem fair.

126

WALK IN HIS FAVOR

The good news is this – you can walk in God's favor. In fact, it's already yours!

Before you can fully experience the benefits of God's favor, you must know that they are yours. As with every other spiritual blessing, you receive favor by faith.

Think about your salvation. It's by grace alone. It's offered to everyone the same:

"God so loved <u>the world</u> that he gave His only son..." (John 3: 16)

God gave His son to save the whole world. His forgiveness is available to every single person.

But what does the rest of the verse say?

*"...that **whosoever believes in him**, might not perish, but have everlasting life."*

Yes, eternal life is available to everyone.

But who receives it?

Only those who believe in Him.

God holds out this incredible gift and our part is to believe and receive. We take it. We accept it.

God's favor is exactly the same.

It's free. We don't deserve it. We can't earn it.

But we receive it by faith and then live out of that new identity of being favored by God.

We see a great example of this in the life of Abraham (formerly Abram), the Father of our faith.

In Genesis 13, hostility develops between the herdsmen of Abram and his nephew Lot. Abram has a solution:

"Let's part company. If you go to the left, I'll go to the right; if you go to the right, I'll go to the left." (v. 9)

Notice, Abram didn't pray about the decision. He didn't even check out the quality of the land in different locations.

He was so convinced that God's favor rested upon him and not his surroundings that he essentially said:

"Lot, you choose whatever piece of land you like. It doesn't matter to me because I know I'll be blessed wherever I go."

Imagine how having a core belief like this would impact your life.

How would you walk if you knew, deep in your heart, that the favor of God rests upon you?

How would you carry yourself if, every time you enter a room, you were confident that you are covered in the favor of God?

Would you feel the need to compete or compare?

Would you be striving or trying to gain approval from people?

No. Because you know that you are highly favored.

Often, God does give us very clear direction about moving to a specific place or taking on a certain role. Our response is simply to obey what He says.

However, there are other times when I believe God says:

"You choose. I'll bless you wherever you go or whatever you do. As long as your deepest desire is to please me, you'll find my favor there."

128

I recall listening to a message from Pastor Paul Scanlon years ago. At the time, he was leading one of the largest and most prominent churches in the UK. It was located in a city known for crime, deprivation, and a large Islamic population. Someone had asked him:

"Why Bradford? Why not London or one of the larger, more affluent metroplexes?"

His response went something like this:

"I thought about it. But I decided to try Bradford. I knew God's favor rested upon me, not necessarily the location. So, wherever I planted a church, I was sure that God would bless it."

That probably comes across to some people as arrogance.

People might ask: *"Who do you think you are? How can you be so confident of God's blessing and favor?"*

I'm sure some people thought the same about Abraham. He didn't mind. He was too busy enjoying God's favor to worry about the opinions of others.

As I reflect on my own life, I can see the fingerprints of God's favor all over it.

Of course, I have had many challenges and difficulties like everyone else. I've shared them openly.

But I have also always carried a deep sense that I am favored by God. I believe that His goodness, blessing, health, and provision follow me into every season and situation. That core belief has shaped my life and decisions.

YOU ARE FAVORED

My dear friends Pastors Paul and Priscilla Reid have four grown-up daughters. Every time one of their daughters celebrates a birthday, Paul posts a picture on social media and writes: *"Happy birthday to ___, my favorite daughter."*

A few months later, he does the same for a different daughter.

Is he lying? No! They are all his favorite daughters. He loves them all the same.

If you are a believer, you are a child of God, a son or daughter of Most-High. And you are His favorite.

Do you believe that? Really?

God looks at you today and He says: "You're my favorite."

Imagine what fully grasping that would do to your life.

How would it change the way you see yourself?

How would you interact with others?

What would you expect from life?

If you struggle with this, begin to study and contemplate these truths about God's favor.

Understand that His favor is available to you right now.

You are a beloved, blood-bought, chosen child of God.

His favor touches every area of your life and surrounds you continually. All you have to do is accept it by faith.

A moment of God's favor can do more than a lifetime of labor.

His favor will open doors to rooms that you're not qualified to enter.

His favor will bring opportunities before you that you don't deserve.

His favor will allow the right people to enter your life at the perfect time.

His favor will enable you to flourish in even the harshest environments.

His favor will empower you to speak with authority to those who are in positions above you.

The favor of God is yours - today and forever. Believe it and receive it.

PROPHETIC ENCOURAGEMENT

YOU'RE GOING TO TAKE YOUR PLACE. YOU'RE GOING TO FIND YOUR SEAT.

The Lord gave me a short vivid vision of someone boarding an airplane. I believe this person represents you.

Every time you tried to take a seat, you were informed that the seat was already taken or that it belonged to someone else.

You were growing increasingly frustrated because you knew you had a ticket. This was a journey that you had to take.

But you couldn't find your place. It seemed as if there was no seat for you.

Then a member of the cabin crew came along and said: *"Follow me. I've found your seat. There's a place for you."*

And they led you into the first-class section.

The seat was perfect.

As you looked around there were lots of smiling faces. People said *hello*. You couldn't believe it because you knew some of them.

Others, who you didn't know, called you by your name. They knew you even though you didn't know them.

Today, the LORD would tell you:

I HAVE A PLACE FOR YOU.

Some of you have been really struggling to fit in.

You've been finding it difficult to find your place.

Every time you think that you have found your seat, it doesn't work out, it doesn't fit, you know it's not right, and you're even supplanted or replaced by someone else.

And you've grown increasingly frustrated. Because you know the Lord has a specific call on your life.

But you are struggling to find your place.

The LORD is saying:

You're going to take your place.

You're going to find your seat.

And it is so much better than you could ever have imagined or expected.

I have people waiting for you.

There are resources and relationships in place for you.

There are already people there having conversations behind your back (in a good way).

And when you get there, you're going to be surprised because it may not be the seat that you expected.

It's an upgrade to your original plan.

It's His plan. It's perfectly prepared. Designed just for you.

The waiting will have been worth it.

YOU'RE GOING TO TAKE YOUR PLACE.

YOU'RE GOING TO FIND YOUR SEAT.

DAY 15

WHEN GOD INTERRUPTS YOUR LIFE

BIBLE READING

Now Moses was keeping the flock of his father-in-law, Jethro, the priest of Midian, and he led his flock to the west side of the wilderness and came to Horeb, the mountain of God. And the angel of the Lord appeared to him in a flame of fire out of the midst of a bush. He looked, and behold, the bush was burning, yet it was not consumed. And Moses said, "I will turn aside to see this great sight, why the bush is not burned." When the Lord saw that he turned aside to see, God called to him out of the bush, "Moses, Moses!" And he said, "Here I am." Then he said, "Do not come near; take your sandals off your feet, for the place on which you are standing is holy ground." And he said, "I am the God of your father, the God of Abraham, the God of Isaac, and the God of Jacob." And Moses hid his face, for he was afraid to look at God.

The LORD said, "I have indeed seen the misery of my people in Egypt. I have heard them crying out because of their slave drivers, and I am concerned about their suffering. So I have come down to rescue them...
...So now, go. I am sending you to Pharaoh to bring my people the Israelites out of Egypt."

(Exodus 3: 1-10)

DEVOTIONAL

I'm a planner. I book all our family trips. When we go anywhere, I tend to be super organized. I have all the documentation printed and in order. I check that we have our passports (several times). I like everything to run smoothly. And normally, there are no problems. Because Mr. Planner takes care of everything.

However, some things are beyond even my control.

Last summer we took a family vacation in Portugal. As we sat in the taxi to the airport to catch our return flight, I suddenly felt quite anxious. I couldn't understand where the unease had come from. We'd had a very relaxing two weeks. But I couldn't shake the feeling of apprehension.

When we arrived at the airport it all became clear. The air traffic control system for the entire UK had crashed. This had never happened before. No flights could enter or leave UK airspace. Like tens of thousands of others across the world, we were stranded. Our plans had been abruptly interrupted.

We scrambled to book alternative flights and went to stay at a hotel near the airport. It was almost three days later before we finally made it home.

Did I mention that I'm a planner? Interruptions irritate me. Disruptions bother me. Interferences are an inconvenience.

If everyone would just stick to my plans, the world would be a much happier place.

The problem with people like me is that we serve a God who interrupts us. He messes with our best-laid plans.

Have you found that?

He sometimes brings delays and detours into our lives.
He closes one door and then opens an unexpected opportunity.
He reroutes, redirects, and reorientates us.
He calls us to fresh assignments and unfamiliar places.
He draws (or snatches) us out of the old and sends us into the new.

Just when we're getting settled and comfortable, He shakes up our predictable existence.

We see that throughout Scripture and history. And we experience it in our own lives. God is an interrupter and a disruptor.

BETWEEN TWO WORLDS

Moses had been the Prince of Egypt. Born a Hebrew, he was protected by the providential hand of God and raised as royalty. For the first 40 years of his life, he was caught between two worlds.

Moses was too Hebrew for the Egyptians. And he was too Egyptian for the Hebrews.

He didn't really fit anywhere.

He was a misfit.

A square peg in a round hole.

Never really feeling as if he belonged here or there.

Maybe you can relate.

Yet, that was exactly how God intended it.

Because in His sovereignty and omniscience, God had looked into the future and knew that one day His people would cry out to Him for deliverance from slavery and oppression in Egypt.

And Moses was exactly the sort of leader He would need for the job – someone who understood both cultures. A man who knew the protocol of the palace and the plight of his own people.

So, all through Moses' early life, God was busy answering prayers that hadn't yet been prayed.

Isn't that incredible? Eighty years before the people even cried out to God, He started raising up a deliverer – the answer to their prayers.

God is so intentional in your life. He sees where you're going. He knows where history is moving. So, He begins to prepare and align you now – far in advance - so that you can be most effective in whatever lies ahead.

That's why we often look at our lives and they don't make sense. We thought we would be somewhere else, doing something different.

Yet, we are only seeing such a small part of the whole picture. One paragraph or chapter in an entire book. God, who is authoring the book with us, sees the end from the beginning:

"I make known the end from the beginning, from ancient times, what is still to come. I say, 'My purpose will stand, and I will do all that I please." (Isaiah 46: 10)

We make mistakes and get it wrong. He doesn't. His plans are perfect.

However, Moses rushed ahead of God. He tried to skip some chapters.

One day, he witnessed a Hebrew slave being beaten by his Egyptian taskmaster.

Frustration and anger that had been simmering beneath the surface for years spilled over. He lashed out and murdered the Egyptian slave master. Terrified that Pharoah would find out what he'd done, Mose was forced to run for his life.

He was trying to do the right thing. His sense of anger towards the injustice his people were experiencing was good. His desire to rescue them was noble.

But the way he went about it was all wrong.

Rather than wait on God's timing, he tried to force that which God hadn't yet endorsed.

THE WILDERNESS YEARS

Moses then spends the next 40 years living in the backside of the desert - in the middle of nowhere - working as a shepherd for his father-in-law.

Overnight, his old, familiar life has been completely interrupted and turned upside down.

His existence in the wilderness was the opposite of everything he'd ever known.

No more privilege, servants, status, or silver cups. Just smelly sheep and the scorching sun.

He's gone from being a somebody to being a nobody. From the limelight to the wasteland.

At least he's safe from Pharoah. Plus, he's got a wife and family. There's predictability and routine.

This is Moses' new normal.

It might appear that God has removed His blessing from Moses' life.

But I have found - and Scripture shows us - that **it's often in the deserts of our lives that we encounter God.**

It's in the wilderness times - when we are hidden away; when it seems like it's all fallen apart; when everything has been stripped back – that God is doing His deepest work in our lives.

The deserts are places where we encounter God in a way we never could in the busyness and noise surrounding us when everything is going well.

The desert is also where God shapes and molds us backstage, so we are ready for what He has prepared for us.

We see this in Moses' life:

"Now Moses was tending the flock of Jethro his father-in-law, the priest of Midian, and he led the flock to the far side of the wilderness and came to Horeb, the mountain of God." (Exodus 3: 1)

When we find Moses here, he's been leading stubborn sheep in the desert for 40 years.

He doesn't know it yet, but what is he about to spend the next 40 years doing?

137

Leading God's stubborn people through the desert.

To an outside observer, this may have looked like wasted decades in Moses' life. It was, in fact, the greatest possible preparation for everything God was calling him into.

Nothing is wasted with God.

If you're in a desert place right now - if life feels barren, dry, and unfruitful - ask yourself: what might God be doing in my life?

What is He stripping away?

How is He preparing me?

And know this: **the desert doesn't mean that God has finished with you.**

That's what Moses probably thought. After 40 years in the desert, Moses saw himself as 'a has been.'

His best days were behind him.

His memories were greater than his dreams.

He was too old to be used by God again.

He was destined for a life of insignificance and obscurity.

But God had other plans.

Because it's here, in the desert, that God interrupts Moses again:

There the angel of the LORD appeared to him in flames of fire from within a bush. Moses saw that though the bush was on fire it did not burn up. So Moses thought, "I will go over and see this strange sight - why the bush does not burn up." (Exodus 3: 1-3)

INTERRUPTED AND RE-ASSIGNED

It was just an ordinary day. Nothing special about it. Just like every other day, Moses woke up, dressed, and began his 12-hour shift of herding Jethro's sheep.

But then something very strange happened.

Moses noticed that a bush was on fire.

In children's books, this scene is usually illustrated with a large tree blazing. But the original language indicates that it was just a small thorny shrub.

There's nothing too unusual about the fire. In the desert sun, Moses often saw fires/

But as he looks at it for a few moments, Moses notices something strange. The shrub continues to burn without being consumed by the flames.

A little side note here: **God wants us to be on fire, but he doesn't want us to burn out.** Sadly, it's often the Christians who start with the most passion and zeal for the Lord who end up burning out. I've seen it many times. People start well but don't finish well. Through exhaustion, compromise, or getting side-tracked, it's easy for the fire in your life to burn out. Keep fuelling the fire. Don't allow anything or anyone to extinguish the passion in your life.

Anyway, Moses sees this strange bush burning and moves closer to check it out:

"When the Lord saw that he had gone over to look, God called to him from within the bush, 'Moses! Moses!'

And Moses said, 'Here I am.'" (v. 4)

Notice, it was only when Moses stopped and looked more closely, that God spoke to him.

The burning bush was simply God's way of getting Moses' attention. I get the sense that Moses could easily have kept on walking here. If he hadn't paused and paid attention, he could have missed what God was seeking to communicate.

How many times has God been trying to get my attention, but I haven't realized it? Or I've been too busy to stop?

Or perhaps it's all appeared too ordinary. It's not been dramatic or supernatural enough. It appears random or meaningless. I mean, a burning bush in a scorching desert is not that exciting.

Increasingly, I am noticing that God speaks most profoundly through ordinary and insignificant ways.

He's always been doing it. I'm only just starting to pay attention.

God does the extraordinary in the common, everyday moments. Or through the most normal people.

But we often miss it because it's not dramatic or exciting enough.

For example, I frequently wake up in the morning with a song going around in my head. Over the past year or so, I realized that many of these were songs I hadn't heard in years, sometimes decades. When I finally began to pay attention and started to Google the song lyrics, I was amazed. God has spoken powerfully through the words.

Or, when I'm prophesying over someone, increasingly God will draw my attention to some insignificant piece of jewelry or a piece of clothing they're wearing. This becomes the springboard for a powerful and accurate word from the Lord.

Let me give you a recent example.

Recently, I was prophesying over some of my Prophetic Transitions Mentorship Community. Over Zoom, a lady appeared on the screen. I knew nothing about her. So, I asked the Holy Spirit to speak to me. Immediately my attention was drawn to what looked like a miniature guitar on a stand behind her. I began to prophesy that God was giving her

140

back her song. She had been through a painful season and had lost it, but He was now restoring it. I then thought of a songbird and began to prophesy about that, emphasizing the word 'bird'. There were many other things but that was the gist.

I finished and asked her if it made any sense.

Apparently, it did. This lady had been through a very difficult year and had asked God just the previous week to "give me back my song". Also, she had an unusual last name: Blackbird.

Pay attention to the small things.

Notice what God is placing in front of you.

It could be song lyrics, a road sign, slow traffic, something written on the side of a passing truck, a line in a movie, or numbers that you keep seeing.

It may appear ordinary or insignificant, but that's often how God communicates. These are divinely placed in your path for a reason.

Through this interruption of the ordinary, Moses' life takes a completely new trajectory. God calls him to return to Egypt and deliver the Hebrew slaves.

Sometimes, what appears to be an interruption is God's intervention.

It would be easy to mistake it as merely an inconvenience. But if, like Moses, you are willing to pause and pay attention, you may discover that **the interruption is an invitation to step into something new.**
Paul Tripp puts it like this:

"You and I don't live in a series of big, dramatic moments. We don't careen from big decision to big decision. We all live in an endless series of little moments. The character of a life isn't set in ten big moments. The character of a life is set in ten thousand little moments of everyday life."

When I think about our family vacation last summer, do you know what my favorite memory is? Those last two days when we were 'stranded'. I'm not kidding. We found a beautiful hotel close to the airport and enjoyed every moment of our extended stay. (And the airline completely reimbursed the cost!)

It was also during those few days of delay that God began to speak to me about writing a new book, a daily devotional for the start of a new year. He even gave me the title: The Threshold.

My plans were disrupted. But God always has a greater plan.

Don't miss the interruptions. Those unexpected events that upset your carefully crafted plans.

They may appear to be an inconvenience.

But, if you are willing to pause, look, and listen, you might discover that God is trying to get your attention.

Your plans might be put on hold or even canceled. But there's an invitation to step into a bigger and greater plan.

PROPHETIC ENCOURAGEMENT

I HAVE *PLANS* FOR YOU

"For I know the plans I have for you," declares the Lord, "plans to prosper you and not to harm you, plans to give you hope and a future." (Jeremiah 29:11)

Notice that I have 'plans' for you - plural - not just one single plan.

In other words, you cannot thwart my plan for your life through one wrong turn or a bad decision.

My plans are flexible, not set in stone.

I take account of the multitude of choices you can make.

Yes, you can delay your progress or take a detour.
But if the deepest desire of your heart is to please Me, you can always be restored.

My grace is greater than any mistake or mess you could make.

I know the plans I have for you.

Don't think of my will as a tightrope or a balance beam.
It is more like a field with boundary lines.
There is freedom to roam and explore without stepping outside of my purposes.

You don't need to stress about every little decision.
My plans for you are not designed to be restrictive.

They bring hope, joy, fulfillment, and a future filled with freedom.

Stop worrying about the future.
You don't have to rush.
Nor do you have to force anything.

I know the plans I have for you.

This isn't a competition.
Stop looking at those around you and comparing your progress to theirs.
Your calling is not like theirs.
I have you on a unique and bespoke timeline.

I have many plans for your life - but only one purpose - that you would know me.

I want above all for you to experience intimacy with Me.
To live in My presence.
To have My Word dwell within you.

If you do this, you will be in my will and experience the abundant life I long to give you.

I know the plans I have for you.

DAY 16

NOT EVERYONE CAN GO WITH YOU

BIBLE READING

After six days Jesus took with him Peter, James and John the brother of James, and led them up a high mountain by themselves. There he was transfigured before them. His face shone like the sun, and his clothes became as white as the light. 3 Just then there appeared before them Moses and Elijah, talking with Jesus.

(Matthew 17: 1-3)

Then Jesus went with his disciples to a place called Gethsemane, and he said to them, "Sit here while I go over there and pray." He took Peter and the two sons of Zebedee along with him, and he began to be sorrowful and troubled. Then he said to them, "My soul is overwhelmed with sorrow to the point of death. Stay here and keep watch with me."

(Matthew 26: 36-38)

Greater love has no one than this: to lay down one's life for one's friends.

(John 15: 13)

DEVOTIONAL

As I've grown older, my circle of friends has gradually become smaller. There are all sorts of reasons for this. People move away. Marriage and family commitments make it more difficult to spend time together. As you change, you sometimes have less in common with people. Relationships naturally grow distant if not intentionally nurtured.

But I've also discovered that, **if you are passionately pursuing God, there are some people who simply can't go where the Spirit is leading you.**

They might not have the capacity or the desire to journey where you are going.

That's okay. It doesn't make them bad people. You're just on different paths.

We see this throughout Scripture, the most obvious example being with Jesus and his followers.

CIRCLES OF FRIENDS

Throughout his ministry on earth, there were large crowds who surrounded Jesus. They usually had a need they wanted him to meet such as healing, deliverance, provision, etc.

Then there was a significant group of followers. For example, in Luke 10: 1 we read:

"After these things the Lord appointed seventy others also, and sent them two by two…"

And in Matthew 27: 55, we read about *"…many women who followed Jesus from Galilee, ministering to Him…"*

The seventy and the women had a closer connection than the crowd. They didn't only receive from Jesus. They also sought to serve him.

145

Then, of course, we have the twelve:

"Then He appointed twelve, that they might be with Him and that He might send them out to preach..." Mark 3: 14)

These disciples were carefully chosen and appointed by Jesus to learn from him and carry on his mission once he departed.

Then there were the three: Peter, James, and John.

They were his 'inner circle'. We don't know why these three were specifically selected. What we do know is that they had access to certain key events in Jesus' life that the other nine disciples were excluded from.

And Jesus never seems to apologize or explain to the others why they weren't picked.

For example, in Matthew 17:1 we read:

"Jesus took with him Peter, James and John the brother of James, and led them up a high mountain by themselves."

The principle is this: **As God takes you further and higher in your journey with Him, not everyone will be able to go with you.**

Some people will naturally exit your life as the difference and distance between you grows.

And others will try to keep you where they are and as you used to be.

It's important to understand that relationships changing and transitioning doesn't mean that they have failed. It just means that their time or the way they have functioned has come to an end.

They may have fitted who you were. But they no longer fit who you are. Or who you are becoming.

If you remain tethered to relationships that have reached their expiration date, you will become stuck, stagnant, frustrated, and resentful.
Resolve to keep moving forward with Jesus.

If others don't choose to join you on the journey or they're not part of the Father's plan for your future, that's okay. Gracefully release them to continue along their own path.

YOUR INNER CIRCLE

Then there is your inner circle. These are the small group of people who are there for the long haul. 'Come hell or high water', they will remain by your side. We sometimes call these 'covenant relationships'. These are the people who stick with you, no matter what. They are with you through every season of life. They tell you the truth, even when it hurts. And they are open to hearing the truth, even when it's uncomfortable for them.

These relationships have a vulnerability, a durability, a level of commitment that is able to weather the storms of life.

This kind of relational allegiance is exemplified by Ruth in the Old Testament. She implores her mother-in-law Naomi:

"Don't urge me to leave you or to turn back from you. Where you go I will go, and where you stay I will stay. Your people will be my people and your God my God. Where you die I will die, and there I will be buried." (Ruth 1: 16-17)

Your inner-circle commitments may not always be expressed as explicitly or verbally as this one. But there will be some understanding on both sides that this person has been placed in my life by God for the long-term. I will not treat this relationship casually or lightly.

The thing is – you usually don't know who these people are going to be in your life. At least, not at first.

Rarely will a 'covenant friend' show up as such. They may start as part of the crowd. Then, over time, you grow closer. There's an unusual bond. A deep affection. A steadfast loyalty. A common purpose. An ease around them. An enjoyment of their company. A growing transparency. A greater openness. An unwavering commitment. After a while, you can't imagine life without them.

147

We see this type of deep, unwavering friendship modelled in the lives of David and Jonathan. Shortly after David defeats Goliath, we read:

"Now when he had finished speaking to Saul, the soul of Jonathan was knit to the soul of David, and Jonathan loved him as his own soul...Then Jonathan and David made a covenant, because he loved him as his own soul." (1 Samuel 18:1, 3)

Don't expect to develop many of these 'covenant' relationships. Outside of the unique marriage bond, you're blessed if you have more than one or two in your lifetime. And please don't be discouraged if you don't have one of these in your life right now. These connections are so special because they are so rare.

I recall hearing Kris Vallotton of Bethel Church describe his relationship with Pastor Bill Johnson in these terms. Even though he could start his own church or ministry, Kris has committed to serve the vision of Bill for the rest of his life. He would lay down his life for Bill, and he knows Bill would do the same for him. Even in Christian ministry, its unusual to hear an expression of devotion like this.

It's significant that Ruth's declaration of devotion happened at a time when everything had been stripped from Naomi's life. Her husband and sons were dead, and her other daughter-in-law, Orpah, had returned to Moab. There was very little to be gained from an attachment to this older widow. Yet, Ruth expressed her loyalty so beautifully and without reserve.

RECOGNIZE THE GIFT

In this last season, so much has been stripped back in your life.
You have experienced loss.
Some relationships have fractured or died.
You have walked through deep valleys of grief.
And often, there has been no one there to hold you.
Maybe, you can't imagine that anyone would ever be drawn to you in covenant relationship.

In this next season, God is going to bring key individuals alongside you who are aligned with your destiny.

You may not initially sense their 'specialness'. So be careful not to write off those who enter your wider circle.

However, over time, you will see that this is not merely another acquaintance.

They are a gift to you from the Father. Value them as such.

When God brings these new alignments into your life, there will be exponential growth and advancement. As Deuteronomy 32: 30 states:

"...one can chase a thousand, and two put ten thousand to flight..."

These new connections will resource you to break through barriers and cross thresholds.

They will strengthen and sustain you in the face of obstacles and opposition.

They will hold up your arms when you are weary and carry your burden when you feel overwhelmed.

Your purpose requires people. You need more than people who simply provide you with company; you need people who help you carry out your calling.

Therefore, look around and see the presence of certain people in your life not as an accident; see them as an expression of God's providence.

God sends them, but you must see them.
God releases them, but you must recognize them.
God assigns them, and you must align them.

PROPHETIC ENCOURAGEMENT

CHOOSE YOUR CLOTHES CAREFULLY.

I heard the LORD say that His people are moving from 'UNDRESSED to RE-DRESSED'.

The undressing happened in this past long season where there was a continual stripping back and pruning in our lives.

There was dismantling and disruption, intense shaking, and relentless warfare.

However, many are still waiting and waiting for the 're-dressing' - for a new, clear sense of direction.

You know what you've taken off and left behind - you've just not entered the next 'putting on' stage.

In a sense, you are left feeling naked, vulnerable, and uncertain about the future.

The Lord is now bringing you into a time of 're-dressing'.

I believe He would say three things:

1. You have a choice about what to put on in this next season.

Your re-dressing isn't set in stone. The garment isn't completed yet. You can be part of the design and creation process.

As you look ahead, there are dreams and desires percolating in your heart. As long as they are God-honoring, pursue them. Put them on. Try them out. See if they fit.

150

2. Don't try to put on the clothes from the past season.

As we enter this new era, don't be tempted to wear what suited you just a few years ago. They won't fit you and they're no longer in style. They're simply not useable.

You need a completely new wardrobe for where you're going.

3. Dress for where you're going, not where you are right now.

Size up. You've grown more than you realize and will continue to grow.

We have an 11-year-old son. We buy him clothes that are too big because he's growing so quickly. They might be a little large now, but he will soon 'grow into' them.

It's the same with you.

You are entering a time of enlargement and expansion.
Don't limit yourself.
Don't shrink down.
Dress for increase.
Dress for promotion.
Dress for greater levels of influence and impact.

Incidentally, when I looked up the definition of 'redress' after I received this word, I discovered it meant:

"to remedy or set right an undesirable or unfair situation".

That is significant. The LORD is going to bring 'redress' for some of you where there has been injustice, unfair treatment, betrayal, lies, or loss.

You will experience His restoration, recompense, and restitution. His justice is perfect.

THIS IS A SEASON FOR 'RE-DRESSING'.

CHOOSE YOUR CLOTHES CAREFULLY.

151

DAY 17

THE BLESSING OF CLOSED DOORS

BIBLE READING

Paul and his companions traveled throughout the region of Phrygia and Galatia, having been kept by the Holy Spirit from preaching the word in the province of Asia.

When they came to the border of Mysia, they tried to enter Bithynia, but the Spirit of Jesus would not allow them to. So they passed by Mysia and went down to Troas.

During the night Paul had a vision of a man of Macedonia standing and begging him, "Come over to Macedonia and help us."

After Paul had seen the vision, we got ready at once to leave for Macedonia, concluding that God had called us to preach the gospel to them.

(Acts 16: 6-10)

DEVOTIONAL

Have you ever stepped out in faith because you believed that God was leading you to do something – but then it didn't work out?

Maybe you were certain that a job or promotion was yours – but someone else got it.

Or perhaps you started a business expecting it to grow and flourish. You put everything into it. But it didn't succeed.

It could be a relationship. You met someone and you were so sure this was 'the one'. You told your family and friends. You were secretly planning your wedding. Then they abruptly broke things off and six months later they were engaged to someone else.

Maybe it was purchasing a house. After searching for months, you eventually find the perfect property. It was the perfect location and within your price range. Then the sale fell through.

You've wasted time and energy.

Emotionally, you're spent.

You're disappointed, frustrated, maybe embarrassed.

And it feels like you're out of options. Where do you turn now?

You were only trying to do the right thing – what you thought God wanted you to do – but it fell apart.

We've all been there at some stage.

WHEN IT LOOKS LIKE GOD HAS OPENED A DOOR

In 2017, during our major transitional year as a family, we were constantly praying that God would open a door for our next stage of ministry. We were on staff at a church we loved, but we knew it was a short-term assignment. God was using this beautiful community as a holding place for us to heal and find fresh direction.

Then it happened. I was made aware that a particular church was seeking a new Senior Pastor.

But this wasn't just any church. It was my dream church.

For over a decade I had been praying that God would make a way for me to pastor this congregation one day. Every time I drove past the building (which was frequently), I would pray, "God, please let me lead that church."

Occasionally, I would even park my car on the church grounds and ask God to open a door for ministry in that place.

So, when the news came through that their pastor was retiring, you can imagine how I felt. It appeared that all my prayers were being answered. Plus, the timing couldn't be more perfect.

I began to openly tell family and friends that this was likely to be our next assignment.

The pastoral search committee contacted me and asked me to consider applying for the role.

Could this be any clearer?

Then something unexpected happened.

As Becky and I began to engage with the long recruitment process, we both felt some unease. It was difficult to pinpoint, but something wasn't right. Call it a gut feeling, intuition, or the leading of the Holy Spirit - but we almost had a sick feeling in our stomachs every time we would meet with the church board.

Finally, after a process that lasted several months, I received a phone call from the church board. They had appointed another candidate.

The door was closed.

I felt a mixture of deep disappointment and intense relief.

Disappointment because of the rejection I felt. My pride and ego were dented. I would have to tell everyone that I didn't get the job. Plus, we were back to square one with nowhere else to go.

But also, I felt relief. Because deep down we knew this wasn't where God wanted us to be. Yet, if I had been offered the role, I would probably have accepted it.

As believers, we love it when God clearly opens a door for us. Those opportunities that come along and there are green lights all the way.

It's so easy. Everything runs so smoothly. It all goes as planned.

Open doors are great.

But what do you do when every door you push is shut?

Or when what looks like an open door closes in your face?

It can be incredibly confusing, discouraging, even heartbreaking.

It's also humiliating if, like me, you told everyone that this was the door that God was opening.

It can even shake your faith, raising all sorts of doubts and questions:

Did I not hear God right?
Did I do something wrong?
Why did God allow this to happen?

GOD OPENS AND SHUTS DOORS

Isaiah 22: 22 says this about God:

"What he opens no one can shut, and what he shuts no one can open."

Our God is a God who opens doors.

But He's also a God who closes them.

And we must learn to trust that closed doors can be as much a sign of His blessing and goodness as open doors.

In Acts 16, Paul and Silas are on what is known as Paul's second missionary journey. Their desire is to preach the Word, reach the lost, and establish churches.

These are good, Godly goals and ambitions. You would assume that God would bless them at every turn. But look at what we read:

"Paul and his companions traveled throughout the region of Phrygia and Galatia, having been kept by the Holy Spirit from preaching the word in the province of Asia." (Acts 16: 6)

They decide to make an evangelistic visit to the province of Asia – modern-day Turkey. Here they can reach new people with the Gospel. But look at what happens. They were *"...kept by the Holy Spirit from preaching the word in the province of Asia."* (Acts 16: 6)

The word *kept* in the original Greek means: *prevented, forbidden, denied, withheld.*

That's frustrating. They change course and make new plans.

Next, they attempt to enter the region of Bithynia. But the same thing happens:

"When they came to the border of Mysia, they tried to enter Bithynia, but the Spirit of Jesus would not allow them to." (v. 7)

Once again, the Holy Spirit wouldn't permit them to go that way.

I could understand it if the enemy hindered them or blocked their advance. This happens elsewhere. For example, in 1 Thessalonians 2: 18:

"For we wanted to come to you – certainly I, Paul, did, again and again – but Satan blocked our way."

At times the enemy will attempt to disrupt our plans by placing obstacles and opposition in our way.

However, there are other situations where we give the devil more credit than he is due. We assume that Satan is opposing us when, in fact, God is holding us back – sometimes even from things that appear good, Godly, and are likely to advance the Kingdom.

That's what happens Paul and Silas.

Notice, in both cases the Bible never explains how the Spirit stopped them.

Was it a strong inward impression?

Or maybe a gut feeling - a deep sense that something wasn't right.

Perhaps it was outward circumstances like illness or opposition from others.

It could have been a clear prophetic word. Silas was recognized as a prophet in the early church (Acts 15: 32).

In considering this, ask yourself: *How has the Holy Spirit stopped me in the past?*

Sometimes He simply doesn't give you inner peace about something. The apprehension might not make sense. On the surface, what you are moving towards appears to be the right thing. But still, you can't shake the unease and feelings of anxiety each time you try to progress.

Other times you keep hitting unusual obstacles and roadblocks. It shouldn't be this difficult. But each time you take a step forward, you encounter another problem.

God might warn you through the advice or wisdom of others. Their experience enables them to see potential pitfalls that you might be missing. Or they have inside knowledge of the situation that you aren't privy to.

157

God will also speak through prophetic words, visions, or dreams. He warns you directly or speaks through someone else.

Whatever way the Holy Spirit works, the message is clear – do not press on with this course of action.

With Paul and his companions, we don't know how God stopped them.

All we are told is that Paul had his own plans. Practically, they made sense. But the Holy Spirit had different plans.

Common sense is important. Especially in a world where it is so uncommon. God gives us wisdom and natural reasoning to weigh options up and make decisions.

But there are times when something might make perfect logical sense - but it's not God's will for you.

It (or they) may look perfect on paper. But the Holy Spirit says 'no'.

WHEN A DOOR CLOSES

So, what do you do when God closes a door?

You slow down, step back, and ask: "God, what are you doing here?"

That's what Paul did?

He didn't get angry with God. He didn't throw a temper tantrum or assume that God had finished with him.

He paused, refocussed, then kept moving.

Paul knew with certainty that his calling was still to preach the Gospel. The specific location wasn't the most important thing.

He also knew God's character. He believed that God was still good, even if He didn't do things the way Paul would have preferred. If God was saying 'no' He must have another plan.

When you find yourself in a similar situation - pause, step back, and ask:

- *What could be the other side of this 'no'?*
- *What does this closed-door open up to me right now?*
- *What is the next best thing I can do?*
- *How can I keep moving forward, even if I'm not sure where God is leading me?*

Remind yourself of God's goodness to you.
Recall His faithfulness in your past.
Remember that He is God, and you are not.

You might pray something like this:

"God, I don't know what's going on here. This is hard. But I am choosing to trust You. I'm not going to take this closed door as rejection – I'm choosing to believe that it's Your protection or your redirection. I believe that You're closing this door because it's not right for me – or it's not right for me at this time. I submit and surrender to Your plans."

What happened with Paul?

"During the night Paul had a vision of a man of Macedonia standing and begging him, 'Come over to Macedonia and help us.' After Paul had seen the vision, we got ready at once to leave for Macedonia, concluding that God had called us to preach the gospel to them." (vv. 8-10)

Paul and Silas keep moving forward until they come to the coastal town of Troas. There's nowhere else for them to go.

So, they pause, seek God, and wait for re-direction.

I've discovered that sometimes God has to slow us before He can turn us.

At major transition points in your life, try not to rush or push things. Step back, seek God, take time out, and listen.

How long did Paul wait?

We aren't told. However, when God did speak, it was clear, supernatural, and unmistakable.

Paul had a dream. A man from Macedonia was begging him for help. So, they immediately get moving.

As a result of two closed doors, the good news of Jesus was preached in Europe for the first time.

THANKING GOD FOR UNANSWERED PRAYERS

In 34 years of following Jesus, I have encountered many closed doors.

I have walked through seasons of disappointment when plans haven't worked out.

I have had dreams that fell apart and desires that were left unfulfilled.

I have been in relationships that were perfect on paper, but the Holy Spirit wouldn't allow me to move forward.

I have watched as most of my friends got married and had kids while I remained single until I met my wife when I was 34.

At times, I have felt contained, hidden, and stuck while watching others advance with relative ease.

I'm not going to pretend it's easy. Rejection, failure, and broken dreams always hurt. It's embarrassing when you feel so sure about something – then it falls apart.

However, I have also come to believe that closed doors are as much a sign of God's closeness and involvement in my life as open doors.

I can see now that if God hadn't closed some doors, I would have wasted years in rooms that I was never supposed to be in.

And I would have missed out on incredible experiences, places, and people that God ordained to be a part of my life.

In our own story, shortly after the door closed for ministry at the church that I had been so sure about, we received a call asking if we'd consider leading a new congregation called HOPE Church that had recently been planted in the area where I grew up.

At first, we politely declined the offer. This wasn't something we desired or imagined for our future.

However, God had other plans. He began to speak very clearly through visions, dreams, input from other trusted leaders, and unusual circumstances. This was the door He was opening.

We are now in our seventh year of leading HOPE Church and have found great favor, friendship, and fruitfulness. We are more sure than ever that God brought us here.

I occasionally drive past the other church that turned me down. And each time I still say a prayer. I thank God that He closed that door and didn't allow us to go somewhere that wasn't His best for us.

PROPHETIC ENCOURAGEMENT

THE WILDERNESS IS NOT YOUR HOME.

Those of you who aren't completely sure who you are anymore - don't be discouraged or dismayed.

It's okay to feel a little insecure, uncertain, and vulnerable right now.

You have been through a deliverance much greater than you realize.

God has been intentionally dismantling, removing, stripping back, and pruning those things (and people) in your life that aren't compatible with your next season. You can't take them with you.

161

Transition and transformation always go together.

But in the 'messy middle' it's hard to find anything to hold on to.
Little seems clear. It's hard to discern direction.

You know who you're not. You're just not completely sure who you are.

You're no longer sure where you fit.
You feel like a square peg in a round hole.
You want to belong somewhere.

Take heart. You're coming through to the other side.

The LORD is rebuilding you.
He is remantling you.
He is reclothing you.
He is realigning you.
He is re-assigning you.
He is re-appointing you.
He is re-anointing you.

I know it's been too long. But don't stop here. And don't look back.

In the wilderness, even Egypt looked attractive. But the promised land was already theirs, if they would only keep going.

Manna is okay. But there is milk and honey on the other side.

I know you can't see it yet – but what lies before you is so much better than anything you have left behind.

God is with you.
God is for you.
You will cross over.
You will occupy the land.
You will receive your inheritance.
You will have rest from warfare.
You will see His abundant provision.

You will walk in His promises.

It's taken longer than you expected. But you are still a possessor of every promise.
The in-between is not your habitation.
Temporary is not your permanent situation.

THE WILDERNESS IS NOT YOUR HOME.

DAY 18

WHEN GOD GOES QUIET

BIBLE READING

The boy Samuel ministered before the Lord under Eli. In those days the word of the Lord was rare; there were not many visions.
One night Eli, whose eyes were becoming so weak that he could barely see, was lying down in his usual place. The lamp of God had not yet gone out, and Samuel was lying down in the house of the Lord, where the ark of God was. Then the Lord called Samuel.
Samuel answered, "Here I am." And he ran to Eli and said, "Here I am; you called me."
But Eli said, "I did not call; go back and lie down." So he went and lay down…
…A third time the Lord called, "Samuel!" And Samuel got up and went to Eli and said, "Here I am; you called me."
Then Eli realized that the Lord was calling the boy. So Eli told Samuel, "Go and lie down, and if he calls you, say, 'Speak, Lord, for your servant is listening.'" So Samuel went and lay down in his place.
The Lord came and stood there, calling as at the other times, "Samuel! Samuel!"
Then Samuel said, "Speak, for your servant is listening."
And the Lord said to Samuel: "See, I am about to do something in Israel that will make the ears of everyone who hears about it tingle."

(1 Samuel 1: 1-11)

DEVOTIONAL

I'd love to tell you that I always hear God speak with clarity and precision. But that's simply not true. I go through periods where I struggle to discern what He is saying. I pray and press in and listen – but it feels as if God's gone quiet. It's both disconcerting and frustrating.

Sometimes I fear that I've done something wrong. Maybe God has finally had enough of my weaknesses, flaws, and failings. So, I confess every sin I might possibly have committed. Yet, nothing changes. Heaven still seems silent.

Then - maybe a few days, or a week, or a month later – something shifts.

Sometimes suddenly. Other times, slowly.

But I can hear Him clearly once again.

It's as if a wall has come down or my spiritual ears have been unblocked.

He starts speaking through words, pictures, dreams, Scripture, songs, movies, and conversations. I love those times. There's nothing better than communing with my Creator.

A THRESHOLD MOMENT

At the beginning of 1 Samuel 3, it seems that Israel was going through a 'quiet season' with God:

"In those days the word of the Lord was rare; there were not many visions." (v. 1)

At this stage God's people were living in the Promised Land but, but spiritually they were at a very low ebb. They were stuck in a continual cycle of sin, defeat, misery, repentance, and deliverance. Sadly, it's a destructive cycle that many believers know all too well.

Eli is acting as both a priest and a judge in the nation. However, he's getting old and losing his edge. His sons and supposed successors were corrupt and immoral. Things look hopeless for Israel. It's difficult to see how the moral and spiritual decline can be reversed.

However, unbeknownst to everyone (except God) a major shift is about to take place. God's people are about to transition into a completely new era. God is about to bring a great turnaround.

The parallels with the church in the 21st century are obvious.

For decades, much of the modern church has gradually lost its way. Increasingly, we have become indistinguishable from the world around us. We have compromised our convictions and watered down our message. Many of our leaders have 'fallen' into sin and immorality. Spiritually, the nations are at a low point. It's difficult to see many signs of hope.

But God always has a redemptive plan. A turning is coming. A shift is stirring.

POSITIONED TO HEAR GOD

As I've already mentioned, at this threshold of change, God has gone quiet. The word of the LORD was rare. Few are hearing His voice or seeing prophetic visions.

But then, the silence is broken:

"Then the Lord called Samuel." (v. 4)

It happens in the middle of the night. A boy called Samuel, an apprentice to Eli, is lying down in the tabernacle. Only a curtain separates him from the holy of holies, where the Ark of the Covenant was kept.

In other words, **Samuel had positioned himself as close to the presence of God as possible.**

We cannot force God to speak. But we can choose to posture ourselves in places where we are most likely to hear His voice.

How do you do that?

You can be intentional about getting around individuals who are gifted in discerning the voice of the LORD.

You can visit churches and gatherings that are known to have a strong prophetic anointing.

You can watch prophetic leaders on YouTube and follow them on social media.

That's what I do. Particularly in seasons where I'm struggling to hear God's voice for myself.

I try to get around those who are hearing Him. I tune into established prophetic voices that I respect. I watch their YouTube broadcasts. I attend their gatherings. I join their online mentorship groups. I read their books. I sow into their ministries.

It's amazing how proximity (in-person or online) to their anointing can stir something inside me. Often my own prophetic gift begins to flow more freely again.

Currently, I lead a monthly mentoring community called *Prophetic Transitions*. However, I am also a member of two online mentorship groups with seasoned prophets. Being connected to them stirs up the gift of God inside me.

HE TALKS MOST AT THE TURNS

Most of us know the story. Three times God speaks to Samuel. And on each occasion, he runs to old Eli, assuming that it's him who is calling. Eventually, Eli catches onto what's happening:

"Eli told Samuel, "Go and lie down, and if he calls you, say, 'Speak, Lord, for your servant is listening.'" So Samuel went and lay down in his place. The Lord came and stood there, calling as at the other times, "Samuel! Samuel!"
Then Samuel said, "Speak, for your servant is listening."
(1 Samuel 3: 9-10)

Let me share a few insights about how God speaks.

(i)   He wants you to hear Him.

I am so thankful that God didn't speak to Samuel once and then give up. He called the boy four times in total. And He would have kept calling until Samuel discerned the source of the voice.

People often come to me concerned that they have missed God's will for their life. They're afraid that God has spoken but they didn't hear Him, and now they're destined for a life of misery.

Of course, it is possible to go through a season of rebellion and harden your heart against God. You will live with the consequences of your wrong choices.

But, most often, these concerns come from people who genuinely love God and want to do His will.

My response generally goes something like this:

"The fact that you're even asking this question tells me that you've most likely not missed God's will. Your concern shows that you have a deep desire to hear Him and do what He wants. God sees that and loves that about you.
When God wants to reveal something important to you, He will make it clear. If you miss it the first time, He will keep speaking to you until you get it."

Isn't that what we see here?

Four times God speaks to Samuel. **He is more willing to speak than we are to listen.**

(ii)   God speaks in the everyday and ordinary.

Isn't it amazing that each time God spoke, Samuel ran to Eli?

Do you know what that tells me?

God's voice sounded normal and familiar. It wasn't some thunderous, booming sound from heaven. It sounded like the guy next door.

We often make it so difficult for ourselves to hear from God because we expect Him to speak in a dramatic and spectacular manner. And occasionally He does. But mostly, for me, God speaks in very ordinary ways - through a thought, a picture, a song, a Scripture verse, a movie, a book, a billboard, a friend.

Don't miss how God is speaking to you today because it's not dramatic or spectacular. Discern His voice in the mundane routines and the normal flow of life.

(iii)   **God speaks most clearly at times of significant transition.**

That's what we see here in 1 Samuel.

While life continued as normal, the word of the LORD was rare. However, massive change is coming. The nation is about to transition from a loose confederation of tribes led by judges to a fully formed nation ruled by a king.

That was a significant shift!

And so, God begins to speak more clearly and with greater frequency. By the end of the chapter, we read:

"The Lord was with Samuel as he grew up, and he let none of Samuel's words fall to the ground. And all Israel from Dan to Beersheba recognized that Samuel was attested as a prophet of the Lord." (vv. 19-20)

In my own life, I have found that God tends to speak with greater frequency and clarity as I am moving into a time of significant transition and change.

I might already be sensing a shift, and God then brings increasing clarity and confirmation over a period of time.

It's not a perfect analogy, but I think of it like the GPS (or Sat Nav) in my car.

When I am driving on a long, straight road, the GPS tends to be silent.

However, when I am approaching a turn, that's when the GPS begins to communicate. It gives some initial warning a mile or two in advance.

As I get closer to the junction, it gives more and more direction.

When God is relatively silent in a particular season, the best course of action is to keep moving forward and remain faithful where you are. Try to avoid making any drastic changes.

However, when you start to have more prophetic dreams or receive an increasing number of prophetic words, it is often a sign that a turn is coming up. Some sort of change is imminent.

The more major the shift, the more He will clarify and confirm it through other prophetic input, trusted friends, and life's circumstances.

Maybe God has been speaking to you. But, like Samuel, you haven't been able to discern it was Him.

In this pivotal season of global and personal transition, I pray that He would direct your steps and lead you forward with confidence and clarity.

And if He seems silent today, don't despair.

Position yourself in His presence.
Get around others who are hearing His voice.
Discern His voice in the everyday and ordinary.

And get ready for a shift.

This year things are going to move for you. You will not stand still or stay stuck.

It is starting slowly. But in the next few months you will begin to experience acceleration and advancement.

You will see answered prayers and promises fulfilled.

You will hear His voice.

Things will start to turn.

So, keep persevering and pressing in.

This is a breaking-through year.

PROPHETIC ENCOURAGEMENT

YOU HAVEN'T MISSED IT. THE LORD HASN'T PASSED YOU BY.

I know you might feel invisible right now.
Overlooked and undervalued.
Unnoticed and unappreciated.
Isolated and lonely.

At times, it has felt that everyone is advancing while you're being left behind. Or that you have become stuck in a rut.

They have all the favor, while you seemed forgotten.

Know this - the LORD has you on a unique schedule and timetable perfectly timed to position you for His purposes.

It is unique and bespoke to your individual personality and destiny.

You might have been through pain, rejection, even betrayal by those you trusted.

You were seen as 'too intense' by some. But the LORD could see the passion and purity in your heart.

Be assured - no one who left your life is necessary for your future. None of what's happened will be wasted.

The Lord has been digging deep foundations so He can build something strong and enduring.

Any pressing or crushing has only served to produce fresh, pure oil.

You don't have to rush, push, or force things.

Simply stay faithful with what He's placed in front of you. Little things are big to God.

God is calling His sons and daughters in from the outside.

Those who have been forged in the wilderness are being drawn in from the sidelines.

The war-wounded are being healed and called back into battle.

The weary in waiting are receiving sustaining strength.

Those who have been hidden are being strategically positioned into place.

His hand is upon you.
Clarity is coming.
Doors are opening.
New assignments are being released.
You will be fruitful and flourish.

YOU HAVEN'T MISSED IT. THE LORD HASN'T PASSED YOU BY.

DAY 19

WHY DOES GOD LEAD YOU INTO TRANSITION?

BIBLE READING

When I was a child, I spoke and thought and reasoned as a child. But when I grew up, I put away childish things.

(1 Corinthians 13: 11)

Again, it will be like a man going on a journey, who called his servants and entrusted his wealth to them. To one he gave five bags of gold, to another two bags, and to another one bag, each according to his ability. Then he went on his journey. The man who had received five bags of gold went at once and put his money to work and gained five bags more. So also, the one with two bags of gold gained two more. But the man who had received one bag went off, dug a hole in the ground and hid his master's money.

After a long time the master of those servants returned and settled accounts with them.

(Matthew 25: 14-19)

DEVOTIONAL

I love traveling. Let me rephrase that. I love visiting other countries. The traveling part – I'm not so fond of that. Especially when it involves airports. The long check-in line, having my suitcase weighed (knowing that it's almost always too heavy), and then the most dreaded part of all – airport security. It stresses me out. When I finally take a seat in the departure lounge, I always breathe a huge sigh of relief, even though I still haven't even left home soil!

Unless the Holy Spirit miraculously transports me like He did with Philip in Acts 8, traveling is a necessary component of going anywhere different.

I can't visit somewhere new without taking a journey.

Similarly, transition is defined as *"the process of changing from one state, stage, place, or condition to another."*

The key word is **process**.

Transition is not the change itself – it's all the small steps and stages that bring about a change.

It's the journey of how you get from where you are to where you're going. Hence, the first seven letters of the word *transition* are **transit**. You're passing through somewhere or something as you travel towards a destination.

Not every transition in your life is necessarily personal or initiated by God. Sometimes it is simply a result of your environment or decisions that are outside of your control.

But often transition is internal. It's directly related to what God is doing in your life. It's what's going on inside you.

It's the emotional, spiritual, relational, and psychological journey you take when change is happening.

Transition is when you ask questions like:

- *What is God doing in my life?*
- *Where do I sense change?*
- *How do I feel about it?*
- *What do I need to do?*
- *Where do I need to be?*
- *Who do I need to align with?*

In these unusual times we are living through, many of us will experience significantly more transitions than in the past. We must become comfortable with the in-between. Understanding the reasons behind transition will help us journey through it.

So, why does God lead you through transition?

1. YOU ARE ENTERING A NEW SEASON OF LIFE.

Transition is like a fifth season or a season between seasons. In April, it's often too warm to wear a winter coat, yet too cold to go outside wearing only a sweater. It's difficult to choose what clothes to wear.

Similarly, when you're walking through a transition, you're living in the in-between. **You're not where you used to be, but you haven't arrived at where you're going.** It feels like you're in limbo.

However, just as you can't enter the fullness of the summer season without passing through that late spring stage, so also **God can't bring you into a new season without first taking you through transition** - a period when you'll often feel uncertain, disorientated, and unsure of your next steps.

If that's your experience today, be assured that it's temporary. Just as spring inevitably turns to summer, so you also will pass through transition into a new season.

2. YOU HAVE MORE CAPACITY THAN YOU ARE CURRENTLY USING.

In Matthew 25, Jesus told a parable about a master giving three servants different amounts of wealth to steward and invest. The amount they each received was according to their capacity to produce a return.

Transition sometimes happens when you're a five-talent person living a two-talent life. God knows your capacity and He wants to get out everything he has placed inside you.

Maybe in the past few years you've grown and developed. You've been through a process of preparation and maturing. But in your current place and space, there simply aren't the opportunities or openings for you to express your gifts, talents, abilities, and wisdom. If you remain there too long, you'll stagnate and even begin to spiritually suffocate. Or you'll settle for less than God has intended for you.

To use David as an analogy - on the inside, you're a giant-killing king, but you've never stepped outside of the sheepfold.

Transition is designed to bring you into a wider space where you can fully engage your capacity.

3. YOUR ASSIGNMENT IS FINISHED.

God called you to a particular work. That work is now complete. So, He's opening up a new assignment for you.

When your assignment is complete you usually reach the stage where your work/ministry etc. has become boring and predictable. You've done everything you can do in this place and now you're in maintenance mode, going through the motions to keep things ticking over.

You no longer feel challenged or stretched. Your days become dreary. You have little enthusiasm for what you're doing.

You have no vision for the role. It's hard to see any potential there. You've hit a ceiling. It begins to affect other areas of your life. You begin to lose your passion and spark.

That's why God is leading you into transition. He has a new assignment prepared that will ignite a fresh passion in you.

4. YOU HAVE STOPPED GROWING.

This is related to the previous two points. All healthy, living things are designed to grow – physically, mentally, emotionally, and spiritually.

However, when you plateau in some area of your life, you stop growing. You flatline and then begin to stagnate.

Your life becomes too comfortable and predictable.

You may even become a little depressed. Because you need a challenge. You long for excitement.

The danger is that you begin to look for stimulation or a sense of thrill in the wrong places.

Deep down you know that God has more for you.

Transition is the entranceway to a new season of growth and expansion.

5. GOD WANTS TO REVEAL HIMSELF TO YOU IN NEW WAYS.

This is often the case when God transitions you from one spiritual environment to another.

In your current environment, you've experienced everything of God and the life of faith that they have the capacity to express.

For example, you may have been part of a solid evangelical church with strong Bible teaching. That's fantastic. But God also wants to expose you to a deeper relationship with the Holy Spirit. However, your current church simply doesn't have a paradigm for that. Something is being quenched inside you.

God transitions you into a new environment where there is a much greater openness to things of the Spirit. You begin to encounter Him in new ways. It can almost feel as if you've been born again - again.

6. YOUR CURRENT ENVIRONMENT HAS BECOME TOO LIMITING OR RESTRICTIVE.

Not long ago, my friend, Australian prophet Vicki Simpson, sent me this message:

"I had a dream of you the other night. You were trying to take your jacket off because it was uncomfortable. You didn't want to wear it anymore and it was quite tight. You were struggling to get it off. And you were getting frustrated and angry with it. And wrestling with this dumb jacket. You finally got it off!"

I immediately knew the dream was referring to some aspects of my ministry which I had been wrestling with for some time.

As you read this dream, I wonder if you can relate to that feeling.

Something that used to fit you well, now just seems too tight. You feel as if you can't be yourself in a certain environment, role, or with particular people. The jacket (or whatever it represents) hasn't changed – but you have.

I think this can also refer to new spiritual mantles.

When Elijah was taken to heaven, his mantle was picked up by Elisha. This initiated a new phase of ministry for the younger prophet.

Some of your old 'coats' or 'mantles' have expired. They were God's anointing for a specific assignment or purpose in a previous season. But now He wants to re-mantle you for what lies ahead. Picking up the new requires being willing to release the old.

7. YOUR CURRENT PLACE/POSITION/RELATIONSHIP WAS NEVER SUPPOSED TO BE PERMANENT.

God brought you there for a reason and a season. But now that season is over. The danger is that you settle and stay too long. You allow a temporary stop-over has become a permanent habitation.

In Genesis 11 we read:

"One day Terah took his son Abram...and moved away from Ur of the Chaldeans. He was headed for the land of Canaan, but they stopped at Haran and settled there. Terah lived for 205 years and died while still in Haran."

Terah was called to Canaan, but instead, he settled in Haran and died there. He stopped short of his destiny and finished up in the wrong place.

I have watched many people with great callings and dreams from God get settled and stuck in a place where they were only meant to stay for a limited time. They become too comfortable. They struggled with fear of the unknown. Disappointments and hurts from the past kept them from pioneering and taking new risks.

In Deuteronomy 1: 6-7, God tells Moses:

"You have stayed at this mountain long enough. It is time to break camp and move on."

That's a word for some of you today. You've been here long enough. It's time to move on.

8. IT ISN'T THE RIGHT FIT.

Maybe the place or role was once perfect for you. But you have changed - or it has changed - and it just isn't working like it used to.

Or perhaps it was never a great fit, but you stuck around hoping something would change. It hasn't, and at this point, it's unlikely that anything is going to shift.

You've begun to feel like a square peg in a round hole.

Don't change your shape to fit in the wrong place.

Allow God to transition you to a place or role where you don't feel the constant pressure to squeeze into a mold not made for you.

9. YOUR CURRENT PLACE/POSITION HAS BECOME DAMAGING OR HARMFUL.

Sadly, not everything that starts well, ends well.

When Jacob and his eleven sons moved to Egypt during a famine, they initially experienced great favor and honor. However, years later, a new Pharaoh who knew nothing about Joseph began to severely mistreat the Hebrews. Therefore, God called Moses to deliver His people from this oppressive and abusive environment.

Sometimes God transitions you because something has changed in your environment. A place that was once safe and welcoming has become toxic and destructive.

A relationship has become abusive.
A boss demeans and mistreats you.
A job has become too isolating.
A church or ministry has become controlling.

To remain there will be damaging or detrimental to your well-being.

Of course, I'm not talking about leaving just because something is difficult. Everywhere has challenges and bad days. I'm referring to when it has become harmful or detrimental to your physical or emotional health to remain there.

Move on. Do whatever you need to do. You must protect yourself and those under your care.

10. IT'S JUST TIME TO CHANGE

Again, Ecclesiastes 3: 1 tells us that *"there is a time for every activity under heaven."*

Maybe God is saying to you: "Your time here is up." And you can't change God's timing.

This most likely doesn't mean that you immediately resign and walk away.

But you can start to plan and prepare for your exit.

Quietly pack your bags as you determine to leave as well and honorably as you can.

As you reflect on your personal journey, can you relate to any of the above points? Do you see God's sovereign hand in your own significant transitions?

What about today? Do any of the above apply to your current situation? If so, take some time and bring it before God in prayer.

Here are some questions you might ask Him:

- *What are you doing in my life right now?*

- *Am I entering a new season?*

- *Why do I feel so much discomfort or boredom in my current environment?*

- *Have I stopped growing and being stretched in this place?*

- *Is there much more inside me that I'm unable to express in this place/role?*

- *Do I constantly feel contained and stifled?*
- *Where are you leading me?*

181

- *What is the next step I should take?*

You could be in the middle of a transition but, until now, you haven't realized it.

If you discover that you're in between two seasons, here's my advice: **Start to dress for the season you're entering, not the one you're leaving behind.**

PROPHETIC ENCOURAGEMENT

YOU HAVE BEEN IN A LONG LABOR.

It feels as if you've been pushing and pushing - but nothing is happening.
Life has been so slow and arduous.
Prayers appear unanswered and promises have been delayed.
You're weary. Confused. Uncertain. Close to giving up.

Yet, you know that something inside you needs to be birthed!
You sense it in your spirit.
You are pregnant with a word from God.
You're carrying a weighty promise.
You're 'expecting' the fulfillment of a prophetic word.
The enemy has tried to abort it - but you have protected it.

Through it all, you have been stretched to your limits.
The LORD has been growing your capacity to carry His purpose.
He's been enlarging your ability to steward His gift.
You don't know exactly what it looks like, but you know it's there.
It's been growing, gestating, forming, developing, taking shape inside you.

At times you wondered if all of this was leading anywhere.
The weariness and waiting. The delay and discouragement.
You kept expecting change, but nothing shifted.
You felt so close, only to experience emptiness.

But now, the shift has come. The waters have broken.
Your new life is beginning to emerge.
The present discomfort is simply the final contractions - the transition point.
It won't be long now. Your due date is here.

In this delivery season:
PUSH! Against any doubts and fears...
PUSH! Against any weariness and pain...
PUSH! Against any frustrations and delays...
PUSH! Against any disappointments and discouragement...
PUSH! Against any opposition and critics...
PUSH, PUSH, PUSH!

When you see the life that emerges, you will know that this last season wasn't in vain.

YOU HAVE BEEN IN A LONG LABOR.
NOW BRING IT TO BIRTH.

DAY 20

CREATED TO HEAR GOD'S VOICE

BIBLE READING

"But the LORD God called to the man and said to him, "Where are you?"

(Genesis 3:9)

"Very truly I tell you Pharisees, anyone who does not enter the sheep pen by the gate, but climbs in by some other way, is a thief and a robber. The one who enters by the gate is the shepherd of the sheep. The gatekeeper opens the gate for him, and the sheep listen to his voice. He calls his own sheep by name and leads them out. When he has brought out all his own, he goes on ahead of them, and his sheep follow him because they know his voice. But they will never follow a stranger; in fact, they will run away from him because they do not recognize a stranger's voice." Jesus used this figure of speech, but the Pharisees did not understand what he was telling them.

Therefore Jesus said again, "Very truly I tell you, I am the gate for the sheep. All who have come before me are thieves and robbers, but the sheep have not listened to them…The thief comes only to steal and kill and destroy; I have come that they may have life, and have it to the full.

(John 10: 1-10)

DEVOTIONAL

Recently, I had a mini epiphany: **Adam and Eve never struggled to hear God's voice.**

They never had difficulty in discerning His will.

It wasn't mystical, spooky, or even spiritual.

It was completely natural and normal.

They were made for communion with their Creator.

To speak with Him. To listen to Him. To enjoy life in His presence.

Maybe that is obvious to you. But it was a revelation for me.

Hearing God is humanity's default setting.

You were created to hear God speak.

I'm aware that The Fall changed things.

Our first parents sinned and hid from God. They were banished from The Garden.

The intimate, beautiful bond between the Creator and the created was broken.

A barrier was wedged between God and those formed in His image and likeness.

Our distance brought dullness of hearing.

But God never stopped speaking. Through prophets, the Law, angels, dreams, miracles, a burning bush, and even a donkey.

185

Even the chasm of our sin didn't stop Him from communicating with His beloved creation in every way possible.

He missed our company.

He longed to have His kids come home.

He wanted us restored to our privileged position.

The greatest expression of God's desire to cross the divide and reunite with humans was in sending His only Son, Jesus.

Here's the best news of all: **everything that was broken and undone by the fall has been restored and reconciled through Jesus Christ.**

The cross and resurrection reversed the curse.

We are no longer excluded from the presence of God. There is no distance between us. The gulf is gone. The chasm has been crossed. We have been brought close to Him:

*"But now in Christ Jesus you who once were far away have been **brought near** by the blood of Christ."* (Ephesians 2: 13)

As a blood-bought child of God, it should be as natural to hear God speak as it is to hear the voice of your best friend.

You have been chosen and adopted as His child (Ephesians 1: 4-5).

And what parent doesn't speak to their kids?

We make hearing God's voice so much more difficult than it needs to be.

He is always speaking.

The thoughts that He has about you outnumber the grains of sand (Psalm 139: 18).

And He wants to share those thoughts with you. He wants you to know what He's thinking about. He desires that you would hear His voice with greater clarity and frequency.

Jesus himself made this abundantly clear. In describing himself as *the Good Shepherd*, he says:

"The sheep hear his voice, and he calls his own sheep by name and leads them out. When he has brought out all his own, he goes before them, and the sheep follow him, for they know his voice." (John 10: 3-4)

The sheep *hear* his voice.

The sheep *know* his voice.

The sheep *obey* his voice.

Jesus is saying that it is the birthright of every believer to hear and understand the voice of God.

No exceptions. No exclusions.

If you are a Christian, born again by the Spirit, you can hear God's voice.

It is not so much a matter of giftedness as it is of relationship.

The question isn't: *Can I hear God's voice?*

It has become: *How is God speaking to me?*

HOW DO YOU HEAR GOD'S VOICE?

I talk to my son Elijah differently to how I speak to anyone else.

Of course, I still mostly use words and sentences.

But we have a unique connection, a special bond, that is the foundation for how we communicate with each other.

It's the same with you and God.

He is your Father. You are His son or daughter.

You are not exactly like any other human on the planet.

Therefore, how you hear from God and how you share His heart with others will not be like anyone else.

It will be specifically tailored to your personality.

There are four primary ways that people tend to receive prophetic revelation: *knowing, hearing, feeling, and seeing.*

Let's briefly explore each of them.

(i)   KNOWERS

Knowers just 'know' in their mind or 'gut' that something is true and right.

They are highly intuitive and perceptive. They can't really explain how they 'know' - they just do.

Knowers will frequently have 'a-ha' or lightbulb moments when something just clicks or suddenly becomes clear. They have a deep conviction about how something will turn out. And they're usually right.

In Matthew 9: 4, we read:

*"But Jesus, **knowing their thoughts**, said, "Why do you think evil in your hearts?"*

The word *knowing* here means "perceiving". Jesus perceived their thoughts. He had a supernatural intuition.

In February 2020, just before COVID, I was the guest preacher at a church that is located around two hours from where we live. This was my first visit and the only people I knew were the Senior Pastor and his wife.

Following the evening service, I was briefly introduced to another couple who were part of the church.

Immediately I just *knew* that this couple would play a key role in leading this church into the future.

I can't explain how I *knew*. I didn't hear God's voice or see a vision. But as I looked at them, an unshakable conviction rose up inside me.

Without getting too specific, I prophetically declared that God was moving them into a greater leadership role.

Not long after that the husband was offered a part-time position on staff at the church. He gradually took on increased responsibility until, in 2023, he became the Senior Pastor.

(ii)   HEARERS

Hearers tend to 'hear' God speak in words, phrases, and sentences. Very rarely will this be audible. Most often, it will be an inner, inaudible voice, sometimes described as the "still small voice of God".

There are many examples of Hearers in the Bible. The most obvious is Samuel who heard the voice of God so clearly that he assumed Eli was speaking to him:

"Then the LORD called Samuel.

Samuel answered, "Here I am." And he ran to Eli and said, "Here I am; you called me." (1 Samuel 3: 4-5)

As a hearer goes about their day, God's distinct voice will often interrupt their thoughts. Over time, they learn to distinguish these God-inspired thoughts from their own thoughts. They develop the ability to dialogue with the Holy Spirit.

Sometimes these words and phrases are personal. Other times they for someone else and require courage on the part of the hearer to share them.

Hearers use phrases like, *"I heard God say..."* or *"God told me...".* The message tends to be clear and without much need for interpretation.

This is the most common way that God speaks to me. Most of the words I share through *Daily Prophetic* begin with God speaking a word or phrase.

Hearers often keep journals to record the revelation they receive. In my own private devotions, I often sit with a notebook or journal and write down any words and phrases that come into my mind.

(iii)   FEELERS

Feelers tend to experience the emotions of God. It is as if the Father expresses His heart through theirs.

They feel things deeply and are very sensitive to the emotions of other people. Their heightened sensitivity causes them to notice what others don't notice.

Feelers also have unusual sensitivity to their surroundings. When they walk into a physical environment, they can often 'pick up' on what is going on. They find it difficult to explain, but 'feelers' intuitively discern the spiritual atmosphere – positive or negative.

Feelers can't explain why they feel something. They just do. God often interrupts them throughout their day so they can partner with Him. They perceive spiritual nuances that most people miss.

Often, but not always, Feelers also have the gift of intercession.

(iv)   SEERS

Seers tend to be very visual. God communicates with them through mental images, pictures, visions, and dreams. They see *what* is doing and will do, but not necessarily *how*.

Seers often see the world differently – as it could be, not as it is. They tend to be highly expressive individuals who are faith-filled. They dream big and have an eye for the future.

Seers also tend to be very certain when God has shown them something and will act on it without a lot of hesitation or deliberation.

In 2017, when we were initially asked to lead HOPE Church, we politely declined. It wasn't somewhere we had envisioned as being part of our future.

However, God had other ideas.

Within a few weeks of declining the invitation from HOPE, something in our hearts began to shift. Perhaps we needed to be more open to the possibility. Still, this inner stirring wasn't enough to convince us to change our minds.

Around the same time, my wife, Becky, kept sharing pictures and dreams she was having in which she would see a large white house with a treehouse in the garden.

Becky has a lot of pictures and dreams. So, initially, I didn't give these a lot of attention.

A few weeks later, a couple I knew from my high school days posted on Facebook that they were moving to New Zealand for one year and that their house would be available to rent. This house was 1 mile from HOPE Church.

Guess what color it was? White.

And what was in the garden? A huge treehouse.

Within two months we had moved into their property and began leading the church.

There are many examples of Seers in the Bible. Joseph had dreamed of a future when his parents and brother would bow down to him. Jacob dreamed of a ladder stretching into heaven. And the entire book of Revelation is a vision the Apostle John received from the Lord.

Do any of the above forms of hearing from God especially resonate with you?

Of course, you might hear God in a number of different ways. **Most people are a combination of two or three of the above.**

191

However, you will probably find that there is one dominant way that God most frequently speaks to you.

Develop that area. Give it your attention. Grow in your discernment of His voice.

And take risks in sharing what you see, sense, hear, and feel.

AMID THE NOISE, GOD IS SPEAKING

It is interesting to note that all of the major prophetic books in the Bible were written during times of crisis and upheaval for God's people.

Our Old Testament books of Isaiah, Jeremiah, Ezekiel, Daniel, etc. show us that God is not inattentive or unconcerned about what is going on in our lives and our world.

In fact, **in seasons of turbulence and disruption, God communicates with greater clarity and frequency.**

He shows His people the way forward through the mayhem and confusion.

His voice reminds them of their true identity and points them toward their destiny.

Like the prophets of old, we too are living in tense and tumultuous days.

Everything is shifting and the future feels increasingly uncertain and unpredictable.

Amid all the other voices competing for our attention, God's people must be very intentional about discerning what the Father is speaking at the beginning of this new era.

That is the only way we will find security and stability in a world that is being shaken and reshaped in ways unimaginable just a few years ago.

Today, God wants to speak *to* you and *through* you.

He is not simply looking for a voice – He wants to speak through *your* voice.

Prepare to receive downloads from Heaven of wisdom and revelation for this hour.

Anticipate that you will hear the Father's voice with increased clarity and frequency than ever before.

Open your mouth and speak.

Mountains will move.

Dead things will come to life.

Barrenness will be broken.

Darkness will be illuminated.

Diseases will be healed.

Captives will be set free.

The Word of the Lord is inside you. Let it out.

PROPHETIC ENCOURAGEMENT

I AM REMOVING THE STING OF THE LAST SEASON.

I see Jesus tenderly pulling sharp thorns out of people's skin.

Some of them are lodged deep.
Others are shallow.
Some are large. Others are not so big.

But Jesus is removing every one of them with great intentionality and gentleness.

The thorns represent the wounds you have picked up in this past season. Not necessarily the big losses and hurts that cause others to notice your pain.

Rather, each thorn represents:

the small disappointments,
the unnoticed rejections,
the weariness of waiting,
the unanswered prayers,
the spiritual battles,
the secret struggles,
the broken promises,
the lack of appreciation,
the feeling that nobody really cares,
the frustration and boredom,
the words that cut you,
the shame of failure,
the pain of regret,
the loss of innocence,
the plans didn't work out,
the diminishing of dreams.

As each thorn is extracted, there is a moment of pain.

Then Jesus reaches out again and touches the little red wound that remains.

He holds his hand there for a moment.

When he lifts it, the wound has completely disappeared.

Some people have only one or two thorns.

Others, it appears, are covered in them.

That doesn't matter to Jesus.

He takes his time to carefully and purposely remove every single thorn and heal every individual wound.

I then see Him look at each person with eyes full of such love, grace, tenderness, and compassion.

He says the words:

"You are free. Now that I have healed your wounds, go and heal the wounds of others."

As each person turns around and walks away, they are filled with a profound sense of freedom and peace and lightness and gratitude and joy.

They can't remember the last time they felt so free. So loved. So known. So whole.

They go out to every place and space to start lovingly removing the thorns and healing the wounds that others have been carrying.

Today, experience His grace and healing.

I AM REMOVING THE STING OF THE LAST SEASON.

DAY 21

DON'T GIVE YOUR BEST ENERGY TO THE WRONG PEOPLE

BIBLE READING

When word came to Sanballat, Tobiah, Geshem the Arab and the rest of our enemies that I had rebuilt the wall and not a gap was left in it - though up to that time I had not set the doors in the gates - Sanballat and Geshem sent me this message: "Come, let us meet together in one of the villages on the plain of Ono."

But they were scheming to harm me; so I sent messengers to them with this reply: "I am carrying on a great project and cannot go down. Why should the work stop while I leave it and go down to you?" Four times they sent me the same message, and each time I gave them the same answer.

Then, the fifth time, Sanballat sent his aide to me with the same message, and in his hand was an unsealed letter in which was written:
"It is reported among the nations - and Geshem says it is true - that you and the Jews are plotting to revolt, and therefore you are building the wall. Moreover, according to these reports you are about to become their king and have even appointed prophets to make this proclamation about you in Jerusalem: 'There is a king in Judah!' Now this report will get back to the king; so come, let us meet together."

I sent him this reply: "Nothing like what you are saying is happening; you are just making it up out of your head."
They were all trying to frighten us, thinking, "Their hands will get too weak for the work, and it will not be completed."
But I prayed, "Now strengthen my hands."

(Nehemiah 6: 1-9)

196

DEVOTIONAL

"You will never be criticized by someone doing more than you."

I'm not sure where I first heard that quote, but I have consistently found it to be true.

When you obediently live out God's calling on your life and seek to make a real difference in the world, it will always arouse the critics.

Some might be people you know, even close family and friends.

But today, many of them will be 'keyboard junkies' or 'heresy hunters' who spend their days scouring social media for someone with whom they can find fault.

It's sad. But it's true. The haters you will always have with you.

And it's hard not to take it personally. Because criticism stings your soul. Even if you know it's unfounded or if you don't even know the person behind it.

Criticism can shake you.

It causes you to doubt yourself, your abilities, and your motives.

It can even make you shrink back, hide, and live below God's calling so you don't draw attention to yourself.

I know from experience. I've got the receipts. I could show you the emails I've received through the years – most of them anonymous – attacking my ministry and my character.

I have also received hundreds of positive emails and encouraging comments.

But the ones that stick in my mind are those that pointed out where I was deficient or failed in some way.

It's funny that, isn't it?

I recall one particularly nasty email. It was three pages long (I printed it out). Its sender was a female seminary student who didn't like a sermon I preached at a Christmas carol service that took place in a prison.

My crime?

I told the inmates that we are all sinners, but no matter what we have done, Jesus came to save us and make us new. Buy we must repent and bring our sin to the cross.

She started by meticulously tearing my sermon apart - how dare I make those men behind bars feel worse about themselves!

Then she moved onto assassinating my character and every aspect of my ministry.

Every sentence pierced my heart. It sent me into a mild depression for days.

Did I mention that this happened over a decade ago? Or that I had never met the sender before this incident? Or that I have never heard of her since?

Yet, I remember those words and how they affected me.

It's ridiculous, I know. And I've definitely become better at not letting these types of criticisms bother me so much. I've had to. But they still sting.

It comes with the territory. As Aristotle said,

"There is only one way to avoid criticism: do nothing, say nothing, and be nothing."

Of course, there are times when I need correction. We all do. It would be the height of arrogance to assume that no one can ever point out some area of our lives where we've messed up or have a blind spot.

But there is a difference between correction and criticism.

Correction seeks to make you better. It comes from a place of genuine care and concern for your well-being.

Criticism seeks to make you miserable. It rarely comes from a loving place.

Back to the quote at the beginning.

Criticism rarely comes from above – from someone doing more than you. It usually comes from spectators who sit on the sidelines and never step into the game.

The people who are making a real difference in the world are too busy getting on with their calling and assignment to waste their time looking around at what everyone else is doing.

Think about your own critics. You'll realize it's true.

BROKEN WALLS AND A BROKEN HEART

In 446 BC, the walls of Jerusalem had been lying in ruins for over a century. A city without walls was vulnerable and defenseless to enemies. It was a shameful and pitiful sight.

Yet, in all that time, no one thought to do anything. Everyone saw the problem but chose to ignore it.

However, when Nehemiah heard about their situation, he was profoundly impacted:

"When I heard these things, I sat down and wept. For some days I mourned and fasted and prayed before the God of heaven." (Nehemiah 1: 4)

But Nehemiah did more than shed a few tears. He moved beyond prayer and fasting. He took massive effort to repair the walls.

It's one thing to get emotional when something isn't how it should be. It's important to talk and pray about it.

199

But sadly, that's where most people stop.

Even with most well-meaning believers. Only a tiny percentage are willing to roll up their sleeves and take responsibility for making things different.

Nehemiah was such a man of action.

He gathered resources, mobilized workers, and set about the momentous task of rebuilding the walls.

THE OPPOSITION ARISES

Before a brick was even laid, the criticism began. The opposition was aroused:

"Sanballat the Horonite and Tobiah the Ammonite official…were very much disturbed that someone had come to promote the welfare of the Israelites." (Nehemiah 2: 10)

These two career politicians were enraged that someone would seek to change the status quo.

A weak Jerusalem promoted their personal interests. So they began a concerted campaign of discrediting Nehemiah and all associated with him.

It started subtle with words of ridicule and mocking. But when that failed, they increasingly became more forceful.

That's how it usually happens. There is a progression:

Subtle negativity.
Underhand comments.
Innuendo and accusation.
Gossip and gathering allies.
Thinly veiled threats.
Outright attacks.

Nehemiah was undaunted. He simply kept working. But as the walls neared completion, his critics became desperate. They co-ordinated a plan to get rid of him, to cancel him once and for all:

"...Sanballat and Geshem sent me this message: "Come, let us meet together in one of the villages on the plain of Ono." (v. 2)

That all sounds very reasonable and harmless, doesn't it.

Why don't we just sit down, see can we iron things out.

Let's just have a chat.

Talk it through.

Maybe we can come to a compromise.

Get rid of all this hostility.

Where they wanted to hold this meeting is fascinating. It was exactly halfway between Jerusalem where Nehemiah lived and Samariah where Sanballat governed.

Why don't we meet halfway? Let's find some middle ground.

Why don't we all just compromise? Some give and take.

And there are many times when the right course of action is to it down and talk things through.

But this isn't one of those occasions.

How do I know that?

Because I look at Sanballat's history. And everything about him reveals that he can't be trusted. Every previous encounter and experience with this man shows that his only goal is oppose and destroy the work of God.

(Incidentally, even the name of the place where he wants to meet should raise red flags - *Ono*. Does that sound inviting? Oh no!)

So, while his words might sound harmless and appealing – let's just have a talk – his actions show that that is not where his heart is at.

I would say the same to you: **look at their history.**

Is this person for you?
Have they shown that they can be trusted?

Or has every interaction you've ever had with them shown that they're not someone you want to be around?

DON'T GIVE IN

Look at Nehemiah's response:

"But they were scheming to harm me; so I sent messengers to them with this reply: "I am carrying on a great project and cannot go down. Why should the work stop while I leave it and go down to you?" Four times they sent me the same message, and each time I gave them the same answer." (vv. 2-4)

He sees through their plots and plans.

He knows their intent is always the same – to harm and to hurt.

He's not naive or stupid.

To meet with them would mean traveling a full day to get there and a full day to return. And the likelihood is that he would never come back. He would disappear and Sanballat would say: "I don't know what happened to him, he never showed up for the meeting."

The enemy knows that if he can destroy the leader, he can discourage all the people and destroy the entire project.

KEEP YOUR FOCUS

Read Nehemiah's response again:

"I am carrying on a great project and cannot go down. Why should the work stop while I leave it and go down to you?"

I love that.

It might sound somewhat arrogant and boastful.

But it's not.

It's confidence in knowing that **any work for God is a great work. Because the work is being done for a great God.**

Any work that honors and glorifies God is a great work. There is a significance and an importance attached to it.

It might not always be highly visible or nation changing. But when you fulfil God's calling on your life, it is a great work.

So, Nehemiah says: "No. I'm not stopping this great work to go down to you. That would be a waste of my time."

This is too important.

This is my priority.

This requires all my focus, time, energy, and attention.

I will not be distracted by your negativity.

I will not be deterred by your opposition.

I will not be discouraged by your criticism.

What I am doing matters more than anything you could have to say to me.

Nehemiah kept working with tireless commitment. And the walls were completed in 52 days.

His results finally shut the mouths of his critics.

I've found that often happens.

Stay focused on your calling and your work will speak for itself.

Eventually, even some who were against you will realize they were on the wrong side.

Are you committed to Jesus' Kingdom?

Are you set on making a difference in the world?

Do you desire to do great things for God?

Then you must be prepared for criticism. It will come.

Sometimes from those in the world. We expect that. Darkness and evil will always oppose light and truth.

But sadly, the most painful criticism often from those who you assumed would be on your side. From other believers. From family and friends. From people you looked up to and admired.

Determine today:

I will complete the assignment God gives me.
No matter what is said about me.
And no matter who says it.
Only one opinion matters.

Recognize that if Jesus has called you to do something, then it is a great work.

You simply cannot descend to the level of the critic or be distracted by those on the sidelines who will have plenty to say but never really make an impact on the world.

Don't give your best energy to the wrong people.

PROPHETIC ENCOURAGEMENT

PROTECT YOUR TERRITORY.

You have a sphere of influence over which the LORD has given you spiritual authority.

It could be your home, workplace, ministry, tribe, community, etc. Your territory has boundaries and borders. It has different inhabitants, allies, and opposition.

In this season of important transition and change, there will be a concerted attempt by the enemy to usurp your authority in your territory.

It can happen in some subtle ways - through distraction, disappointment, and misunderstanding.

But it could also happen in more blatant ways - through assaults on your character, reputation, and integrity.

You may even find old temptations, weaknesses, and wounds coming to the surface.

There is also a deep sense of weariness in many of God's people.

You're tired.
This past season has taken its toll.
You just want a rest from warfare.

And yet, you can't afford to neglect the responsibility you have to protect your territory right now.

You cannot retreat, shrink back, or go into defensive mode.

Assert your Kingdom authority in that area. Be proactive, press forward, take ground.

Use your spiritual weapons of warfare - prayer, prophetic decrees, declaring God's Word, worship, acts of service, and generosity.

Don't underestimate the significance of this current season.

Territory that you give up now will be very difficult to get back.

Lost ground will not be easy to regain.

Be aware that small decisions now may have great ramifications for your future.

Make careful choices. Ask for wisdom. Pray for discernment.

PROTECT YOUR TERRITORY.

DAY 22

THE SIX STAGES OF TRANSITION

Stage One: Disruption

BIBLE READING

Samuel said, 'Send for him [David]; we will not sit down until he arrives.'

So he sent for him and had him brought in. He was glowing with health and had a fine appearance and handsome features.

Then the LORD said, 'Rise and anoint him; this is the one.'

So Samuel took the horn of oil and anointed him in the presence of his brothers, and from that day on the Spirit of the LORD came powerfully upon David. Samuel then went to Ramah.

(1 Samuel 16: 10-13)

In the sixth month of Elizabeth's pregnancy, God sent the angel Gabriel to Nazareth, a town in Galilee, to a virgin pledged to be married to a man named Joseph, a descendant of David. The virgin's name was Mary. The angel went to her and said, 'Greetings, you who are highly favored! The Lord is with you.'

Mary was greatly troubled at his words and wondered what kind of greeting this might be. But the angel said to her, 'Do not be afraid, Mary, you have found favour with God. You will conceive and give birth to a son, and you are to call him Jesus. He will be great and will be called the Son of the Most High.

(Luke 1: 26-32)

DEVOTIONAL

Since 2017, when I began thinking seriously about transition, I have sought to simplify and put some structure around what is often a very confusing, and even messy, season of life. My contemplation and conversations led me to develop what I call 'The Six Stages of Transition':

- *Disruption*

- *Detachment*

- *Separation*

- *Disorientation*

- *Discovery*

- *Emergence*

I'm fully aware that transition is not always linear and is usually not predictable.

For example, some transitions immediately begin at Stage 3: *Separation*. These are usually what I call *involuntary transitions*. Unexpectedly, you get fired from your job. A loved one dies in a tragic accident. You discover that your spouse is cheating. You have a heart attack.

These are the significant and sudden transitions that you didn't see coming. They shake you to the core and change your world irreversibly.

Other transitions are voluntary and more gradual. You have time to make choices and devise plans. You get to navigate your way through the time of change. These transitions are the most likely to go through all six stages.

Today I want us to think about the first stage: **Disruption**.

WHEN YOUR SETTLED WORLD GETS DISTURBED

Disruptors. It's a term used to describe innovative and unconventional startups that have subverted and challenged entire industries in the 21st century. Think about what Amazon did to traditional bookstores. Or Airbnb to the hospitality sector. Or Uber to taxi firms. Or Spotify to the music industry.

Just last week, I was pointing out to Elijah, our 11-year-old, where the local Blockbuster store was once located. I described how we would excitedly wait for new movies to be released on VHS video cassettes. We would then rush down to the store and compete with others to be the first to rent them for one night. My son looked at me like I was a dinosaur. All he has ever known is Netflix and Amazon Prime.

We are living in an age of disruption - in technology, retail, science, the media, politics, and the church. The pace of change is accelerating. And the experts are now predicting that AI is going to disrupt pretty much every aspect of life as we currently know it. Time will soon tell.

Disruption isn't just 'out there'. It also happens in our personal lives and is often the precursor to a significant transition.

We had been leading a church for three years. It was hard work and there were many challenges, but we loved it. God was moving powerfully in our midst. We honestly thought we would spend the rest of our lives ministering there.

Then, around the beginning of year four, we started to become unsettled. Nothing major happened. There were some disappointments and hurts. But none seemed significant enough to make us want to leave. However, gradually, we began to wonder if God maybe had other plans for us.

Initially, these thoughts disturbed us. We didn't even want to contemplate moving. So, we tried to ignore them and push them away. But we couldn't. More and more, my conversations with Becky started to drift toward what the future might hold. We began to ask God what doors He was opening for us.

Our settled world had become disrupted.

Disruption enters our lives in many ways. They can be positive, negative, or neutral. Here are some examples:

Relationships: Emily has been dating John for two years. They appear to be a happy and committed couple. Everyone's expecting that they'll soon be engaged.

Then, one day, a new guy called Steve begins working alongside Emily. Instantly, the two of them click. There's compatibility and chemistry. Unexpectedly, her steady, stable relationship with John is disrupted.

Work: Bryan is 28. He has been working in his corporate job as an insurance broker for six years. It's steady and secure. Plus, it pays well. He plans to purchase his first house soon. In the long term, Bryan would like to meet someone, get married, and raise a family.

Then, one Sunday morning, a visiting speaker in Bryan's church shares about the work their organization is doing in Mozambique. Bryan's eyes fill with tears as he is moved by the images of smiling kids on the screen. He has no idea why he is so emotional. But even imagining doing work like this makes him feel more alive than he has done in years.

After the church service, he makes his way to the front to chat with the visiting speaker. His world has been disrupted.

Family: Tom and Susan have been married for almost 40 years and have three daughters. Their eldest is married and is a stay-at-home mom. The second is about to graduate from college and start working for a graphic design firm three hours from her parent's home.

Now, the third is packing up, preparing to move across the country and begin her first semester at law school. Tom and Susan have poured so much of their lives into raising these three girls and they're immensely proud of them all.

Increasingly, the reality of becoming 'empty nesters' is dawning on them. Susan currently works two days a week in a local real estate office. Tom is due to retire next year from a senior management position.

What will their lives look like in 12 months from now? How will they spend their time? Should they move? They can't think of any reason to stay living where they are. But where would they go? Their lives are being disrupted.

Church: Jen has been leading the women's ministry in her church for the past five years. She has always loved her church family. The blend of traditional and contemporary worship, solid Bible teaching, and a strong sense of community were aligned with her theology and personality.

However, over this past year, Jen has started to hunger for a deeper experience and encounter with God. Increasingly, she's watching other churches and ministries online. She senses the presence of God in the worship. There's an anointing upon the teaching that she doesn't experience in her home church. She's also started reading more books about the Holy Spirit and her appetite for the things of God is growing.

While she still loves the people in her church, increasingly she's feeling unsettled. The worship feels a bit dull and the people around her seem to lack passion. The teaching sounds like it's been lifted straight out of a Bible commentary. And the people…they're lovely. But it feels like she has less in common with most of them than before.

Jen doesn't know what to do. She feels a deep sense of loyalty to this place. But her heart is being drawn elsewhere. Her life has been disrupted.

Can you relate to any of these stories of disruption?

Yours, of course, will be different in the details.

But it will share similar elements of unsettledness, discomfort, disturbance, change, tension, and indecision.

You know something is shifting.

You sense a change inside you.

Your desires are changing.

Your heart is drawn to new things.

Your world is opened to possibilities that you never considered before.

The future that was once so clear, has now become a little blurry.

When David was out in the field, looking after his dad's sheep, he probably thought his life would look like that of his brothers. He'd work on his dad's land, fight in Saul's army, and, one day, raise a family of his own.

Then, out of the blue, the renowned prophet Samuel showed up. David was called in from the field, and before he knew what was happening, a horn of oil was being poured over his head. Apparently, God had chosen this kid as the future king of Israel. From that moment onwards, his life was disrupted.

Nehemiah had a good life. Yes, he was living as an exile in a foreign nation. But his diligence and loyalty had positioned him as one of the King's most trusted staff. Now and again, he thought about the city where he was born, Jerusalem. But he quickly pushed those thoughts away. This was his home now. He would make the most of this situation.

Then, one day, some relatives return from a visit to Jerusalem. They report that the city is in a desolate state. The walls are broken down and the people are living in constant fear of attack. Unexpectedly, Nehemiah is overwhelmed by a rush of emotion. He finds himself uncontrollably weeping over the condition of the city he loves. His life has been disrupted.

Mary lived a simple but satisfying life. A small-town girl, she was preparing for her marriage to Joseph, a decent, hard-working local carpenter. Her future was all mapped out. Until one day, an angel named Gabriel appeared. His message completely disrupted her world and Mary's life would never be the same again.

DISRUPTION CREATES FRICTION

Marketers today talk a lot about reducing friction. They want to make the customer experience as smooth and seamless as possible. The less friction there is, the quicker and easier it is to purchase their products. And the more sales and revenue they make.

Unfortunately, it's not as easy to eradicate friction from our everyday lives as it is from a retail experience.

Just when we think that things are finally under control and life is settling down, something happens to disturb and upset the tranquillity we had been hoping for.

Our lives get disrupted.

The disruption could be God working in your life. He shakes our world to refocus or reorient us.

It could come from others. They make choices and decisions that impact our lives and impinge upon our futures.

Or the disruption could be something that happens in the wider world. Some external factor - a virus, a war, a natural disaster, an economic crisis, political and social instability - has consequences that directly or indirectly affect our lives.

Disruption creates a stirring, agitation, even an irritation inside you. Something that was settled and smooth becomes bumpy and full of friction.

Maybe, there's a growing dissatisfaction. You're bored. You feel underutilized. You know you're capable of more. Your passion is gone.

There's a misalignment. Something just isn't working like it used to.

It takes more effort to get fewer results. You can't keep doing this.

Your relationship has changed. You once loved spending time with them. Now they drain you. The conversation is strained. You begin to pull back.

You have an argument. It wasn't about anything important. But it brought issues to the surface that have been hidden or pushed down for a long time. Things were said that can't be unsaid.

Maybe you've changed. But your surroundings have stayed the same. People still relate to you the way they did in the past. But you're struggling to relate to them. It's like they're speaking a different language.

Increasingly, you're imagining being somewhere else. Living life differently. Creating new rhythms and routines. Spending more time doing things you love with the people that matter most.

COVID brought major disruption to many areas of life. For the first time, people were able to work from home. They stepped back from the hustle and grind of life and reassessed their priorities. That led to what has been called 'the great resignation'. People discovered there was more to life than what they had previously known or experienced.

Sometimes, like David when he was anointed, **disruption comes in the form of a prophetic word.** A prophecy is spoken over your life, and it unsettles you. But it also causes you to envision possibilities and opportunities that you would never have imagined. Your future isn't as set in stone as you previously thought. Your destiny starts to look different.

Some friends had been leading a large and influential church for almost 20 years. I recall the evening when, during a large conference, the guest speaker prophesied over them from the stage, declaring: "The LORD says, it's time to pioneer again." This prophetic word shook them. But it also unlocked something within them. Deep in their hearts, they had been sensing change for some time. This was the clear confirmation. Within 18 months of that event, they had moved to the other side of the world and were pioneering in a different nation.

In our own situation, when we began to experience disruption, the Holy Spirit spoke to me through the parable of the fig tree in Luke 13:

"Then he told this parable: "A man had a fig tree growing in his vineyard, and he went to look for fruit on it but did not find any. So he said to the man who took care of the vineyard, 'For three years now I've been coming to look for fruit on this fig tree and haven't found any. Cut it down! Why should it use up the soil?'

"'Sir,' the man replied, 'leave it alone for one more year, and I'll dig around it and fertilize it. If it bears fruit next year, fine! If not, then cut it down.'" (vv. 6-9)

I believe the Lord was telling us: "Don't rush or make hasty decisions. Give it time. Things will become clear."

This was helpful as there can be a tendency for us to respond to disruption by making rash decisions. We think we need to move or change everything immediately.

If you are able, slow down and step back.

Ask God to speak and confirm what you sense Him saying.

Talk to one or two trusted friends about what is happening.

Not everyone will get it. That's okay. But God will lead, guide, and direct your path. He will order your steps. Slowly, things will become clear.

As I finish today, let me ask you to consider:

- *Are you currently sensing disruption in any area of your life?*
- *Where is it coming from?*
- *Is there somewhere that you have become too settled and God is increasingly allowing friction or agitation to provoke you to make a change?*
- *Looking ahead into the next 12 months, what disruption do you foresee in the wider world? How might this affect you personally? Is there anything you can do now to prepare for what might happen?*

Why now take time with the Holy Spirit, asking Him to give you insights into what lies ahead and what you can do to get ready?

PROPHETIC ENCOURAGEMENT

BREAK OUT OF THE BOX

In this new season, the Spirit is calling you to step beyond self-imposed boundary lines and religious restrictions.
There is freedom to lift off old labels that have limited you.

Break out of confinement…
Shake off containment…
Step out of old ruts and routines…
Open up options…
Push back perimeters…
Shatter glass ceilings…
Enlarge your territory…

There is blessing beyond your previous borders.
There is favor outside the field.
You have permission to explore the land.

Things don't have to be done the way you've seen them in the past. Not everything is as black and white as it first appears.

Previously, many of your decisions had to be *either/or*.
You had to choose *this* or *that*.

You are entering a hybrid season.
You have permission to do *both/and*.

David was a shepherd, *and* a musician, *and* an armor bearer, *and* a warrior, *and* then a king. In each new environment, the *more* on the inside of him was drawn out.

You too are much more than how you have been labeled or defined.
Why limit yourself to one narrow lane when God has given you a broad range of diverse gifts?
Don't be forced to fit into preconceived notions and expectations.

216

Try the new. Innovate and experiment.
Give it a go. Embrace the shift.
Holy living and creative thinking will be a powerful combination in these days.

A new breed of Kingdom pioneers, entrepreneurs, and creatives is emerging.
Men and women with holy boldness and Christ-like humility.
These prophetic trailblazers will forge new paths, break new ground, push back frontiers, and take back enemy territory.

They won't slot neatly into a category.
They don't fit religious stereotypes.
They break the mold.
They are hard to label and difficult to define.
They are neither *this* nor *that*.
They are so much *more*.
Their identity is firmly rooted in Christ.

Follow the wind of the Spirit into wide open spaces and uncharted places.
Explore and express all that the Father has woven within you.
A new level of favor, fruitfulness, and fulfillment will be found on unfamiliar paths.

Ask for wisdom to make the right strategic adjustments and pivots in this rapidly changing season.

The rewards will be great for those who will embrace the new and step into the unknown in response to the call of God.

BREAK OUT OF THE BOX.

DAY 23

THE SIX STAGES OF TRANSITION

Stage Two: Detachment

BIBLE READING

Then Saul sent messengers to Jesse and said, 'Send me your son David, who is with the sheep.' So Jesse took a donkey loaded with bread, a skin of wine and a young goat and sent them with his son David to Saul.

David came to Saul and entered his service. Saul liked him very much, and David became one of his armour-bearers. Then Saul sent word to Jesse, saying, 'Allow David to remain in my service, for I am pleased with him.'

…David went back and forth from Saul to tend his father's sheep at Bethlehem.

(1 Samuel 16: 19-22; 17: 15)

Joseph had a dream, and when he told it to his brothers, they hated him all the more.

…So Joseph went after his brothers and found them near Dothan. But they saw him in the distance, and before he reached them, they plotted to kill him.

(Genesis 37: 5; 17-18)

DEVOTIONAL

During my 20s, I lived in Cleveland, Ohio for almost two years. There, I had a good friend called Josie who fell in love with a guy called Brad. Everything was going smoothly for this great couple and soon they were talking about marriage and building a future together.

Brad secretly arranged to meet Josie's father to seek his permission to propose to the love of his life.

This is where things got interesting.

Josie's dad didn't say *"no"*. Neither did he give his unequivocal blessing.

He said, *"Yes, under one condition."*

Brad had to move out of his parent's house and live on his own for one year before he could ask Josie to become his wife.

You see, even though he was almost 30, Brad had only ever lived with his parents. They were a close family, and his mom did (almost) everything for him – cooking, cleaning, laundry, ironing, etc.

Josie's dad was concerned that, should the couple get married immediately, Brad would either treat Josie like his mom and expect her to do everything for him *or* he would run home to his mom any time he had a problem.

This year of living on his own would give Brad time and space to detach from his mom so he could develop some independence and learn to do things for himself.

I'm pleased to say that Brad moved into his own place. He still went home often and maintained a close relationship with his parents. But he also became less reliant on his mom and learned to do laundry, iron a shirt, and even cook a few basic meals.

Exactly 12 months later, he went back to Josie's dad. This time around, he was more than happy to give Brad his complete blessing.

At the time, some friends thought Josie's dad was being a little harsh or over-demanding. I think he was being incredibly wise and protective of his daughter.

He understood that biblical marriage involves both 'leaving and cleaving' (Genesis 2: 24). Before Brad could properly leave or separate from his parents (or more specifically, his mom), he needed a period of detachment. There had to be physical, emotional, and psychological space created between his old life (as a son) and the new life he was about to begin (as a husband).

In the stages of transition we are looking at, we have seen that the first stage, *disruption,* unsettles how things have been.

Something (or someone) interferes with the status quo. It could be an external event or a personal shift. But our 'normal' life gets interrupted in some way.

Often, the next stage after *disruption* is *detachment.*

In the beginning, this is often emotional and psychological. You sense a change coming and begin to prepare yourself. You slowly begin to pull back. You aren't as invested as you once were. You realize that something you thought was permanent might actually be temporary.

I often think of the words of John the Baptist when it was clear that the ministry of Jesus was becoming more popular than his own ministry:

"He must increase, but I must decrease." (John 3: 30)

During the detachment phase, the old version of you begins to gradually shrink and decrease as the new version slowly begins to emerge and increase.

You still show up and perform the role. You do the job. You spend time with the person. But your heart isn't fully in it.

220

You're not ready to let go or walk away. Not yet.

You don't want to make a mistake. Or do something you later regret.

But as time goes on, you know that something has shifted. And it can't be undone.

Again, we see this detachment in the life of David.

Following his anointing by Samuel, things begin to shift in the life of this shepherd boy:

"...David went back and forth from Saul to tend his father's sheep at Bethlehem." (1 Samuel 17: 15)

David is still looking after his dad's sheep. But more and more, he's spending time away from the pasture and instead is found working at the palace. He's between two worlds, fully engaged in neither.

We also see this in the story of Joseph.

As a young man, he has two vivid prophetic dreams that disrupt how he sees himself and his future. Unintentionally, they also affect his relationship with his family. While he's still living at home, the emotional chasm between Joseph and his brothers is growing wider. Eventually, there will be a complete separation.

QUIET QUITTERS

Recently, the media have been reporting about a trend known as 'quiet quitting'. Employees are doing just enough to fulfill their job description and keep their positions. But they are putting in no more time, effort, or enthusiasm than is absolutely necessary. In fact, Gallup's 2023 "State of the Global Workplace" report states that 59% of the global workforce consists of quiet quitters.

While I understand the sentiment of 'quiet quitting' in a job that lacks purpose or satisfaction, as believers we should follow the words of Paul:

"Whatever you do, work at it with all your heart, as working for the Lord, not for human masters, since you know that you will receive an inheritance." (Colossians 3: 23-24)

That might not require that we work late or take on extra responsibilities that will cause needless stress. But it does mean that, when we are at work, we give it our all. We show up and are fully engaged. Even if we know we're not going to be there much longer. Even if we are quietly packing our bags and preparing to leave.

Detachment will look different in each context.

In a **dating relationship**, you might still see one another. But you are keeping your options open. (It's probably best if you communicate this to the other person!)

In a **friendship**, the text messages become fewer, and meeting up for coffee is less frequent.

In a **church**, you were previously at Sunday worship every week. Now, you attend once or twice a month. You step back from serving 'for a season'. Perhaps you begin to visit other churches.

Again, in **work**, you might start looking at jobs with other organizations. Or you may think about doing something completely new and different. This may involve going back to school or learning a new skill.

The detachment stage can be exciting. It feels as if you have a blank canvas. You are free to explore options. You begin to dream of what the future might look like, how much better life could be.

DANGERS DURING DETACHMENT

Detachment can also be a difficult time for several reasons.

ᘯᘯᘯ

You may be finding it difficult to get clarity on what to do next. You know that you can't stay where you are. But you're not sure what your next step should be.

You might be paralyzed by having too many options. Or maybe you feel stuck because there don't seem to be any other possibilities.

It's like there's a fog around you and the future is blurry.

The friction and unsettledness that created the initial disruption will usually intensify during detachment, especially if this stage lasts longer than you expected. You can begin to resent the people and place that you want to leave behind. Small issues become increasingly frustrating. Relationships start to fracture.

The longer the delay in something new opening up, the greater the temptation will be to:

(i) Throw in the towel and walk away too soon; or,
(ii) Settle back into your old ways and conclude that this is all that God has for you.

Let's take the dating example.

You've been dating someone for two months. Overall, they're a good person and they tick many of the boxes on your checklist of desired qualities.

However, as time progresses, it becomes increasingly apparent that something is missing. There's a lack of chemistry. You see them more as a friend.

So, you detach. You pull back and tell them that you want to date other people.

They're disappointed but respect your decision.

It feels liberating. You're excited to explore the world of dating again.

223

And so, for the next month or two, you go on various dates with different people. But none of them develop into anything.

After one particularly uninspiring date, you begin to conclude: "Maybe (initial person) isn't so bad after all. They're steady and stable. Plus, does it really matter if there's not much chemistry? I should give them a call."

HONESTY AND OPTIONS

I'm not telling you what the right thing is to do here. What I would advise is that you **get very honest with yourself about what matters most to you.**

If chemistry is really important to you, don't settle for less than that.

If friendship and companionship matter more, this person might be a great fit.

You can apply this to the other areas of your life during the detachment stage.

If you're going to move on, you want to make sure it's towards somewhere or something more fulfilling and satisfying.

Again, be brutally honest with yourself.

Why do you want to leave?

What do you not want/like in your current situation?

If you could do anything, what would it be?

Where do my abilities/skills and passion intersect?

What are the top three things you need in a job/relationship/church etc?

What can you not tolerate? What are your non-negotiables?

It can be helpful to write down or journal your thoughts during this stage. I find that journalling helps me explore all the options and brings clarity to the process.

It's also good to speak to a few people with more life experience than you, especially if they have wisdom about the specific area or situation you're transitioning through.

I've already mentioned how, in 2017, we had left Dublin and were working at a wonderful church on the north coast of Ireland. We loved it but we knew it was a temporary stop for a year. God was using that season to heal us and refuel us for whatever He had next.

The problem was that we had no idea what to do next.

I wrote down eight options or possibilities. Then I met with my friend, Pastor Paul Reid, for lunch. Paul is in his 70s and, along with his wife Priscilla, has been in senior leadership for over 40 years. There are few people I respect more than this couple.

Over lunch, we chatted through the first seven possibilities on my list. I could tell he wasn't overly enthusiastic about any of them.

As we were waiting to pay the check, I casually mentioned a new church called HOPE that had expressed interest in me becoming their pastor.

Immediately Paul looked me in the eye and said: "I think that's what you should do. Try it for a few years. If it doesn't work out, come back to me and I'll support you in whatever way you need."

There were many other factors involved, and God confirmed the move in different ways. But this wisdom from someone I respected empowered us to decide to say *yes* to HOPE. We've been here for almost seven years and I've never doubted that it was the right choice.

RISK AND REWARD

The detachment stage can also be a time of fear.

Depending on your age and personal circumstances there are varying degrees of risk involved in change. It's probably easier for a 24-year-old single person to make a career change than it is for a 45-year-old husband and father with three dependent kids.

That's why not rushing through this stage is important. **You can take time to weigh up all your options.** You can plan and prepare. You can seek the best wisdom and advice. You can wait for God to bring clarity and open new doors.

I would say this: **While there is always a risk in leaving, there is also a risk in staying.**

Sometimes both options are equally scary, so you need to choose your fear.

Like the Israelites standing at the edge of the Jordan River, it's frightening to think of crossing over into the unknown.

But it's also terrifying to think of spending another 40 years wandering in the wilderness.

Let me repeat: Sometimes you just have to choose your fear.

Finally, in the detachment stage, **it's important not to try to see too far ahead.**

If you try to imagine what life will look like in five years, you will likely become overwhelmed. **It's much less daunting to simply think of the next best step.** You might need to hear the advice Paul Reid gave me: *"Try it for a few years…"*

Don't stress if you're not yet completely clear on your overall calling in life. We'll talk more about this later, but I've found that your calling doesn't typically drop down from Heaven fully formed or fleshed out.

Rather, it slowly emerges and takes shape over time. It's taken me years to figure mine out and I'm still tweaking it as God presents new opportunities and opens doors that weren't on my radar just six months ago.

However, as you look back at your life and experiences, you should begin to see themes and patterns beginning to emerge. As you explore your gifts and passions, you will discover that certain things move you more than others. These are the areas you will probably want to lean into.

At 48, I could never have imagined my life would look like this. There have been plot twists in my story that I could never have anticipated or prepared for.

But what I have sought to do is simply to **take the next best step.** To be faithful where I am while continuing to move forward. Because, as we've already discovered, God rewards faithfulness in the small things.

As I conclude today, it's important not to rush or push too hard through the detachment stage.

But equally, be careful not to stay here too long.

If you are waiting until all your circumstances are perfect or everything is completely clear, you'll never move.

There is always risk involved. If there wasn't, there would be no need for faith. Sometimes you need to choose your fear.

PROPHETIC ENCOURAGEMENT

THE LORD IS BREAKING CONFUSION OFF FROM YOUR LIFE

Many of you have been experiencing a fog over your mind causing a lack of focus, forgetfulness, and disorientation.

There has been a weariness and lethargy that you have struggled to shake off.

When you pray, you lose concentration. You're finding it difficult to hear God's voice.

It feels as if your mind is muddled, and your thinking is messy. Everything seems blurry and hazy.

It's been hard to make decisions or plan for the future.

You keep second-guessing yourself and what you sense God saying to you.

Everything changes now!

Today, I break off every demonic assignment from your life.

I cancel every attack in the spiritual atmosphere around you.
I declare that exhaustion and weariness will no longer affect or afflict you.

In Jesus' name, I command every hindering spirit to leave.

Angels are now being dispatched to war on your behalf and minister to your spirit.

Your eyes will be opened.
Your ears will be unstopped.
Your thinking will be clear.
Your prayers will have potency and power.
Your spiritual senses will be reawakened.

I declare today…

You will go from deplete to complete.
From emptiness to expansion.
From exhaustion to energy.
From stuck to advancement.
From procrastination to progress.
From passivity to promotion.
From blurriness to sharpness of vision.
From lack to abundance.
From delay to acceleration.
From barrenness to breakthrough.

Everything changes now.
Believe it Receive it.
Shake off the slumber.
Align your steps with what Heaven is saying.
Step into God's power and provision.

THE LORD IS BREAKING CONFUSION OFF FROM YOUR LIFE.

DAY 24

THE SIX STAGES OF TRANSITION

Stage Three: Separation

BIBLE READING

So Abram said to Lot, 'Let's not have any quarreling between you and me, or between your herdsmen and mine, for we are close relatives. Is not the whole land before you? Let's part company. If you go to the left, I'll go to the right; if you go to the right, I'll go to the left.'

…The two men parted company

(Genesis 13: 8-9; 11)

So when the Midianite merchants came by, his brothers pulled Joseph up out of the cistern and sold him for twenty shekels of silver to the Ishmaelites, who took him to Egypt.

(Genesis 37: 28)

When Paul had finished speaking, he knelt down with all of them and prayed. They all wept as they embraced him and kissed him. What grieved them most was his statement that they would never see his face again.

(Acts 20: 36-38)

DEVOTIONAL

"I think we're done here. Unless there's anything else?" The chairman of our church board glanced up at the small group who had convened an hour earlier in my office.

He began to stand but I interrupted his exit: *"Well, actually, there is one more thing."*

I could feel my heart thumping as I passed a typed A4 page across the desk. As much as I had prepared for this moment, I still had no idea what would happen next.

The chairman read it slowly. Without saying anything, he handed it to the other board members sitting next to him.

From the expressions on their faces, it was immediately clear that my resignation wasn't expected. Yet, under the current circumstances, I couldn't see how it was a complete surprise.

A place I had loved, a community I had poured my heart into for five years, a city where I thought I would spend the rest of my life, had become a place where I could no longer stay.

That meeting took place at 9.30 on Friday morning.

Two days later, holding my wife's hand, I stood before our entire congregation and announced the news. It was time for us to move on.

We've already explored the first two stages of transition: *disruption* and *detachment*. The next stage is usually *separation*.

Again, let me remind you that not everyone will experience all the stages in this linear order. Each transition is unique. But every person going through any significant transition will walk through many of these stages.

Leaving is rarely easy. Unless you're going on vacation.

Severing ties and walking away from the familiar and known unearths all sorts of emotions. Especially when you don't know what's on the other side. Or when there's some conflict, tension, or pain around your exit.

Yet, to fulfill your potential, protect your well-being, and walk in obedience to the Father, there will be times throughout your life when you will have an awkward conversation, say goodbye, tender your resignation, and move on.

It's not so much a matter of *if* some things will end.

But *when* and *how* will they end?

And what happens next?

MOVING ON

Most people prefer starts over separations. Beginnings are easier than endings. We often struggle to say goodbye.

Yet, without separation, we remain where we are.

In every transition, something, someone, or somewhere is left behind.

There is an exit.

A breakup.

A resignation.

A removal.

An ending.

A departure.

A death.

It may be planned or unplanned. It might be smooth or sharp.

But before we enter *next*, we first walk through *leave*.

Even in healthy transitions, leaving can be hard. There are emotions attached to people and places. We develop connections and friendships. We put down roots and establish patterns. We get comfortable and familiar in roles. We know what to expect. We can make plans.

Separation severs us from at least some, if not all, of that.

We might first journey through the stages of disruption and detachment. That can make separation a little easier.

You know things are changing in the relationship. You've been growing apart for months.

You don't have the same passion for the role that you once had. You're applying for other jobs.

The house you've been living in for 30 years is for sale. You love it but know it's time to downsize.

As difficult as these separations can be, at least you see them coming. You have some time to plan and prepare for them.

Other separations are sharper and more sudden.

Seemingly, out of nowhere, your fiancé announces that they're breaking off the engagement.

The company where you work unexpectedly makes you redundant.

You have a major car accident which leaves you unable to function normally.

It's discovered that the long-time pastor of your church has been having an affair. He is forced to immediately resign.

I've mentioned earlier that Becky's mom recently went to be with Jesus.

In many ways, Rosemary's departure was both gradual and sudden.

Just four weeks before her passing, she had been preparing for a trip to Australia to visit her son and his family. Although she had been living with cancer for several years and had been struggling with pain management, the growth of the tumor had been slow. Her doctor had encouraged her to get on with life as she would likely be around for at least another year.

However, just four days before her trip, overnight Rosemary lost all movement in the lower part of her body. The next week was spent in the local hospital before she was transferred to a hospice.

Those last two weeks were so difficult for her family as they sat at her bedside watching life slowly drain from the frail body of someone they adored.

When Becky received the call to say that her mother had breathed her final breath, she was devastated. And yet, I watched an almost invisible weight lift off from her shoulders. The separation they had been preparing for was now complete. Accompanying the immense sadness, there was a deep sense of relief. Rosemary's pain had ended. She was home.

Endings can bring a whole range of emotions to the surface.

These can include sorrow, regret, confusion, freedom, anger, joy, anxiety, pain, grief, and gratitude.

Often, you feel a mixture of the above.

For example, the relief you experience can also bring a sense of guilt. You know that it's the right thing to say goodbye, but you're also fully aware of the deep loss to others that accompanies this separation.

Maybe you're thankful for a new job but you'll miss your colleagues in your current workplace.

Or perhaps you're moving across the country. While you're excited for a new start, you're sad to be leaving extended family and close friends behind.

In our own situation that I shared at the beginning of today's devotional, my resignation initially brought relief to Becky and me. It was the end of a long process of disruption and detachment that was expedited at the end by some relational breakdowns.

For the church board, it mostly brought surprise and some anger. For the members of the wider congregation, this announcement seemed to bring shock, sadness, and some confusion.

It's important to recognize that not everyone will respond to endings and separations the same way as you. Be sensitive to the emotions of those around you.

NEW BEGINNINGS START WITH ENDINGS

There are many examples of separation in Scripture.

Abram who left his homeland to set out in obedience to God:

"The LORD had said to Abram, "Go from your country, your people and your father's household to the land I will show you." (Genesis 12: 1)

Later, he separated from his nephew Lot when quarreling broke out among their servants.

Moses had to flee from Egypt after he murdered an Egyptian who was beating a fellow Hebrew:

"Moses fled from Pharaoh and went to live in Midian." (Exodus 2: 15)

Ruth had to leave her home with her husband and sons when famine struck the land:

"...there was a famine in the land. So a man from Bethlehem in Judah, together with his wife and two sons, went to live for a while in the country of Moab." (Ruth 1: 1)

God's people, including a young man named Daniel, experienced separation when they were carried off into exile by the Babylonians in 587BC:

"Nebuchadnezzar king of Babylon came to Jerusalem and besieged it." (Daniel 1: 1).

The disciples were separated from the lives they knew before encountering Jesus:

"At once they left their nets and followed him...immediately they left the boat and their father and followed him." (Matthew 4: 20-22)

I love how Gary Thomas puts it in his excellent book *When to Walk Away*:

"Sometimes to follow in the footsteps of Jesus is to walk away from others or to let them walk away from us."

As I have already pointed out, whether voluntary or involuntary, separations are hard.

There is loss.

Emotions are involved.

Relationships change.

The future might be unclear or uncertain.

Our world, as we know it, is turned upside down.

Yet, we simply can't get to a new place or stage without leaving some people or things behind.

Henry Cloud, in his book *Necessary Endings*, says this:

"Getting to the next level always requires ending something, leaving it behind, and moving on. Growth itself demands that we move on."

The separation stage is difficult. But it can also be a time of excitement and anticipation.

When God delivered His people from Egypt, it was to bring them into the Promised Land.

When Jesus called the disciples to follow him, they were embarking on a journey that would change history.

Similarly, if God is calling you out from a place or position, it's because He is leading you somewhere better.

Jesus said that it's only when a seed of wheat is buried and dies that it can bear many seeds. Otherwise, it remains only a single seed.

In other words, you can hold tightly to the life you have and nothing much will change.

Or you can take a risk, make a move, and exit from a place that is no longer right for you, trusting in the goodness of a Father who leads us from glory to glory.

You will usually have to make a clean and complete break from the old to fully embrace the new. You can't have Egypt *and* the Promised Land. It's one or the other.

One of my mentors, Paul Scanlon, expresses it this way:

"Separation is always the first act of possession."

As painful and difficult as endings can be, we can't go through life without letting some things die. To do so only keeps us stuck, stagnant, and can prolong suffering. There will come a point when we all must be willing to say *goodbye*, even if it's with a heavy heart and tear-stained eyes.

Henry Cloud puts it like this:

"Endings are not only part of life; they are a requirement for living and thriving, professionally and personally. Being alive requires that we sometimes kill off things in which we were once invested, uproot what we previously nurtured, and tear down what we built for an earlier time."

While we can't completely avoid the discomfort of change, there are steps we can take to help us move through the separation stage with as little upheaval and upset as possible.

LEAVING WELL

It's been said that people remember your exit more than your entrance.

I would tend to agree.

Even if you've been a faithful, hardworking employee for ten years, if you slack off or become rude during your final few months, that's likely to be the dominant memory you'll leave behind.

From a spiritual standpoint, how you exit one season often determines the level of favor you experience in the next season.

I am very aware that it's not always easy to honor those who have mistreated you or caused pain. However, honor can still be your standard, independent of the actions of others.

The Apostle Paul put it like this:

"If it is possible, as far as it depends on you, live at peace with everyone." (Romans 12: 18)

The key phrase here is: ***"...as far as it depends on you...".***

We might not be able to choose how they treat us, but we can decide how to respond.

237

In our situation, while we had sensed for several years that our time in that church was coming to an end, in those final few months, seemingly out of nowhere, we began to experience major friction in some of our key relationships.

We didn't *have* to leave. We could have brushed everything under the carpet, taken our planned sabbatical, and returned for a few more years as had been discussed.

However, Becky and I both knew that God was moving us on. To stay there would have been disobedience.

On reflection, there are a few things I wish I'd done differently. However, I honestly believe that we exited as honorably as we could, given the difficult circumstances. We protected our family and the church from more unnecessary pain and divison.

I'm also convinced that leaving honorably positioned our family for the significant increase of God's favor that we have experienced in the years since that difficult departure.

I know that God loves me. But I also want Him to be able to trust me.

It's especially in these difficult and painful events, when we are tested, that what's growing inside our hearts comes out.

I also realize that not everyone can plan and prepare for their separation as we did. When you're caught off guard or when emotions are running high, we can all say or do things that we later regret.

At times, you may have to exit without sufficient explanation. That's okay. Do whatever you have to do. But still, the principle remains:

As far as it depends on you, seek to leave well.

Exit honorably.

Don't leave muddy footprints on your way out.

If mistreated or provoked, take the high road. I promise - you won't regret it.

PROPHETIC ENCOURAGEMENT

THIS IS A TIME OF COURSE CORRECTION

It's not that you have wandered off from the right path or taken a wrong turn.
Rather, it's that the entire landscape around you has changed.
Therefore, the Father is making some strategic adjustments to your direction and positioning.

In many cases, what worked just 6 or 12 months ago will soon become unhelpful or ineffective.

The LORD is realigning you so that you stay in sync with His Spirit.

He is imparting innovation and wisdom to bring creative solutions.
He's renewing your mind so that you begin to see things differently.
He's reorienting your heart towards new passions and purpose.
He's anointing you with new gifts and reactivating dormant gifts in your life.
He's removing some hindrances that would trip you up, hold you back, or slow you down.

A Kingdom restructuring is taking place.
A re-ordering of people and positions.
Therefore, between now and the end of the year there will be much movement and repositioning.

Don't cling too tightly to temporary things.
Keep your heart free of distractions or unhelpful attachments.
Don't let your life be encumbered by 'stuff' that will slow you down.
When the LORD moves, it could happen unexpectedly and quickly.

Stay in a posture of surrender.
Remain discerning, alert, and attentive in your daily walk.

The Lord will make the way ahead plain.
Your job is simply to obey.
We are living through an era shift where so much is changing.

You must be willing to change too.

THIS IS A TIME OF COURSE CORRECTION.

DAY 25

THE SIX STAGES OF TRANSITION

Stage Four: Disorientation

BIBLE READING

Remember how the Lord your God led you all the way in the wilderness these forty years, to humble and test you in order to know what was in your heart, whether or not you would keep his commands. He humbled you, causing you to hunger and then feeding you with manna...Your clothes did not wear out and your feet did not swell during these forty years.

(Deuteronomy 8: 2-5)

When I was a child, I talked like a child, I thought like a child, I reasoned like a child. When I became a man, I put the ways of childhood behind me.

(1 Corinthians 13:11)

Brothers and sisters, I do not consider myself yet to have taken hold of it. But one thing I do: Forgetting what is behind and straining toward what is ahead, I press on toward the goal to win the prize for which God has called me heavenward in Christ Jesus.

(Philippians 3:13-14)

DEVOTIONAL

I walked into the conference room and was warmly welcomed by the familiar group of around 20 senior pastors and leaders. We had been meeting together every few months for the previous two years for conversation, prophetic insight, and prayer about what God was doing in our nation. I had always looked forward to these gatherings of like-minded, Kingdom trailblazers. They challenged me to think bigger, live a more consecrated life, and expect God to move mightily.

However, this time, it felt different. No. I felt different.

Deep down, I didn't know if I should be there. Did I really belong in this group if I was no longer leading a church? I wondered if perhaps others were thinking the same.

A wave of insecurity washed over me. I was a pastor without a congregation. A leader without any followers. A spiritual nomad with no idea what the future might hold. I felt like an imposter.

LIVING IN THE IN-BETWEEN

When the Israelites left Egypt, they didn't immediately enter the Promised Land. They had no choice but to journey through the harsh wilderness that lay between their past and their future.

They lived in the in-between. They were no longer slaves. But they hadn't yet entered into the fullness of their inheritance. It was a time of wandering in the desert and wondering what their future might look like.

It's the same for each of us. **Even if we transition well and have solid plans in place, there is always a season of displacement and readjustment.** That's simply the nature of change. In the separation stage, we have stepped out (or been forced out) of the familiar and predictable, and now we must navigate the unfamiliar and uncertain.

This disorientation stage will usually vary depending on several factors.

Usually, the longer we were in our previous place/position, and the more attached we were, the harder the transition will be.

Breaking up with a boyfriend after a month causes much less upset and upheaval than a divorce.

Leaving a family business that you have invested 30 years into is significantly more stressful than resigning from your part-time job at Starbucks.

The Hebrews had been slaves in Egypt for over four centuries. It was all they knew. It's no wonder they found it so difficult to let go of their old life and embrace what God was now making available to them. Every time life became difficult, they wanted to go back to Egypt. They preferred predictable slavery to unpredictable freedom.

Also, the more sudden and unexpected the separation, the greater will likely be our sense of shock, confusion, loss, and debilitation.

A wife who opens an email and discovers that her husband of 35 years has been cheating will experience a greater level of disorientation than a couple who have been drifting apart for decades and mutually decide to go their separate ways.

Don't get me wrong, there's pain in both. But one has had more time to prepare for and adjust to the transition than the other.

The separation process is usually much quicker than the disorientation stage. It's often been said that it took one day for Israel to get out of Egypt, but it took 40 years to get Egypt out of Israel.

Similarly, you might be let go from your job during an hour-long meeting with your boss. But the reverberations of that conversation can last for many months or even years.

Your marriage might end through a separation and divorce process lasting several years. But rebuilding a new life after the divorce can take much longer.

This disorientation stage is also sometimes known as a *liminal* stage, which is derived from the Latin *limen*, meaning a threshold or the bottom part of a doorway that must be crossed when entering a building. Author Susan Beaumont expresses how liminality and disorientation usually go hand in hand:

*"Liminality refers to a quality of ambiguity or disorientation that occurs during transition, when a person or group of people is in between something that has ended and something else that is not yet ready to begin...**During liminal seasons we stand on both sides of the threshold.**"*

In this disorientation stage, we're not who we were. But we're not yet completely sure who we are.

WHO AM I?

A big part of the disorientation we experience centers around our identity.

Unconsciously, over our lifetimes, we build up an internal construct of who we are. We relate to others from our familiar roles of spouse, mom, leader, business owner, teacher, and so on. And that's how others relate to us.

For example, I'm Becky's husband, Elijah's dad, Lead Pastor of HOPE Church, the prophetic guy who writes books and shares content on social media about transition.

What if one or more of those roles are no longer applicable?

We derive more of our self-esteem and security from our roles than we imagine or maybe want to admit. I know that, as believers, ultimately our identity comes from Christ. But let's keep it real here. We all derive some confidence, status, significance, and self-worth from our relationships, roles, and possessions. We just don't realize how much until we are separated from one or more of them. Hence, the imposter syndrome I felt that day with other church leaders. If I wasn't Pastor Craig, the leader of that well-known church - who was I?

In this disorientation stage, our old identity is being dismantled and deconstructed before our new identity has been fully formed. **We know what we're not. But we don't know what we are.** You can feel like you're falling apart. Because, in some sense, you are. A stripping away is taking place of what was 'you'.

If you've ever done a major remodel to your home, you'll have some idea what I'm talking about.

You look around at something that barely resembles what was once your house. Interior walls have been knocked down or stripped down to bare studs, cupboards and closets have been removed, electrical wiring criss-crosses over your head where the ceiling used to be, and the bathroom consists of nothing but pipes jutting out of the floor.

Day by day, how it used to be is being taken apart and dismantled. The old is being cleared away before the new is constructed. You know it's still your house. But, right now, it's barely recognizable. And it's incredibly uncomfortable to inhabit. You might begin to wonder if it's worth all this upheaval. Could you not just have lived with how it was?

Similarly, in the disorientation stage, you're trying to build a new life while still surrounded by the remnants, debris, and ruins of the old. None of it fits what you're trying to construct, but it's all you have right now. It's hard to see any way through the mess.

Perhaps that's why contractors warn that remodeling always takes more time and money than new construction. The clearing of the old is costly. Yet, it must take place before the construction of the new.

Some of our old labels no longer identify us. Yet, they're all we've known. When people ask questions like, "What do you do?" or "Are you married or single?" we fumble over our response. What used to be a simple one-word answer becomes a long, drawn-out explanation. We can talk about what we used to be. That much is clear. What we are now – that's less easy to define.

Marilyn Ferguson describes it well:

"It's not so much that we're afraid of change or so in love with the old

ways, but it's that place in between that we fear… It's like being between trapezes. There's nothing to hold on to."

That's what the disorientation stage of transition feels like – you're between trapezes. It's the unfamiliar, insecure, and uncomfortable place that lies between where you were and where you're going. It's difficult to find much to cling on to.

NAVIGATING THE WILDERNESS

When we left the church we had been leading, we knew it was the right thing to do. God had clearly spoken. And it seemed that the circumstances left us without any other option.

But it was still hard. Much harder than we thought it would be.

Psychologists talk about the five stages of grief: denial, anger, bargaining, depression, and acceptance. Apparently, these stages are our attempts to process change and protect ourselves while we adapt to a new reality.

I think I experienced most of them but certainly not in any linear order. Our emotions aren't that tidy. Just when we think we've accepted our new circumstances, something happens, and buried anger rises to the surface once again.

Also, there was so much uncertainty about the future. We had our sabbatical rest for the next three to four months planned. After that, we had absolutely no idea what we would be doing. We didn't own a house. We had no jobs. Our little boy was due to start preschool. And our savings wouldn't last very long.

God had brought us out.

But into what?

That's where the test of trust began.

In your own disorientation stage, you can expect to experience some of the following:

Dislocation: You don't recognize your surroundings. Physically, spiritually, emotionally – you're not sure where you are or where to go. All of your old landmarks are gone, and you don't know where to get your bearings.

Insecurity: So much of what previously formed your identity has been stripped away. Your crutches have been removed. You feel vulnerable and unsure of yourself.

Imposter Syndrome: You feel like you no longer belong in places and with people where you once felt comfortable. You're not sure where you belong anymore. You might even feel like a failure or a fraud.

Regret: It's not uncommon in this disorientation stage to question your past decisions. Especially when things aren't working out the way you hoped. You begin to wonder if you made the right decision to leave. You might even be tempted to make contact with the place or people you left behind, just in case they want you back.

Resentment: You might find that you feel increasing anger towards the people who mistreated you in the place you left. After all, it's their fault that you had to move on.
Or you might feel animosity towards those who encouraged you to take the step of faith. If you hadn't listened to their advice, you would still be in your safe, secure role.
You may begin to even feel resentment towards God. You've stepped out in obedience and faith, but He hasn't kept His part of the deal.

Fear: You don't feel like you're in control. The uncertainty about your future is causing increasing levels of worry and anxiety.

Grief: I mentioned this earlier. Any time you go through significant change, you will experience losses. It's important that you acknowledge these and go through the process of mourning what has left your life, without getting stuck there.

Overwhelm: Maybe you've too many possibilities and options and you don't know which to choose. Or you feel completely directionless and have no idea which way to turn.

Disillusionment: You can become critical and cynical of your old life. You wonder how you stayed there for so long. How were you so easily manipulated or blinded by them?

You can't rush through the disorientation stage. But you can prolong it.

Scholars tell us that the journey from Egypt to Canaan could have been completed in 11 days.

But it took Israel 40 years.

Why so long?

Partially, it was because they needed time to prepare to enter the new place. Their identity had to be upgraded from slaves to sons. They would have to learn to trust their Father.

But the delay was also because of their unwillingness to let go of Egypt. Any time they encountered pressure or opposition, they reverted to their old ways of idolatry, grumbling, and distrust.

Similarly, in our own season of disorientation, there will be some things we cannot shortcut. God's process of preparation must run its course.

However, we can also shorten or prolong this in-between season by the degree to which we respond in obedience and faith.

This sounds easy and straightforward. But when you're separated from the people or the place that you've known for a long time and the future is uncertain and unclear, it's difficult not to succumb to fear and even dismay.

This is where your trust in God is tested most. Not in the old slavery of Egypt or in the promised land of Canaan - but in the wilderness and barrenness of the in-between.

248

If you will fortify your faith and deepen your dependence on God here, you can avoid unnecessary delays and detours to the next place and stage where the LORD is leading you.

In the middle, when everything is uncertain and unclear - don't look back and don't give up.

I promise you - the details and definition will gradually emerge as you take the next best step forward in faith and obedience.

PROPHETIC ENCOURAGEMENT
(This word is a little different today.)

COME OUT OF THE COCOON

As soon as I awoke, I heard two words: **"cocoon"** and **"chrysalis"**. Honestly, immediately a few thoughts came to mind:

1) Are they not the same thing?

2) I've heard so many prophetic words and sermon illustrations about "becoming a butterfly" and "spreading your wings" that I really didn't want to share this. It feels so generic and overused.

Yet I couldn't shake the thought that this was exactly what God was doing in my life right now, and also in the lives of many of His people.

I sensed that I was to spend some time researching the exact process through which this metamorphosis occurs.

As I read about this radical transformation from a caterpillar to a butterfly, I really sensed the LORD give me clear revelation about the process you and I may well have been going through in this season.

There's nothing wrong with being a caterpillar. In fact, there's never been a butterfly that didn't start off as one of these little green worm-like creatures. However, a caterpillar was never intended to stay down low and in the dirt. **They were created for more.**

I believe that for many of you reading these words, **your life is okay.** It's not awful. There are so many good things which you are thankful for. God has blessed you.

Yet, deep inside, **you can't escape this sense that you were made for more.** There is something inside you that has to come out.

Others around you are very happy to be "caterpillars" but instinctively you know that you were created to fly.

There is a growing **dissatisfaction** and **boredom** with "ground-level" living, which is starting to lead to **frustration** and, in some cases, a sense of **depression**.

Yet you almost feel guilty for wanting more. You think you're being unappreciative and ungrateful for all you have. Others are so much less fortunate and blessed than you.

I believe that for many of you, **in the last season of anything from 6 months to three years, you have been in a cocoon or chrysalis stage. A metamorphosis has been taking place in your life.**

It has been an incredibly difficult time and you've been really struggling to figure out what has been happening. You've been unable to put words around it. Some of you have felt as if you've been going crazy.

250

You see, in the metamorphosis stage for a caterpillar, several things happen.

Firstly, **the caterpillar's appetite changes.** Before this, a caterpillar's existence basically involves eating whatever leaves are around it. It grows very quickly, and its skin is stretched to contain the increase in size. It even sheds its skin a few times to continue its expansion.

However, **just before the transformation begins, it stops eating.** In its current form, it simply can't grow any larger. It has reached its **capacity**.

Some of you are at this stage. You've been fed spiritually on the same food for a long time, and it has nourished you. You have grown spiritually and experienced God in different ways through the seasons.

However, **recently you've been finding that what used to feed you simply isn't satisfying you any longer.** It's all begun to 'taste the same'. It seems bland. You're hungering for more.

Your desires are changing. As a baby moves from milk to solid food, so you too are longing for something more 'meaty' and' substantial'. It's not spiritual arrogance or pride. It's simply that your appetite is changing. **Things that you were once drawn to just don't hold the same appeal any longer.**

The next stage that happens to the caterpillar is that **it finds somewhere to hide,** normally under a leaf or twig, and it spins itself a silky cocoon or chrysalis. This is where it will remain for the duration of the transformation.

Recently many of you have felt hidden. You have experienced **isolation** and even **loneliness**. It almost seems as if everyone has lost your phone number because no one is calling you. Even those closest to you seem to have withdrawn or forgotten about you.

For those in ministry, it can feel almost as if the Lord's hand and favor have been lifted off from you.

Opportunities seem to have dried up.

Doors aren't opening.

Any platform you have seems to be disappearing.

In the past, your problem was that you were too busy. Now it seems as if you're not busy enough!

If this is you, the LORD would have you know that this is because you are in the stage of metamorphosis. **He has deliberately hidden you.** His hand is still upon you, but it has been covering you from being visible to those around you.

In the cocoon stage, if anything or anyone from the outside interferes with the chrysalis, it can kill the new creature being formed inside.

Similarly, **God hasn't wanted outsiders interfering with His precious work in your life. Thus, He has carefully concealed you.**

The other simple thing the Lord showed me was that **there is never more than one creature in any cocoon.**

Metamorphosis isn't a group activity. It can only happen in **isolation**. That is why some of you have felt so alone.

The next stage of transformation sees the **caterpillar almost completely dissolve into a liquid or goo state. Only those parts of it absolutely necessary for its next stage remain.**

This is a time of **great loss** for the creature. So much of what was there before must be **cast off, dissolved, or removed.**

It is the same for us.

There has been **stripping back** for many of you in recent days. **Everything incompatible with where God is taking you is being removed.** You feel **vulnerable** and **exposed**.

Yet, be assured - **He will not take away anything that you need.**

So, the metamorphosis happens in hiddenness, darkness, and isolation when the creature has been reduced to basically a goo or mess.

Does that sound familiar to any of you?

It's not a pleasant or comfortable place to be.

You have to trust the process. The transition is bringing great transformation.

There comes a point where the transformation is almost complete.

The newly formed butterfly stretches and expands, pushing through the chrysalis and emerging into the world.

It is weak, but as its wings dry out and expand, it is now ready to take flight.

I believe many of you are at this final stage right now.

God is calling you out of the cocoon.

253

You're emerging from your shell.

Something is starting to break open.

Divine strength is coming after a season of extreme weariness.

The darkness is lifting, the feelings of containment and restriction are shifting.

You are emerging into a place of freedom and fulfillment.

You will start to see things differently. A caterpillar has a very limited perspective from the ground, but the butterfly has an expansive vision because of its elevated position.

You can still associate with those on the ground, but they can't come up there with you. Therefore, you will find **some realignment of relationships** in the coming days.

Also, recognize that **not everyone will want to go through the transformation.**

Many people choose to remain at ground level because they're not willing to go through the painful process of shedding or letting go.

They admire and respect those who are flying but can't imagine that they could ever do it.

However, the Lord would also say that **you are not alone in this new season.**

He has been taking believers all around the world through this process at the same time.

You will begin to see an emerging movement b shed their old skin and are beginning to fly.

If you're at this last stage, let me encourage you, **push through.**

I know you feel fragile and weary. But you're so close.

Stretch out, spread your wings, let the world see your beautiful colors. And fly!

DAY 26

THE SIX STAGES OF TRANSITION

Stage Five: Discovery

BIBLE READING

My frame was not hidden from you
when I was made in the secret place,
when I was woven together in the depths of the earth.
Your eyes saw my unformed body;
all the days ordained for me were written in your book
before one of them came to be.

(Psalm 139:15-16)

The word of the Lord came to me, saying,
"Before I formed you in the womb I knew you,
before you were born I set you apart;
I appointed you as a prophet to the nations."

(Jeremiah 1:4-5)

Take delight in the Lord, and he will give you the desires of your heart.

(Psalm 37:4)

DEVOTIONAL

"Daddy, when are we moving house again?", our son, Elijah, asked me one morning as I drove him to school.

"What do you mean?", I responded, trying to hide my concern. *"Do you want to move? Are you not happy here?"*

"No, I really like it here," he replied. *"It's just we've moved so much, I figured we would be moving again soon."*

This conversation happened a year or so after we arrived at our current church, HOPE. Elijah was six at the time and had already lived in six different houses during his short life.

Our little boy had become so used to moving around, that he struggled to comprehend staying or settling in any one house for very long. He was always thinking: where next?

Where next?

That's a question you might find yourself asking often throughout your journey of transition.

You have been through the disruption stage and know that something has changed, inside you or around you - perhaps both.

You quietly ponder: *where next?*

You're increasingly detaching from your current job, church, or relationships.

You begin to question: *where next?*

A separation happens – either suddenly or planned. Either way, unless you are stepping immediately into a new place, role, or relationship – the pressure will be in figuring out: *where next?*

You are in the disorientation stage. You've left the old behind. Everything feels unsure and uncertain. You can't go back, but you're not sure how to move ahead.

Every day you ask: *where next?*

Now, you enter the **discovery stage** of transition.

If you haven't done so already, it's in this fifth stage that you figure out: *where next?*

This stage will look very different depending on the suddenness and extent of your transition.

For example, moving from one job to another similar job will likely require much less reinvention or soul searching as would be expected if you went through a difficult divorce or moved to a completely different state or even country.

The more that has been stripped away from you in the previous stages, the more time, space, and work will be required to build a future you desire to inhabit.

WHAT IS IN YOUR HEART?

Desire is an important word here.

As you begin this discovery process, **pay attention to and acknowledge your desires.**

- *What do you want to do next?*

- *What do you love?*

- *Imagine six months from now. How would you like your life to look?*

- *What about five years from now?*

Desire is something many Christians struggle with. We are often implicitly or explicitly told that desires are sinful and wrong. After all, *"the heart is deceitful above all things"* (Jeremiah 17: 9).

Yes, an unsubmitted heart can lead us astray. Absolutely. I get that.
But the Bible also tells us that God carefully crafted and formed you in the womb (Psalm 139: 13).

And God told Jeremiah:

"Before I formed you in the womb I knew you, before you were born I set you apart; I appointed you as a prophet to the nations." (1: 5)

Before Jeremiah was born, God already had a purpose planned for him.

Just as a team at Apple carefully design every new iPhone with the end in mind, your designer and creator, God, looked into the future and carefully crafted you to fulfill a unique purpose here on earth.

He wired you to love certain things.

He shaped your heart to have distinct longings.

He formed you to express yourself in a particular way.

He molded you with passions and emotions.

As a teenager, I remember more than one preacher saying something along these lines: "Don't tell God what you don't want to do. Because that's the very thing He'll call you to do."

Really?

Is our loving Father sitting in Heaven deviously devising ways to make your life miserable? I don't think so.

As a dad, I would never think like that about my son.

I want what's best for him. I want him to experience joy and fulfillment and satisfaction and impact.

259

Of course, there are times when I ask him to do things he'd prefer to avoid. Like brush his teeth. Or stay off his iPad.

But I love him, and I want him to fully express his character, personality, and gifts.

You are a child of God. He loves you more than I could ever love my son. And He created you for relationship and purpose. He gave you specific desires and passions. He wants you to be fully alive and fulfilled. Psalm 37: 4 tells us:

"Take delight in the Lord, and he will give you the desires of your heart."

The discovery stage is a time to dream again. To reimagine what your life could look like. To reinvent yourself. To get fresh vision. To reset your rhythms. To shape the future. To explore options. To try new things.

If you are able, don't rush through this stage. Linger here for a while. It can take a while for the next stage to emerge and become clear.

You might find it helpful to take a blank page and write down your desires.

Don't filter them by writing what you 'should' want. No one else has to see this list. But you should dig deep and unearth what's in your heart.

God appeared to Solomon and said:

"Ask for whatever you want me to give you." (2 Chronicles 1: 7)

Imagine if God asked you that today. How would you respond?

Most of us would struggle to answer this question.

We either aren't clear on what we desire, or we don't think it sounds spiritual enough.

If you are going to build a new future, make sure it's one that you actually want to inhabit. Don't settle for inferior options just because they ease your sense of uncertainty and vulnerability.

Related to desire, other helpful questions to ask in this discovery stage are:

- *What would I not want to do?*

- *Was there anything in my past role/place/relationship that really annoyed me?*

- *What bothers me most?*

- *What can I not tolerate?*

- *What are my non-negotiables?*

Our frustrations can point to our future. When Nehemiah was told that the walls of Jerusalem were in ruins, we read:

"When I heard these things, I sat down and wept..." (Nehemiah 1: 4)

It broke his heart to discover that the Holy City was in such a state of desolation and vulnerable to attack.

However, he didn't just *feel* bad about it. **His emotional reaction became a strategic response.** He obtained permission to return to the city and mobilized the people to rebuild what was broken.

As a teenager, I recall enduring many long, boring, church services that were full of ritual and religious traditions. Amid my growing frustration, a seed was planted in my heart. I determined that I would one day lead a church that was full of life and where people could encounter Jesus.

- *What breaks your heart?*

- *Where do you see a problem that needs to be solved?*

- *In what situations or environments do you see things that could or should be done better?*

- *Could you carry a solution?*

261

In the discovery stage, you're paying attention to your thoughts, emotions, and passions. It can feel as if you're re-introducing yourself to yourself.

There's the version of you that everyone, including you, has experienced up until this point.

But is there another version 2.0 that has yet to fully emerge?

THE GOD WHO EXCEEDS EXPECTATIONS

When we left Dublin and were walking through the disorientation stage of processing all that had happened, we were forced to begin to ask: *where next?*

After all, we had no home or jobs to return to. Everything we owned was in storage.

Obviously, we prayed about the future. But God wasn't giving any clear direction about what our next step should be.

So, we asked ourselves: "Where would we love to live?"

That was easy to answer: a small town called Portstewart on the north coast of Ireland.

We had spent many wonderful summer vacations in that beautiful beach community. Plus, it was located ten minutes away from the Causeway Coast Vineyard (CCV), a church that had impacted us deeply during our time in Dublin. I had even preached there once the previous summer.

So, I went online, found a summer rental that we liked, and emailed the owner to ask if she'd consider an extended rental agreement for six months. She agreed and didn't even ask for a deposit or down payment! It turned out to be the perfect house for our family.

With accommodation sorted, the next question I asked was: *what will I do* for work? Our bank account was almost empty, and I needed a job.

I got very practical, making a list of all my skills and the potential jobs I could apply for.

I contacted people who owned businesses in the area to see if they needed help.

I also accepted any openings to preach that came my way.

But I was also praying very specifically about what I would *love* to do. As I dreamed about what might lie ahead, I wrote in my prayer journal: *"Teaching Pastor at CCV."*

If you have read *The Tension of Transition*, you will know what happened next.

With just a few days of our sabbatical remaining, Becky and I were both offered jobs at this wonderful church. Unknown to us, months before this, God has prompted the leadership to set a full-time salary aside "just in case Craig and Becky ever move to the area."

Our desire brought us there. But God had already made plans for our arrival! How good is our Father?!

WHERE PASSION MEETS GIFTING

It's one thing to desire to do something. However, having competence and ability is a different matter. Just watch a talent show like American Idol. Some people deeply desire to be pop stars. And they may even think they have what it takes. Until they open their mouths...

We tend to veer in one of two directions here. We overinflate our abilities. Or we underestimate our competence.

As you consider the future, think not only in terms of what you *can do*, or what you *have done* up until this point.

Also, consider - *what do you have the potential to do?*

Before 2016, I never imagined that I would write an essay much less six books.

However, while we were living in Portstewart for one year, I had space to try new things. Soon, I found myself writing two devotionals every day, one for the church and the other for a few hundred people who had signed up through a Facebook post. Most surprising for me was that people seemed to find what I was saying helpful.

The discovery stage is a time to try new things. Test yourself. Push past your previous boundaries. Be willing to fail.

You're almost trying to diagnose your soul. What's inside you trying to come out?

This might involve taking an ability you already have but repurposing it somewhere new.

Perhaps you have given a talk in church. Could you use your public speaking skills in business or in teaching a class?

Often, we devalue what we already have. We think, *"I'm just a..."* That might be a part of your identity, but it is certainly not the totality of who you are.

TRY IT ON

I think about this discovery stage a little like I think about fashion.

Most of us know what clothes we prefer and what doesn't suit us. But have you ever seen something that you'd never normally wear but somehow, you're drawn to it? You try it on, and it looks and feels great.

The discovery stage is where you try things on. Give them a go. Be curious. Take a few risks.

Often, I think we make our calling too narrow.

Ten years ago, I would have told you my calling was to preach God's Word. Now, I would say it is to *communicate truth*.

Of course, that primarily involves preaching and teaching the Bible. I am still so passionate about that.

But my calling is broader than *only* that. I want to speak and write truth on many subjects and in different spheres from a Christian perspective.

Usually, there are clues to your future in your past. What do people say you're good at? Where have you experienced success? What do you do easily that other people seem to struggle with?

Where does there seem to be unusual favor in your life?

What does God appear to be blessing?

Joseph had unusual favor in dream interpretation. Leaning into this favor caused him to be promoted from the prison to the palace and saved a nation during a famine.

I started Daily Prophetic in 2018 to learn how to use Instagram. Very quickly I realized that God was breathing on it and I simply followed His favor.

Really, what you're doing in the discovery phase is mining for gold. **You're seeking to discover the intersection of passion and gifting.** What you would love to do and your ability to do it.

TAKE ACTION

It's one thing to *dream*. It's totally different to *do*.

The difference between dreamers and doers lies in *taking action*.

Many of the people who are doing what you'd love to do aren't more gifted or talented or blessed than you.

They just took action. And didn't give up when things got tough.

Life is short. The Bible says that our time on earth is like a mist or vapor that appears for a little while and then vanishes (James 4: 4). And the Psalmist prayed:

"Teach us to realize the brevity of life, so that we may grow in wisdom." (Psalm 90: 12 NLT)

When you're in your 20s or 30s, it feels like you're going to live forever. But the truth is, life passes by much more quickly than we imagine or expect. Don't aimlessly drift through the next ten years. Make the most of everything God has given you.

Ask yourself:

- *As you look into your future, are you excited?*

- *Do you believe the best is yet to come?*

- *Or do you think that you're past it? That your glory days were somewhere back there?*

Can I encourage you today - **dream again**.

Your God is able to do exceedingly, abundantly *more* than you can ask, or even imagine.

I'm 48 now. Older than many of you reading this. Younger than some.

I choose to believe that God has so much more planned for me than I have seen or experienced up until now.

Unless Jesus returns or calls me home, I am going to see more of His goodness, experience His fullness, impact the nations, reap a harvest, walk in abundance, and raise up world changers.

And that's just in the next five years!

Dream again and discover that God is more excited about your future than you are.

PROPHETIC ENCOURAGEMENT

GOD WANTS TO HEAR YOUR VOICE

Many of God's people have been muzzled by intimidation, muted by insecurity, and silenced by shame.

Because of disappointment, discouragement, hurt, and weariness, you have stepped back, shrunk down, and decided to play it safe.

The enemy knows how powerful your faith-filled words are in shifting spiritual atmospheres, breaking strongholds, cancelling curses, and displacing demons.

Therefore his assignment against believers has been simple: To shut you down. To cancel your voice. To silence your shout.

His mission is to fill the 'airwaves' with voices of fear, negativity, despair, and hopelessness.

You have been called to be a voice in the wilderness calling out: "Prepare the way for the Lord."

The Spirit is waiting for you to speak.

In Genesis 1, God's Spirit hovered over the waters. When God spoke worlds were created, chaos was ordered, darkness was dispersed and new life came into being.

Similarly, God's Spirit is hovering over your life, your community, your future, your family, your finances, your relationships, your job, and your ministry.

He's waiting for you to speak God's Word.

When you speak, things around you will start to shift.
Bondages will break.
Hearts will be healed.
Darkness will be dispersed.

Blessing will be released.
Hope will be restored.

The LORD is calling you from the sidelines back onto the frontline.
Like Isaiah, He is touching your lips and commissioning you.

Your words carry authority in both the spiritual and natural realms.
Hell will shake and strongholds will break when you declare the Word of
the Lord.

The world needs to hear your voice.

You have something inside you that needs to come out.

Unmute yourself.
Raise a shout.
Release the Word of the Lord.

GOD WANTS TO HEAR YOUR VOICE.

DAY 27

THE SIX STAGES OF TRANSITION

Stage Six: Emergence

BIBLE READING

Now the priests who carried the ark remained standing in the middle of the Jordan until everything the LORD had commanded Joshua was done by the people, just as Moses had directed Joshua. The people hurried over, and as soon as all of them had crossed, the ark of the LORD and the priests came to the other side while the people watched. The men of Reuben, Gad and the half-tribe of Manasseh crossed over, ready for battle, in front of the Israelites, as Moses had directed them. About forty thousand armed for battle crossed over before the LORD to the plains of Jericho for war.

That day the LORD exalted Joshua in the sight of all Israel; and they stood in awe of him all the days of his life, just as they had stood in awe of Moses.

(Joshua 4: 10-14)

Therefore, if anyone is in Christ, the new creation has come: The old has gone, the new is here!

(2 Corinthians 5: 17)

DEVOTIONAL

When we arrived to lead HOPE Church in late 2017, there were around 70-80 wonderful, committed members who had sacrificed so much to start this new community of faith. I was the only paid member of staff. We were very rough around the edges, but the future was wide open, and we were ready to go wherever God might lead us.

Fast forward seven years.

Last Sunday, hundreds of people gathered in HOPE for worship and to celebrate fifteen baptisms. Each week people are driving for up to an hour to be part of our services. We are increasingly seeing salvations and healings. I lead a Godly, gifted staff team and there is a growing sense of unity, momentum, and God's manifest presence in our midst.

Once seen as the fringe 'breakaway church' that might not survive, we are now very much established in the heart of our community as a Spirit-filled house where God's Word is unapologetically preached.

Of course, we are far from perfect. There have been many challenges and some painful moments along the journey. And I'm sure there will be more.

However, it's important for me to stand back at this juncture and acknowledge all that God has done.

I am so incredibly thankful for it all. If you'd asked me what I longed to see when I first arrived at HOPE, the picture would have looked something like what we are walking in today.

But there's also a real sense that we're just getting started.

This feels like a crossover season into something beyond anything we could have imagined. We're not sure exactly what that looks like, but we believe that God doesn't want to just meet our expectations – He is going to far exceed them.

So, we stop and give thanks for a moment.

But we don't settle. Or become too comfortable.

As we step across this threshold, we are more dependent upon the Spirit than ever. Recently, I've often found myself praying these words from the worship song Oceans:

Spirit lead me where my trust is without borders
Let me walk upon the waters
Wherever You would call me
Take me deeper than my feet could ever wander
And my faith will be made stronger
In the presence of my Savior

CROSSING OVER INTO THE LAND

The sixth stage of transition, *Emergence*, is when you cross the Jordan and take your Promised Land.

You have stepped into our dream job.

You are surrounded by the family you've longed for.

You are comfortable and confident in your new role.

You accomplish your goals and see your dreams fulfilled.

Your prayers are answered.

You are walking in the promise and not looking back.

In some ways, it's like a rebirth. And like any birth, the process of getting there is usually messy and painful. But what emerges is beautiful and makes all the labor worthwhile.

It's vital that you take a moment and acknowledge: I am here.

See how far you've come.

Remember what you've overcome.

Recall God's goodness.

Praise Him for His faithfulness.

271

That's what Israel did when they crossed the Jordan:

"Each of you is to take up a stone on his shoulder, according to the number of the tribes of the Israelites, to serve as a sign among you...These stones are to be a memorial to the people of Israel forever." (Joshua 4: 5-8)

God told Israel to set up physical monuments as a reminder to future generations of how far He had brought them and how good He had been to them.

While you'll probably not set up huge rocks in your yard, it's important to stand back in transitional seasons and recall all that God has done – in you and through you.

Consider how far He has brought you. And give Him thanks.

Pause and praise for a moment. But don't get too settled.

ENTER, THEN ESTABLISH

Even when Israel entered the Promised Land, there were still battles to fight. There was territory to take.

They would develop and cultivate the land. Build houses and plant vineyards. Establish communities. Appoint leaders.

Yes, in one day they had stepped into the promise. But it would take time to fully grow into and inhabit the new reality they had entered.

It's the same with you.

Emergence is an event. But it is also a process.

There is a difference between entering the new and becoming established there.

Between starting a new job and feeling confident in your role.

Between getting married and growing together as a couple.

Between having a child and feeling competent as a parent.

Don't expect to feel at home immediately.

Or for everything to come naturally to you.

Or that everything will be perfect from now on.

Everything new takes time to grow into.

You need to acclimate to the new environment.

So, be patient and gentle with yourself. And kind to others.

This might be new – but it's not yet normal.

You have entered. Now take time to get established.

IT'S NOT HOW I IMAGINED

Our son, Elijah, has developed a love for sneakers to the point where he kind of obsesses over them. When a new pair of Nike Air Jordans is released, he hands me all his savings and asks me to order them online. Then, every day he hounds me to track where they are in the postal system.

When they finally arrive, he carefully opens the box like it's the Ark of the Covenant. He lifts each shoe out and examines it closely. At first, he hardly wants to wear them in case they get dirty. Each evening, he cleans off every speck of dirt.

A few weeks later, Elijah can usually be found running through the muck in his 'old' shoes and has already been searching online for the next new release.

I've come to realize that the anticipation of the new shoes is greater than the reality of actually owning them.

The waiting is more exciting than the fulfillment.

I think many of us are the same.

We have a picture in our minds of what life will be like when we attain a certain goal or reach a particular stage of life.

We imagine what it will be like to meet the love of our life and get married.

Or how it will feel when we get that new job or promotion at work.

Or to reach some milestone or marker that we have worked hard to achieve.

Or to live in that new place or attain a certain level of financial success.

It's good to have goals, dreams, and ambitions. We should desire better things for our lives, families, and future.

But let me offer a word of caution here.

Don't be surprised if you reach your goal or get what you always wanted and now feel a little disappointed or deflated.

You might think, "Is this it?"

You can wonder if it was really worth all the effort, sacrifice, and prayers that got you here.

Of course, you're grateful.

But it's not how you expected it to be. You feel different than you thought you would.

In your head, you pictured 'perfect'. Instead, you were given reality.

Let me give an example.

Some of you would love to write a book. You've had it in your heart for years to put your life experiences and encounters with God onto paper. You know it would help other people. Plus, it might become a bestseller. You imagine yourself leaping out of bed full of enthusiasm each morning, pouring a cup of hot coffee, and sitting behind a computer (or an old typewriter) as you express yourself with eloquent and expressive words.

That's kind of how I pictured it.

The reality is somewhat different.

Right now, I'm typing these words in a deserted hotel lobby while on vacation with my family. While everyone else slept, I quietly tip-toed out of our room at 6.00am. It's still dark outside and I'm feeling tired. But I want to get today's devotional completed without it overly disrupting our time together. Tomorrow I'll do the same. And the next day.

I'm not trying to give you a sob story. I genuinely can't believe I get to do this. I am so thankful that you're reading these words.

But sometimes the reality of life in your 'Promised Land' is harder or more challenging than you could ever have imagined.

Or maybe, it's just different than you had pictured or anticipated.

You have the child you have longed and prayed for – but you really struggle with being a parent.

You get the relationship you've always wanted – but find yourself getting bored or feeling smothered.

You land your dream job – but feel totally unqualified and incompetent.

You grow the ministry platform you've worked so hard for – but everyone else you follow on social media still seems so much further ahead.

You complete the book you've dreamt about writing – but no one, except for your family and close friends, is interested in reading it.

There is often a gap between expectation and reality. And that gap can be filled by disappointment and disillusionment.

You can begin to wonder if you'll ever be content. Maybe there's something wrong with you.

You don't want to admit your dissatisfaction or struggles.

After all, this is what you've wanted for so long. You should be over the moon.

But it's not how you thought it would be.

Maybe that's because it's not supposed to be.

You see, it's not about the destination.

It's always about the journey.

We get so focused on where we're going.

God is more concerned with who we become along the way.

How we grow and mature. How we surrender and submit to His process.

How we learn to trust and depend on Him for everything.

That's what matters more to Him.

The Promised Land was wonderful. But it was far from perfect.

Crossing over the Jordan was the completion of one stage of their journey.

But it was also the beginning of a new era with different challenges to face, battles to fight, and obstacles to overcome.

What they had learned in the wilderness would, in large part, determine the level of victory and blessing they enjoyed in the Promised Land.

It's the same with you.

Your life is not about arriving at some place of perfection or a state of bliss.

That doesn't exist.

It's about who you are becoming each day. It's about the work of the Spirit in your heart. It's about your character, your relationships, your devotion, your trust, your surrender. It's about becoming more like Jesus.

Because soon, at some stage, the process of transition will start all over again.

Maybe in a different area of your life.

Or in a way you can't even imagine right now.

But there will be **disruption**. Something will be shaken.

There will be **detachment**. Relationships will change.

There will be **separation**. People will exit your life.

There will be **disorientation**. You'll feel uncertain or vulnerable.

Then, again, there will be **discovery** and **emergence**.

I'm not being negative or trying to burst your bubble.

It's simply a reality that change is constant.

The world and the people around you will keep changing.

And so will you.

God will surprise you.

Doors will open and opportunities will come that you could never imagine.

Relationships and connections will be formed that you can't even conceive of right now.

There will also be challenges and obstacles that you can't foresee.

But if you will posture your heart in surrender and submission to the Spirit, you will journey through the next transition and emerge more resilient, mature, effective, and Christ-like than before.

PROPHETIC ENCOURAGEMENT

IT'S TIME TO START BOOK TWO

Recently, I was preaching from 2 Samuel 21. This is a record of a period later in David's life. He's probably around 40. He's finally stepped into the promise and has been anointed as king over Israel and Judah. He's experienced much blessing and success.

However, look at what we read:

"Once again there was a battle between the Philistines and Israel. David went down with his men to fight against the Philistines, and he became exhausted. And Ishbi-Benob, one of the descendants of Rapha, whose bronze spearhead weighed three hundred shekels and who was armed with a new sword, said he would kill David." (vv. 15-16)

Look at those first words, *"Once again..."*

There's a pattern. Something keeps happening. This isn't new.

What is it?

David is still fighting Philistine giants.

277

The same Philistine giants that made him famous all those years before as a shepherd boy when he struck down Goliath.

Now, maybe 25 years later, he's still out fighting the same battles.

Some of us know what that is like.

There are some struggles that just won't go away. Even though our circumstances and surroundings have changed, there are battles inside us and around us that are persistent.

Up until now, David has known success in every battle. He's fought and he's won.

But not this time.

We are told that as he battled Ishi-Benob, David became exhausted. He's worn out and almost gets killed. His nephew Abishai sees what is happening, steps in, and kills the giant.

However, this was the verse that impacted me deeply:

"Then David's men swore to him, saying, "Never again will you go out with us to battle, so that the lamp of Israel will not be extinguished." (v. 17)

It seems that others perceive David differently than he sees himself.

Even though he was king, David still saw himself as a giant killer. He felt compelled to go out to battle. That's where he had experienced success before now. It probably gave him a sense of identity. Maybe he thought it was what others expected from him.

But his men see him as "the lamp of Israel."

In other words, David illuminates the entire nation through his life and leadership.

And that lamp was nearly snuffed out in a battle he no longer needed to fight.

His giant-killing days were behind him.

From that day forward, David would focus on what he was anointed to do: lead Israel as their king.

As I reflected on this passage, I sensed God say:

"It's time to begin Book Two.

You are trying to write another chapter of Book One, but you're struggling and weary. That's because Book One is finished.

It's time to start Book Two.

The main characters are the same. It builds upon what has gone before. But it's not simply a continuation of the same story. It's a totally new book in the series."

That made sense to me because each night I've been reading through a series of books with my son. They are all centered around the same main character. But each book is a completely new story. Each book has a beginning, different chapters, and an ending.

The ending is a demarcation line. This story is over. Another one is beginning.

Similarly, for David, Book One had brought him to this point. It had been a great story of a shepherd boy who killed a giant and went on the run until he was finally installed as King.

But Book One was over.

In trying to write another chapter, David was exhausted and almost got himself killed.

It was time to start Book Two.

I believe it could be the same for you.

You're trying to write another chapter of a story that's ended. But you're getting nowhere.

You're exhausted. It's draining you.

Your light is in danger of going out.

Maybe it's because you're trying to be the old you in a new season.

You're doing what used to work.

It brought you success.

You were effective at it.

People praised you for it.

It's what you think others expect from you.

But it's not what you're anointed to do.

You are still anointed – just not for that.

The grace has lifted.

You're still in Book One when it's time to move on to Book Two.

Like David, you need to stop perceiving yourself through the lens of your history and start seeing yourself according to your destiny.

Book One was good. It got you this far.

But it's finished.

IT'S TIME TO START BOOK TWO.

DAY 28

NEW SEASONS BRING NEW PROVISION

BIBLE READING

When the dew was gone, thin flakes like frost on the ground appeared on the desert floor. When the Israelites saw it, they said to each other, "What is it?" For they did not know what it was.
Moses said to them, "It is the bread the Lord has given you to eat.
...The Israelites ate manna forty years, until they came to a land that was settled; they ate manna until they reached the border of Canaan.

(Exodus 16: 14-15; 35)

On the evening of the fourteenth day of the month, while camped at Gilgal on the plains of Jericho, the Israelites celebrated the Passover. The day after the Passover, that very day, they ate some of the produce of the land: unleavened bread and roasted grain. The manna stopped the day after they ate this food from the land; there was no longer any manna for the Israelites, but that year they ate the produce of Canaan.

(Joshua 5: 10-12)

DEVOTIONAL

Your walk with God will not look the same in every season.

Of course, some things remain constant – the centrality of worship, prayer, Scripture, community, reaching others with the Gospel.

However, as you progress and grow in the Christian life, some things are supposed to change.

Something that was positive and productive in the past may become unhelpful or even a hindrance today.

A person, place, or ministry that brought life and growth five years ago might not be as much of a blessing or benefit now.

It was good. Maybe it still is. But it's just no longer for you.

It was God's gift in your history. But it's no longer aligned with your destiny.

That's what we see with the children of Israel in Joshua 5.

After 40 years of wandering in the wilderness, God's people have finally crossed over the Jordan into Canaan. Their feet were finally on the soil of their promise. The was is behind them.

 Look at what happens next:

"The day after the Passover, that very day, they ate some of the produce of the land: unleavened bread and roasted grain." (Joshua 5: 11)

It's easy to underestimate the significance of this sentence:

"...they ate some of the produce of the land..."

For 40 years, they had basically survived on only one type of food called *manna*.

In the wilderness, nothing much grows. There were no crops or animals that they could consume. So, God met their need for food. He supernaturally produced this substance on the ground. It was white and flaky, and it tasted like wafers made with honey.

Each morning, for 14,600 days, manna appeared on their doorstep. They gathered just enough for that day. One day each week, they collected twice as much to feed them on the Sabbath.

For an entire generation, this supply of manna was all they knew. Morning, noon, and night – it was the only food on the menu.

However, as soon as they enter the Promised Land there is a sudden shift:

"The manna stopped the day after they ate this food from the land; there was no longer any manna for the Israelites, but that year they ate the produce of Canaan." (v. 12)

The manna stopped.

Just like that.

The daily delivery of food ceased.

They never tasted manna again.

What was happening? What was God doing?

1. THE MANNA STOPPED AS A SIGN THAT THEY HAD TRANSITIONED INTO A NEW ERA.

For 40 years, manna had been God's supernatural provision to keep them alive in a dry, barren place.

But it was only ever intended to be their desert diet.

Now, they have crossed the Jordan.

They have passed through this major transition from the wilderness into the Promised Land.

This shift is so much more than simply a new physical location. They have crossed over into a completely different way of living.

The most obvious immediate sign of this shift is that manna is no longer on the menu. Their old supply has been cut off.

And there will be new means of provision and a new strategy for sustenance in this new season.

In our own lives, transition always brings change. And the more significant the transition, the greater the changes will be.

Since late 2019, I believe we have been walking through the most significant transition in our lifetimes.

We haven't just entered a new season. We've crossed over into the first season of a completely new era.

And as we continue to move forward into this uncharted terrain, there will be many more substantial changes – in our lives, relationships, churches, communities, and the wider world.

The shaking isn't stopping.
The shift is continuing.
Change is ongoing.

Many things will never be the same as they were just a few years ago.

Like the manna, God has taken them off the menu.

More personally, when an area that was once abundant and fruitful suddenly dries up, it's often a sign that God is leading you into something new.

When a source of provision or supply that you depended on is taken away, you are probably transitioning into a new way of living.

284

When you are suddenly forced to face a change and you have to find new ways of being, God is shifting you beyond your old normal.

It usually feels confusing and disorientating for a while. But you adapt and pivot. And you come to realize that the upset is actually an upgrade.

I think back to March 2020. I had always maintained that I would never do church online. Then, overnight, we were faced with a new reality. We adapted quickly. We had to.

Just a few months later, when we re-opened for in-person gatherings, I couldn't even imagine discontinuing our online services. They had become an immense source of outreach, growth, and blessing for the church.

But the change only happened because, as we entered a new era, the old way of doing things suddenly dried up. We were forced to make the change.

Why else did the manna stop?

2. **THE MANNA STOPPED BECAUSE GOD WANTED HIS PEOPLE TO DEVELOP A TASTE FOR THE NEW.**

Look again at verse 12:

"The manna stopped the day after they ate this food from the land..."

As soon as they consumed the food in the Promised Land for the first time, the manna ceased. The old was to be replaced by the new.

I've always been a fussy eater. I eat a very limited range of food. Mostly some variation of beef or chicken.

Occasionally, when I'm feeling adventurous, I'll try something different. But I usually revert to my old diet. Why? Because it's familiar and readily available.

I think that if the manna hadn't stopped, there would have been a certain group of people who would have been happy to live on manna for the rest of their lives.

Even though there was now a new variety of other food available, there would have been some who would have said:

"I think I'll just stick to manna. There's nothing wrong with manna. It's been good enough for the last 40 years. Why would I change now?"

So, God takes manna off the menu. It's no longer an option. They have no choice but to leave behind the old and try the new.

Manna might have been good - it might even have been from God - **but it was only ever meant to be temporary.** This supply was only ever supposed to be for a season.

We often encounter problems when we take something that was intended to be provisional, and we try to make it permanent.

There are times when God will strategically remove things, people, and situations from your life.

They may have been there for a long time.

And they could have been good.

They brought great blessings and benefits.

But they have served their purpose. Now your season has shifted, and God is making new resource and provision available.

For something new to enter, something familiar often has to depart.

Sometimes things need to be removed from your life, not because they're bad. They're just old, and God wants you to step into the new.

3. THE MANNA STOPPED BECAUSE GOD HAD MORE FOR HIS PEOPLE.

Some might have assumed that the manna stopping was a punishment from God. After all, it had been His supernatural provision for so long. This could have been their thinking:

"God always gave me this. Now He's withholding it. What have I done wrong? Is He angry with me?"

However, the opposite was true.

The manna stopped because it was survival food for the wilderness. Now they had entered a land of plenty and abundance.

The manna didn't cease because God wanted to give them less. It was because He now had so much more available for His children.

Manna might have been off the menu. But now there was fruit and vegetables and meat and fish and milk and honey and so much more for them to enjoy.

Sometimes God will stop the supply of something we've enjoyed for a season, and it can feel like punishment.

We assume He's withholding something from us.

The truth is usually the opposite.

He's inviting us to step into the more that He is now making available to us.

I shared a story earlier in this book about God providing supernaturally for us during a season when we had no money. Within the space of 36 hours, two people we barely knew each gave us £500 ($650).

Here's the thing. That has never happened since. It didn't become the norm.

Of course, we've experienced generosity from others. But never in such an obvious God-ordained way.

Does that mean God doesn't care about us like He did back then?

Or have we done something wrong?

No! It's simply that in the next season He provided us with jobs and incomes where we didn't require emergency provision.

We've moved beyond living paycheck to paycheck.

The 'more' that we now enjoy is as much a sign of God's goodness as the supernatural provision was during a time of shortage.

Perhaps there are things, people, resources, or provision that were once always there for you – and now they exited your life. Could it be that God is saying:

"You don't need that any longer. You've grown, matured, and healed enough to handle this yourself. They were my supply in your wilderness season. But now you're stepping into your Promised Land."

When God removes something from you it's usually because He has got so much more for you.

It's not a downgrade, but an upgrade.
It's not a punishment, but a promotion.

In the land of milk and honey, don't settle for manna.

Don't keep living with a survival wilderness mindset in your land of promise and abundance.

4. THE MANNA STOPPED BECAUSE GOD WASN'T DOING IT THAT WAY ANY LONGER.

God never changes. He's the same yesterday, today, and forever.

But the way He does things will change.

Here, in Joshua 5, God says to His people:

"I'm not doing it like that any longer.
I supernaturally met your needs in the desert with manna.

That means of provision served its purpose. But it always had an
expiration date.

Now you have fertile farmland available, I'm enabling you to feed
yourselves. Follow the laws of sowing and reaping. Learn to plant gardens
and grow crops.

In this new season, there's a new strategy and a new means of supply.
You're shifting from gatherers to growers."

There are some areas in our lives and in His church where God would say:

"I'm not doing it that way any longer. I know it's what you're used to. I
know it's what you're comfortable with. I know it's how you like it.

But the landscape has changed. The season has shifted. I'm not doing it
that way any longer.

The way I dealt with you in the last season is not how I'm going to deal
with you in this new place.

The source is the same. Everything comes from me. But the means of
supply has changed."

Many believers struggle to move on from the way God used to do things.

I'm not talking about forcing change.

But we must learn to co-operate with the Holy Spirit as He removes some
things and reveals new methods and means of doing things.

Don't resist them because they're uncomfortable.

Don't cling to the old because it's familiar.

The manna might have stopped, but God's provision continued in a different way.

Ultimately, His purpose was to move them from being dependent on the provision, to developing a deeper relationship with the Provider.

He wanted them to transition from being former slaves who only knew survival mode to mature sons and daughters who learn responsibility and live in abundance.

It's the same with you.

In transition seasons, when the resources and people you have come to depend on are no longer part of your life, trust that the Father will still supply everything you need, even if it's in a new way.

The old might have been good. But now it's time for an upgrade.

It's time to cross over from the wilderness manna into your Promised Land of abundance.

PROPHETIC ENCOURAGEMENT

THIS IS A TIME OF 'UNLOCKING'

As I worshipped, I had a picture of a large old padlock clicking open. It looked like it had been closed for a very long time.

The key that opened it was very small. There was little effort required. Just a small turn and it was unlocked.

I believe that the LORD is unlocking things that have been closed or sealed for a long time.

Doors that have been tightly shut will suddenly and, in some cases, miraculously open.

Some of you will receive 'keys' enabling you to open them for yourself.

Small shifts and changes;
Seemingly insignificant conversations;
Tweaks in your method or strategy;
A slight adjustment of direction or effort
- these will bring about the unlocking.

Positions, roles, and opportunities that have been closed off are going to open up.

Finances and title deeds to properties are going to be released.

Broken relationships that have been deadlocked - in some cases for many years - are going to be restored and reconciled.

Gifts and callings that have been lying dormant inside you are going to be reawakened and used powerfully for great fruitfulness and fulfillment.

Some are going to receive very clear and specific prophetic words. These 'announcements' from Heaven will unlock a completely new season.

The 'stalemate' will be broken.
The impasse will be lifted.
The blockage will be removed.

THIS IS A TIME OF 'UNLOCKING'.

DAY 29

SEIZE THE MOMENT

BIBLE READING

That night all the members of the community raised their voices and wept aloud. All the Israelites grumbled against Moses and Aaron, and the whole assembly said to them, "If only we had died in Egypt! Or in this wilderness! Why is the Lord bringing us to this land only to let us fall by the sword? Our wives and children will be taken as plunder. Wouldn't it be better for us to go back to Egypt?" And they said to each other, "We should choose a leader and go back to Egypt."

…Early the next morning they set out for the highest point in the hill country, saying, "Now we are ready to go up to the land the Lord promised. Surely we have sinned!"

But Moses said, "Why are you disobeying the Lord's command? This will not succeed! Do not go up, because the Lord is not with you. You will be defeated by your enemies, for the Amalekites and the Canaanites will face you there. Because you have turned away from the Lord, he will not be with you and you will fall by the sword."

Nevertheless, in their presumption they went up toward the highest point in the hill country, though neither Moses nor the ark of the Lord's covenant moved from the camp. Then the Amalekites and the Canaanites who lived in that hill country came down and attacked them and beat them down all the way to Hormah.

(Numbers 14: 1-4; 40-45)

DEVOTIONAL

Several years ago, I was traveling in the States. I flew into Boston and had a connecting flight four hours later. I figured I'd make the most of the wait. I ordered food, read for a while, listened to music, watched a movie on my iPad, and then caught up on replying to emails. At some point, I glanced at my watch and was shocked to discover that it was only fifteen minutes from my departure time. I sprinted to the gate and, after much persuading (and possibly begging), was permitted to board the plane.

I had become so relaxed and preoccupied with other things in the waiting area that I almost missed the whole purpose of the wait - to get to my destination.

When a delay in any area of our lives lasts too long and we see little change, we can begin to lose our expectancy and readiness.

We become so settled in the waiting that, when God does open a door, we're unprepared or apprehensive to walk through it.

In my experience, **there are certain *kairos* seasons of opportunity where God gives a supernatural grace and enablement for accomplishment, advancement, acceleration, and breakthrough.**

It's not that you can't be blessed or promoted at any other time.

But there are certain set times when His divine empowerment brings an unusual ease to accomplish His will and bear much fruit.

It's as if the wind is at your back, propelling you forward.

There is a unique favor for flourishing.

There are abundant resources available for building.

There is an unusual momentum for growth.

There is a rare alignment of the right people, in the right place, at the right time.

293

We see this in the story of Nehemiah. He seizes a divine moment of opportunity and rebuilds the walls of Jerusalem in only 52 days.

We see it in the book of Esther. There was an awareness that she was strategically positioned in the palace *"for such a time as this"* (Esther 4:14).

The Apostle Paul recognized such a moment in his ministry:

"Now when I went to Troas to preach the gospel of Christ and found that ***the Lord had opened a door for me...*** *"*
(2 Corinthians 2: 12)

We see these *kairos* moments throughout Scripture and history. They are turning points, pivotal seasons, times of accelerated change.

I believe we are living in such a time of appointed favor.

God is giving us a moment of unusual grace.

In late 2019 and into 2020, we crossed over into the beginning of a new era. It was the beginning of a decade of major global shaking, sifting, and shifting.

Now, I believe that 2024-25 is the pivot point, the hinge of this major transition - for the nations - but also for you personally.

Amid the accelerated change, there is an unusual opportunity for advancement and innovation.

You are living in a unique and unprecedented season for:

- *Building new businesses.*
- *Pioneering strategic ministries.*
- *Releasing new products.*
- *Launching community programs.*
- *Forming key alignments and partnerships.*
- *Initiating entrepreneurial endeavors.*
- *Developing creative solutions.*
- *Expanding into a new territory.*

- *Growing on a new platform.*
- *Getting started on your passion project.*
- *Writing a book or starting a podcast.*
- *Investing in land or property.*
- *Moving into a new industry or field.*
- *Stepping into positions of influence and impact.*

Don't miss your moment of grace.

Don't procrastinate because of fear or uncertainty.

Don't wait until your plan is perfect and every detail is clear.
Don't hold off until all the resources are available.

Don't postpone moving forward until everyone is in agreement with you.

Don't delay until the environment around you is more settled and stable.

Don't be deterred by obstacles or opposition.

If God opens a door, walk through it.

Because a day will come when that door may close, and that opportunity will be gone. It will be too late.

SOME DOORS DON'T RE-OPEN

When Israel exited Egypt, God presented them with an unprecedented season of opportunity to enter the Promised Land and defeat all opposition.

However, ten spies returned from Canaan with a negative report that drained their faith, diminished their confidence in God's promises, and caused them to shrink back in fear:

"That night all the members of the community raised their voices and wept aloud. All the Israelites grumbled against Moses and Aaron, and the whole assembly said to them, "If only we had died in Egypt! Or in this wilderness! Why is the Lord bringing us to this land only to let us fall by

the sword? Our wives and children will be taken as plunder. Wouldn't it be better for us to go back to Egypt?" And they said to each other, "We should choose a leader and go back to Egypt." (Numbers 14:1-4)

In response to their total lack of trust, God declared that this entire generation would perish in the wilderness. None of them, except for Joshua and Caleb, would inherit the promise.

This sobering judgment from the LORD shook the people. They had a sudden change of heart. We read:

"When Moses reported this to all the Israelites, they mourned bitterly. Early the next morning they set out for the highest point in the hill country, saying, "Now we are ready to go up to the land the Lord promised. Surely we have sinned!" (Numbers 14: 39-40)

They changed their minds. They decided that they were now ready. They should press forward and take the land.

However, it wasn't that easy. The door of grace had closed:

"But Moses said, "Why are you disobeying the Lord's command? This will not succeed! Do not go up, because the Lord is not with you. You will be defeated by your enemies..." (vv. 41-42)

Because they had refused to walk through the open door, the supernatural empowerment for success had lifted.

The opportunity for victory was gone.

The *kairos* moment had passed.

They missed their chance.

Tragically, they spent the next forty years wandering in the desert. An entire generation never took hold of what God had made available to them.

I know the Bible says that when God opens a door, no man can shut it (Revelation 3:8).

But that doesn't mean God won't shut the door if you refuse to walk through it.

You have a choice. Seize the moment or stay where you are.

TAKE HOLD OF THE OPPORTUNITY

I was recently watching a fascinating interview with Pastor Joel Osteen of Lakewood Church in Texas.

As the son of a well-known minister John Osteen, Joel had never wanted to be a pastor or preacher. For 17 years he worked for his father's growing television ministry, shunning the limelight. He was much happier behind the camera, producing programs and supporting those with a more public role.

His father would often ask him to preach, but he always politely declined. It wasn't his thing. He was too shy and introverted for the platform.

When Pastor John was 77, he thought he would try one more time with his son. He called Joel and asked if he would consider preaching the next Sunday.

Instinctively, as always, Joel said *no*.

However, as soon as he set down the phone, he sensed the Holy Spirit stir something inside him. When he called back to tell his father that he'd accept the offer to preach, his whole family was stunned.

That was on Monday.

On Friday, his father was admitted to the hospital.

That Sunday, Joel Osteen stepped onto the platform for the first time. Pastor John listened to his son's first sermon over the phone in the hospital. The nurses told Joel they'd never seen his father so proud.

A few days later, John had a heart attack and went to be with the Lord.

That first sermon which Joel preached only because he was obedient to the nudging of the Holy Spirit made it much easier to transition into the role of leading Lakewood Church after his father's death.

Whatever you think of Joel Osteen's ministry, that is a powerful and inspiring story. He courageously seized the moment and received the reward.

But you can also probably think of people who once had big dreams and great potential.

They were presented with opportunities and open doors.

But, for whatever reason, they didn't respond in obedience to God when He called them to step forward.

They procrastinated.

They made excuses.

It was never the right time.

They were overly concerned with the opinions of others.

They were controlled by fear.

They were distracted by other things.

Maybe they assumed that the opportunity would come around again. Or the door would stay open forever.

Sometimes it does.

At other times, God simply moves on. He finds someone else who will say *yes*. That's why the Bible says:

*"**Today**, if you hear his voice, do not harden your hearts..."*
(Hebrews 3: 15)

I don't want to miss my moment of opportunity.

I know you don't either.

American rapper Eminem (someone I never thought I'd quote in a devotional) asked this poignant question in his track *Lose Yourself*:

"If you had one shot, or one opportunity to seize everything you ever wanted in one moment, would you capture it, or just let it slip?"

Today, if God is speaking to you, don't be deterred by fear or get stuck in a cycle of procrastination because everything isn't completely clear up front.

Of course, if it's a major move, it's right to seek some confirmation. God will bring clarity.

But don't keep holding back because you're waiting for 100 supernatural confirmations!

As the preacher and revival historian Leonard Ravenhill said:

"The opportunity of a lifetime must be seized in the lifetime of the opportunity."

For some, God is placing before you an open door.

But it might not stay open for long.

Don't allow indecision or passivity to keep you from entering into God's best for your life.

Trust His faithfulness.

Take hold of His promises.

Receive His strength and provision.

Seize the moment.

Show up fully.

Step through the door.

And see what God will do through you.

I love what how the late evangelist Reinhard Bonnke expressed this:

"God works with the workers, goes with the goers, but does not sit with the sitters."

PROPHETIC ENCOURAGEMENT

COME OUT OF THE CAVE.

Step out from isolation.
You have endured a long season of barrenness and hiddenness.

Now it's time to re-emerge and step into the new assignment that the LORD is placing before you.
A lot has changed.
Slowly and subtly, a metamorphosis has taken place.
You have shed old skin, letting go of imposter identities and removing hindering habits.

The Spirit has done a significant work within you.
He has healed deep wounds and stripped away hindering attachments.

You have often felt dry and empty, weary and worn out.
Like spiritual surgery, it has been painful, but very necessary.

You have new spiritual eyes.
You will perceive things very differently.
You will see beyond the superficial and shallow.

Things that you once grasped for will hold little appeal.

You will no longer be so easily influenced by those around you.
You are secure in your identity.
You know who you are and Whose you are.

You are going to advance quickly into new territory and take ground.
Detractors and distractions won't slow you down.
Adversity and adversaries can't contain you.

You have been prepared in the wilderness.
Now it's time to move into your inheritance.
You have been stripped back in the barrenness.
Now it's time to receive from His abundance.

Step out of the cave.
Come out of hiding.
Step forward in faith and take hold of everything the Father is placing before you.

COME OUT OF THE CAVE.

DAY 30

DON'T STOP IN THE MIDDLE

BIBLE READING

And the Lord said to Joshua, "Today I will begin to exalt you in the eyes of all Israel, so they may know that I am with you as I was with Moses. Tell the priests who carry the ark of the covenant: 'When you reach the edge of the Jordan's waters, go and stand in the river.'"

… Now then, choose twelve men from the tribes of Israel, one from each tribe. And as soon as the priests who carry the ark of the Lord—the Lord of all the earth—set foot in the Jordan, its waters flowing downstream will be cut off and stand up in a heap." So when the people broke camp to cross the Jordan, the priests carrying the ark of the covenant went ahead of them. Now the Jordan is at flood stage all during harvest. Yet as soon as the priests who carried the ark reached the Jordan and their feet touched the water's edge, the water from upstream stopped flowing. It piled up in a heap a great distance away, at a town called Adam in the vicinity of Zarethan, while the water flowing down to the Sea of the Arabah (that is, the Dead Sea) was completely cut off. So the people crossed over opposite Jericho. The priests who carried the ark of the covenant of the Lord stopped in the middle of the Jordan and stood on dry ground, while all Israel passed by until the whole nation had completed the crossing on dry ground.

(Joshua 3: 7; 14-17)

DEVOTIONAL

We often enter a season of transition with excitement. We've heard God speak. Change is in the air. We're leaving somewhere behind that we'd rather not be. There's movement, momentum, and expectation. Yes, it's scary. But the future is wide open. Our lives are full of possibility and potential.

Similarly, as our transition comes to an end, there's a sense of fulfillment, accomplishment, and new beginnings. We've entered the role or position we had longed for. New, healthy relationships are forming. We're finally starting to feel settled and stable. Life has some semblance of certainty and predictability.

It's in the middle part of transition that we often get a little lost.

When we're in-between where we were and where we're going.

You know you can't go back. But you aren't sure what your next steps forward should be.

Everything seems unclear. It's hard to find a firm footing. Life feels barren and empty.

There's a disconnection with your past. Your former friends aren't around. Your old life has been disrupted and even dismantled. You've been stripped back and feel vulnerable and insecure.

You're weary and you begin to wonder if you made the right decision back there. Maybe you should have stayed. Perhaps things would have changed. Was it really that bad, after all?

That's where the struggle happens – in the middle.

The 'messy middle' is a more accurate term. Because everything is undefined, jumbled, confusing, disorienting, and difficult.

The middle is messy.

I experience that when writing a book.

I begin with a sense of enthusiasm and excitement. The first chapters flow easily. It's like they almost write themselves. It feels great.

Then I come to the middle.

And I hit a wall.

Actually, it normally happens about a third of the way through.

Some call it 'writers block'. Others label it 'resistance'.

Whatever the term, it gets hard. Every chapter is a daunting challenge. I begin to think I was insane to embark on this project.

Should I cut it shorter? Would people notice if the devotional was half the amount of days?

This is my sixth book. And I've experienced this with every one of them. I constantly remind myself of that. I've been here before. I can't stop now. I must keep pushing through the middle.

It happens in life. That's why we joke about a 'mid-life crisis' when the 40-something-year-old dad purchases a red sports car.

Several years ago, I had a conversation with one of the U.K.'s leading counselors. I was pouring out my confusion in regard to my ministry and calling. I was struggling and wondered if it was time to do something else. When I finally was quiet, she looked at me, and in her lovely soft Scottish accent commented: *"Craig, you must be 42."*

"I am", I replied. "How did you know?"

She answered, *"Everyone thinks a mid-life crisis happens at 40. It actually happens to most people at 42."*

That was helpful to know. I was in the middle. I should put away the car brochures and get on with what I was called to do.

It happens in marriage. As couples exchange vows, their hearts are brimming with passion and dreams for their future together. It's in the middle that this commitment is tested. That's why the average age at divorce is 45 for men and 42 for women.

It's the same with work. We start a new job or entrepreneurial endeavor. It's exciting, fresh, and a welcome change from what we were doing before. Three years later, it often feels very different. It's become a slog. Your days are drudgery. Your boss is a jerk. Your colleagues are mean. The market is changing. And you begin to consider a major shift in career.

I could give many more examples. But you can hopefully see the pattern. **The middle is often where we struggle most.**

The middle is where we find God's people in Joshua 3.

After 40 years of wandering in the wilderness, they've come to a major transitional moment. They're standing on the bank of the Jordan River, positioned right at the edge of their promise.

Their future is wide open before them. They can see Canaan on the other side. They're so close to stepping into the life they've been longing for.

YOU HAVEN'T BEEN HERE BEFORE

The challenge is that this is completely unknown and unfamiliar territory. They have never been anywhere like this before. We read in verses 3-4:

"When you see the ark of the covenant of the Lord your God, and the Levitical priests carrying it, you are to move out from your positions and follow it. Then you will know which way to go, since you have never been this way before."

Other than Joshua and Caleb, all the people have ever experienced is the wilderness. They were supposed to pass through the desert. But they got stuck there and it became their home. It's what they know. It's not great, but at least it's familiar and predictable.

Now, on the other side of the Jordan, everything is new and different. There are cities to conquer, inhabitants to displace, and battles to fight.

There's maybe some excitement. But mostly they're feeling fearful, uncertain, and probably overwhelmed.

God knows what they're thinking. He says:

"...you've never been this way before." (v. 4)

That's how life has felt for these past four years. We are entering a new era, living through a major transitional moment in history. There has been so much disruption, volatility, and upheaval. The future is unknown. Everything feels uncertain and unstable.

You haven't been this way before.

That's why we need to give ourselves, and each other, a little bit more grace.

If you've been struggling - as a parent, a spouse, a single, an employee, an entrepreneur, a leader - whatever it is...give yourself a little bit more grace.

It's okay not to have all the answers.
It's normal not to have everything figured out.
It's alright to be feel a bit up and down emotionally right now.

You haven't been this way before.
But also, give others the same grace.

They haven't been this way before either.

In this decade of disruption, we all find ourselves in uncharted territory.

Old maps are obsolete. Previous methods aren't helpful. The former ways of doing things don't seem to be working.

We're all trying to navigate to the other side

We haven't been this way before.

So, the question is: *what do you do in the middle?*

What do you do when you can't go back, but your future is unclear, daunting, and uncertain?

Look at the verses 7-8:

"And the Lord said to Joshua, 'Today I will begin to exalt you in the eyes of all Israel, so that they may know that I am with you as I was with Moses. Tell the priests who carry the ark of the covenant: "When you reach the edge of the Jordan's waters, go and stand in the river."'

1. REFLECT ON WHERE YOU HAVE BEEN.

God tells the priests to stand in the middle of the river carrying the Ark of the Covenant. The Ark represented the presence of God among His people.

That's God's first instruction: Go and stand in the middle.

From the middle, they could see in both directions.

They could look back at the wilderness they had come from.

And they could look forward into the Promised Land – the place they were going.

In our own moments of significant transition, as we prepare to step into the new, it's important to look back and reflect on where we have been.

Take stock. Remember the highs and lows. Recall the special moments and also consider the challenges you've faced.

Think about the people who were with you on the journey. Those who are still with you. And those who, for whatever reason, are no longer a part of your life.

Ask yourself:

What has God taught Me? How have I changed? In what ways have I grown?

What have I lost? What do miss most about the past? What would I change if I could?

Above all, remember the faithfulness of God.

Through every moment - in the love and the losses, the blessings and burdens – God has been with you. He has sustained you. He has strengthened you. He has provided for you. He has protected you.

Use that memory to fuel your faith for the future.
As you prepare to advance, it's important to pause and reflect - on your own journey, and on God's unfailing goodness.

The next thing God would tell His people is:

2. TAKE THE NEXT BEST STEP.

Look at verse 13:

"And as soon as the priests who carry the ark of the Lord – the Lord of all the earth – set foot in the Jordan, its waters flowing downstream will be cut off and stand up in a heap.'"

God instructs the priests to step into the flowing, flooded river. If they do that, the water will stop. But first, they would have to get their feet wet.

I would have much preferred it if God stopped the water first. Then I would step onto the dry ground.

But that's not how God works.

Because our God is a motion-sensitive God.

What do I mean?

In any public restroom, you rarely have to touch anything these days. You stand up, and the toilet flushes. You move your hands under the faucet, the water comes out. You place your hands under the dryer, the air blows on them.

Everything is motion-sensitive.

Our God is also motion-sensitive God.

When we move, He moves.

Often, we are waiting on God, while God is waiting on us.

We are praying: *"God I need you to you move in this situation."*

And God is replying: *"I will. But I want you to move first. I need you to take a step of faith to show that you trust Me. If you will take one step, all of Heaven will back you up."*

How do you avoid getting stuck in the middle?

Take the next best step.

It might not be a big step. It doesn't need to be.

But it's a step of faith that demonstrates to God that you trust Him.

It's a step that signals that you're ready to move forward.

It's a step that makes a statement. You're crossing over. You're not willing to settle for less than God's best.

What might that one step be for you right now?

It could be:

Applying for a different job or position.
Having that difficult conversation in your relationship.
Learning a new skill or registering for a course.
Stepping up to serve in a new area of ministry.
Getting out of the house more often and socializing with others.
Opening up to a trusted friend about your struggles.
Writing the first page of that book.

Whatever it is, take the first step.

You probably already know what you need to do. You don't need more clarity. What you need is courage.

God can't bless what you won't do.

Get your feet wet. Take the first step.

Finally, when you're in the middle:

3. KEEP MOVING FORWARD.

Look at what we read:

"When you see the ark of the covenant of the Lord your God, and the Levitical priests carrying it, you are to move out from your positions and follow it...

...all Israel passed by until the whole nation had completed the crossing on dry ground..." (Joshua 3: 3; 17)

Note the words used: *the people moved...they followed...they passed by...they all crossed over.*

They didn't stop in the middle.

They simply kept moving forward.

That's what God spoke to me at the beginning of the pandemic in relation to the church I lead:

"Just keep moving forward. You might be moving slower than before. But don't stop."

Because here's what can happen: **If you stop too long in one place, you get stuck.**

People often tell me they feel stuck. Sometimes, they've just stopped in one place for too long.

Last summer, as our family took an evening stroll on a local beach, we came across a car spinning its wheels in the sand. The driver and those pushing from behind were giving it their all. But their best efforts were frustrated. Nothing was moving. Normally, another vehicle could have towed them. But the beach was already closed. They had stayed too long. Now they were stuck.

Sometimes you're stuck simply because you stopped too long in one place.

You became too settled.
You ignored the signs telling you it was time to move.
You didn't want to risk change.
You weren't willing to let go of the familiar.

Our God is a God who always leads His people forward. In Scripture, we never see God move His people backward. They keep advancing, taking ground, occupying new territory, seizing fresh opportunities, taking hold of His promises.

Can I encourage you today: **If you're in the middle, keep moving forward.**

You might be weary. That's okay. Catch your breath.

But don't stop for too long. Don't get stuck.

Maybe you have no idea what to do. Just take the next best step.

Whatever it is that God has placed in your heart – don't get passive or procrastinate.

311

Keep moving forward.

One small step can lead to momentum. The next step appears. Then the next one, and so on.

The Father will begin to speak. Maybe in new or different ways than you're accustomed to.

He will start to reveal plans and open opportunities.

You'll begin to get your bearings.
The blurriness will give way to fresh vision.

One day you'll realize - something has shifted.

Your passion has reignited.
A new assignment has been birthed.
New alignments have formed.
Life has started to take on some shape and stability.

You're no longer in the middle.
You've stepped across to the other side.

PROPHETIC ENCOURAGEMENT

BE WARY OF ATTACKS DESIGNED TO DISTRACT.

The enemy is operating a strategy of distraction and discouragement at this time.

He wants to divert your attention and focus away from what matters most and get you overly focused on petty arguments and trivial issues.

Avoid getting drawn into pointless disputes that accomplish nothing.

Don't waste your energy stressing about the negativity or criticism of others.

Save your best strength for the work the LORD has assigned to you.

Like Nehemiah, when he was criticized and opposed by Sanballat and other enemies of Israel, your response must be:

"I am doing a great work and I cannot come down. Why should the work stop while I leave it and come down to you?" (Nehemiah 6:3)

There is a Divine urgency and mandate on your assignment.

That is why the enemy is starting to oppose you so vigorously.

He wants to wear you down through subtle intimidation and blatant attacks.

Stay focused on the calling and ignore the critics.

The LORD's hand is upon you.

He will strengthen and sustain you.

You are completing a great work.

Don't give up or stop short.

BE WARY OF ATTACKS DESIGNED TO DISTRACT.

DAY 31

REPOSITION YOURSELF

BIBLE READING

The Israelites did evil in the eyes of the LORD, and for seven years he gave them into the hands of the Midianites.
Because the power of Midian was so oppressive, the Israelites prepared shelters for themselves in mountain clefts, caves and
strongholds. Whenever the Israelites planted their crops, the Midianites, Amalekites and other eastern peoples invaded the country. They camped on the land and ruined the crops all the way to Gaza and did not spare a living thing for Israel, neither sheep nor cattle nor donkeys. They came up with their livestock and their tents like swarms of locusts. It was impossible to count them or their camels; they invaded the land to ravage it. Midian so impoverished the Israelites that they cried out to the LORD for help.

…The angel of the LORD came and sat down under the oak in Ophrah that belonged to Joash the Abiezrite, where his son Gideon was
threshing wheat in a winepress to keep it from the Midianites. When the angel of the LORD appeared to Gideon, he said, "The LORD is with you, mighty warrior."

(Judges 6: 1-6; 11-12)

314

DEVOTIONAL

Several years ago, I had a prophetic dream. I was the driver of a double-decker (two-tier) bus. However, when I climbed onto the bus to begin the journey, my seat was located on the upper deck, a few rows from the front.

This was completely the wrong position for driving. I should have been downstairs, at the very front of the bus.

I started moving, but as the dream progressed, I became increasingly anxious and concerned. I recall repeatedly complaining: *"I can't see anything. I'm not sure where I'm going."*

However, I kept driving, trying to sense where I was supposed to be. Navigating the large passenger vehicle from where I was seated was both frightening and dangerous.

I was doing the right thing. But I was situated in the wrong place or position to do it most effectively.

At the time, I was struggling to discern vision and see a clear way forward in various aspects of my life and ministry. It was as if God was saying: *"You're doing the right thing, but you're in the wrong position or place. You need to reposition yourself."*

STUCK IN A CYCLE OF DEFEAT

In Judges 6, we find Gideon in a similar predicament. We're told:

"...Gideon was threshing wheat in a winepress to keep it from the Midianites." (v. 11)

Wheat was supposed to be threshed in a designated space called the threshing floor. Threshing floors were hard, smooth, wide-open spaces prepared on either rock or clay. They were carefully chosen for maximum exposure to the prevailing winds. As the grain was tossed into the air together with the straw, the wind would blow the chaff away, leaving only the kernels of grain to fall on the floor.

Threshing floors were not hiding places. They were visible spaces.

Wine presses were the opposite. They were deep holes or pits which were either hewn out of rocks or dug out of the ground. As the grapes were crushed, the juice would be preserved in a stone trough.

Gideon was threshing his wheat in an enclosed winepress, not in an exposed threshing floor.

He was doing the right thing, but in the wrong place.

It was a futile and almost impossible task. There was no wind to blow away the chaff. He was working hard but seeing very few results.

Why was he threshing wheat in a hole rather than out in an open space?

"…to keep it from the Midianites." (v. 11)

Every year, at harvest time, raiders from Midian and Amalek would arrive on a multitude of camels. Like a swarm of locusts, these predatory nomads destroyed Israel's crops, stole their cattle, and terrorized the people.

That's why Gideon is in a winepress, threshing wheat. He's hiding from the prying eyes of his enemies, simply trying to survive by preserving whatever little grain he has left.

What a pitiful picture.

This wasn't how life was supposed to be.

This isn't how God intended it.

This was the Promised Land, a place of abundance and provision. It was meant to be flowing with milk and honey.

God hadn't delivered His people from over 400 years of slavery in Egypt so they could barely survive as prisoners in their own land.

Something had gone seriously wrong.

What happened?

The people of God were stuck in a continual cycle of sin, misery, and defeat.

God had commanded the children of Israel to drive out the enemy from the land that He was giving them.

They only partially obeyed Him, which is disobedience.

Not only did they allow some of the enemies to remain in the land, but they even entered into covenant with them and worshipped their pagan gods.

This was their undoing. Their sin and idolatry removed them from living under the protective hand of the LORD. Thus, we read:

"The Israelites did evil in the eyes of the LORD, and for seven years he gave them into the hands of the Midianites." (v. 1)

God cannot bless sin and He will not bless disobedience.

He permitted Israel's enemies to overpower them, plunder their inheritance, and cause them to live in a constant state of fear. They were in survival mode.

Isn't that what sin does? It robs us of the blessings and benefits that Jesus' blood purchased for us. We might be saved. We're technically living in the land of promise. But we're not enjoying our full inheritance. We're living far below the abundant life promised by Jesus (John 10: 10).

We're told that this cycle of misery had been going on for seven years. They couldn't fully get free. They would repent and return to God for a season. God would raise up a leader or *judge* to deliver them. Life was better for a while. But soon, they would slide back into their old patterns and face the destructive consequences of their disobedience.

Many believers find themselves in a similar situation.

They're in the Kingdom. They have been saved through faith in Christ. But they're stuck in cycles and patterns of sin and misery. They might find freedom for a while, but it's never long before they return to the things they were determined to leave behind. They see others enjoying freedom and fulfillment, and wonder why they never move beyond a place of struggle.

Could it be because they have never put to death the flesh (Colossians 3: 5)? They're keeping things alive that God wants them to kill. As the Puritan John Owen wrote: *"Be killing sin, or sin will be killing you."*

I think this is also a picture of the state of the church.

Instead of reaping a harvest of souls, compromise within the Body of Christ has brought many into a low place where the main goal is survival, not revival.

That's what I see as I look around the church here in the UK and Ireland. I've never seen the church at such a low ebb as it has been from the start of 2020 to the end of 2023.

Maybe it's different where you are.

But here, most of the church retreated into hiding during COVID-19 and became just as fearful as the world. Since the restrictions were lifted, the main goal hasn't been growth or reaching lost people. All of the energy has been focused on trying to get back to where things were before.

While I'm sensing a slight shift in these last few months since we've entered 2024, the majority of the church is still stuck in survival mode, desperately trying to maintain the little they have.

That's what Gideon is doing.

He's in a low place struggling to hold on to what he has.

But he was never going to be effective or productive. Because you can't thresh wheat in a wine press.

It's futile. It's exhausting. It simply doesn't work.

Gideon needs to reposition himself.

He can't stay where he is, doing what he's doing, and expect different results.

MAKE THE CHANGE

That's a word for some of you today. Especially if something isn't working in your life.

You're giving it your all, being diligent, pouring yourself out - but you're seeing little success or fruit.

You're busy and active. Maybe you're exhausted from working so hard. But you're not experiencing the return you expected.

Could it be that you're doing the right thing but in the wrong place?

Do you need to make a shift?

Economist, D. Edwards Deming, once famously said:

"Every system is perfectly designed to get the results it gets."

In other words, **if something isn't working, don't keep doing it.**

This could apply to your job, a relationship, a ministry, a sport, your health - or any other area where something isn't working the way it should - or the way it once did.

Try something different. Reposition yourself.

Or maybe, you're stuck in a cycle of sin and defeat? Like Israel, you're not enjoying the blessings and benefits of your inheritance.

You want to change. You've tried so hard.

But still, you keep finding yourself drawn back to the same destructive habits and patterns.

You're in a low place. A depressed state. Life is miserable.
It's time to try something different. Possibly something that's scary or radical.

Because if you keep doing what you've always done, this cycle is never going to be broken. And that's not the life that God intends for you.

You can find freedom. Things can turn around. You can experience abundant life in Christ.

But not if you stay exactly where you are, doing what you've always done. No matter how hard you try, you're setting yourself up for more failure.

Reposition yourself.

Make a move.

Climb out of the hole.

Don't remain in a place of frustration and futility.

We saw Jesus say something similar in yesterday's Bible reading:

"If anyone will not welcome you or listen to your words, leave that home or town and shake the dust off your feet." (Matthew 10: 14)

In other words, **don't keep trying to force a door that is closed.** You're doing the right thing – preaching the Gospel – but you're in the wrong place. Move on. Try somewhere else. Soon you'll find people who will welcome you and respond to your message.

REMEMBER WHO YOU ARE

God doesn't drag Gideon out of the hole. Instead, He reminds Gideon of his true identity:

"When the angel of the LORD appeared to Gideon, he said, 'The LORD is with you, mighty warrior.'" (v. 12)

320

Gideon saw himself as anything but a 'mighty warrior'.

But how you perceive yourself can be very different from who God says you are.

God speaks to Gideon's real identity, reminding him:

"Gideon, you're not supposed to be hiding in a hole. It's not who you are. I made you for more than this. Stop allowing fear to hold you hostage here. It's time to confront the thing you're avoiding. Climb out of there. Become who you truly are – a mighty warrior. Reposition yourself."

Similarly, today, I believe the LORD would say to you:

"Stop living below your true identity in Christ.
Come out of containment.

Confront the thing you've been avoiding.

Climb out of the hole where you're hiding.

Stop living a small and shrunken existence.

Stop being controlled by fear of other people.

You were made for so much more than this.

It's time to come out of the winepress – the depressed place, the place of crushing. You've been there too long.

What you're doing there isn't working. And it's never going to work.

I want to elevate you. I'm calling you to higher ground.

I want to bring you into a wide, open space where you can experience the refreshing wind of my Spirit.

I will blow away the debris of fear.

I will break the hold of past trauma.

I will remove the things that you no longer need or that can't sustain you.

Stop giving your best time, energy, and resources to things that aren't working.

Stop pouring yourself into people and projects that only drain you.

Make the shift.

Break the cycle.

Disrupt the pattern.

The way things are is not how they have to be.

The way you have been living doesn't represent who you truly are.

It's time to move.

Do the right thing – but do it in the right place.

Reposition yourself."

Following the dream that I shared at the beginning, I made some changes in my life and ministry.

They weren't major. Most people wouldn't have noticed them. But they were significant for me.

I repositioned myself. I moved into the correct seat on the bus.

And, from there, I could see clearly to advance into the good future that God was opening up before me.

PROPHETIC ENCOURAGEMENT

COME UP HIGHER.
Rise above the confusion and swirl.
Pull away from the noise and the crowd.
I want to give you My perspective on where we are going.
I will reveal to you what is to come.
I want to prepare you to stand strong, secure, and steady through the turbulence.
Ascend and abide in Me that you would bear much fruit and flourish in this next season.
Come up higher.

Come up higher.
You are seated with Christ in heavenly places.
Stop looking at things from an earthly viewpoint.
See beyond the surface and superficial.
Look deeper than the distractions and diversions.
There's so much more at stake than you see in the physical realm.
This battle is spiritual. The war is invisible.
But My Kingdom is unstoppable.
Come up higher.

Come up higher.
Step into a position of clarity.
See what I see. Feel what I feel.
The great shaking and sifting looks so different from My Throne.
Everything is right on schedule.
And so are you - you are on schedule.
Come close. Draw near. Lean in.
As you ascend, you will be aligned.
You will see My strategy and My solutions, My purpose and My planning, your alignment, and your authority.
Come up higher.

Come up higher.
I am your shield, your stability, your defender, and your deliverer.

Don't be intimidated by the darkness or silenced by the noise.
It is going to increase and intensify.
Remember - you are Mine. You carry My Kingdom within you.
All of My resources are at your disposal.
Stand on My Word. Speak My truth.
Your prayers and decrees will be backed by the armies of Heaven.
Come up higher.

Come up higher.
Clean your hands. Purify your heart.
Sit with Me. Let me show you hidden things.
In My presence, you will be clothed with fresh power.
In My Presence is supernatural peace.
In My presence is deep rest for your soul.
In my presence is restoration and healing.
In My presence is vision and direction.
In My presence is fullness and provision.
In My presence, you will discover that I am enough.
COME UP HIGHER.

DAY 32

GOD'S PROCESS OF PROMOTION | Part 1

BIBLE READING

Now Jesse said to his son David, "Take this ephah of roasted grain and these ten loaves of bread for your brothers and hurry to their camp. Take along these ten cheeses to the commander of their unit. See how your brothers are and bring back some assurance from them. They are with Saul and all the men of Israel in the Valley of Elah, fighting against the Philistines."

Early in the morning David left the flock in the care of a shepherd, loaded up and set out, as Jesse had directed. He reached the camp as the army was going out to its battle positions, shouting the war cry. Israel and the Philistines were drawing up their lines facing each other. David left his things with the keeper of supplies, ran to the battle lines and asked his brothers how they were. As he was talking with them, Goliath, the Philistine champion from Gath, stepped out from his lines and shouted his usual defiance, and David heard it. Whenever the Israelites saw the man, they all fled from him in great fear.

Now the Israelites had been saying, "Do you see how this man keeps coming out? He comes out to defy Israel. The king will give great wealth to the man who kills him. He will also give him his daughter in marriage and will exempt his family from taxes in Israel."

David asked the men standing near him, "What will be done for the man who kills this Philistine and removes this disgrace from Israel? Who is this uncircumcised Philistine that he should defy the armies of the living God?"

They repeated to him what they had been saying and told him, "This is what will be done for the man who kills him."

(1 Samuel 17: 17-27)

DEVOTIONAL

I have mixed feelings about the word *promotion*. Especially when it comes to the Christian life and matters of God's Kingdom.

Promotion sounds a little too worldly for my liking. It immediately makes me think of people who are power-hungry, overly ambitious, driven, and self-promoting. They will do whatever it takes to get to the top.

Yet, from my reading of scripture and personal experience, I can't deny that God promotes certain individuals.

He chooses to give them greater prominence, position, influence, authority, and resources.

They don't trample on people to get to the top.

Quite the opposite. They are often unassuming, humble men and women who have no desire for visibility or power.

Psalm 75:7-8 tells us:

 "It is God who judges: He brings one down, he exalts another."

In other words, **promotion comes from God.**

Romans 13:1 also says:

"...those in positions of authority have been placed there by God."

All authority is the result of either God's *appointment* or God's *allowance*.

Too often we work only for the approval of man. Or we believe that our lack of promotion is the result of unjust or unfair leaders. If only those above us would recognize our great gifts and talents, we would be much further ahead.

But promotion comes from God, not from man.

And promotion from God Is unstoppable.

We see this best exemplified in the life of David.

For the next few days, I want to explore how we can position ourselves for promotion by God.

1. SEEK GOD FIRST.

When God rejected Saul as King, he told him:

*"But now your kingdom will not endure; **the Lord has sought out a man after his own heart** and appointed him ruler of his people, because you have not kept the Lord's command."* (1 Samuel 13:14)

Saul was more preoccupied with public popularity and people's opinions than He was with pleasing God. So, God found someone who could replace him.

The thing that set David apart from everyone else was that he was *"a man after his own heart"*. That was his dominant and defining characteristic - **he put God first.**

From a human perspective, David was a very unlikely candidate. Even his own father didn't invite him to the dinner with the prophet Samuel.

Yet, God overlooked all of David's brothers and instructed Samuel to anoint the one who was undervalued and unappreciated.

This anointing might have happened with only 10 people present – Samuel, Jesse, David, and his seven brothers.

However, the flowing oil was only a visible representation of the anointing that had already taken place during the many hours that David had spent pursuing the presence of God out in the field. David had built up a history with God in the secret place. **And private devotion brings public rewards** (Matthew 6:6).

2 Chronicles 16:9 tells us:

"For the eyes of the Lord range throughout the earth to strengthen those whose hearts are fully committed to him."

God is always searching for men and women whose hearts are fully devoted to Him. He's thoroughly scanning every nation, city, town, community, and household for someone whose heart reflects His own. There aren't many of them. But when He finds one, He entrusts them with responsibility and resources.

And when God purposes to raise you up, there is nothing man can do to stop it. No unjust, unfair, unrecognizing leader can be your glass ceiling.

Hebrews 11: 6 gives us this promise:

"God...rewards those who earnestly seek him."

Seek God above everything else and allow Him to promote you. You won't have to push, manipulate, cajole, or force anything.

The humility of your heart will attract His favor.
The consecration of your character will draw His attention.
The purity of your life will position you for promotion.

Jesus made it clear:

"Seek first his kingdom and his righteousness, and all these things will be given to you as well." (Matthew 6: 33)

2. BE FAITHFUL WHERE YOU ARE.

Recently, my Associate Pastor, Jamie Bambrick, went viral on social media.

For over a year, he had been faithfully making YouTube videos about important issues affecting the church. A few had done well, garnering several thousand views. Most of them received only a few hundred views.

But, still, he diligently spent many hours scripting, recording, and editing content every week.

Then the 2024 Super Bowl happened.

Jamie was watching the game when, during a break, the ad "He Gets Us" was aired. He felt strongly that this one-minute ad didn't represent Christianity well. I'm sure the creators had good intentions. But overall, it was a woke and weak attempt at expressing the Gospel.

So, the following day, when he had a free hour, Jamie made his own version of the ad.

Within 48 hours of it being uploaded, around four million people had viewed it on Twitter and YouTube. He was subsequently interviewed by media outlets from all over the world.

Interestingly, the day Jamie uploaded it, he was helping with my *Prophetic Transitions* mentorship community. I knew nothing about the video. But during the first session, as I was teaching, I was moved by the Spirit to release a strong prophetic word that God was about to elevate the voices of those who weren't seeking position or prominence. He was going to bring them into greater visibility and enlarge their platform. Little did I know, as I was speaking, Jamie's video was exploding.

The point I'm trying to convey is this: **when you are faithful with little, God can entrust you with much** (Luke 16:10).

Small things are a big deal to God.

Consistency, dependability, and reliability matter much more than charisma, popularity, and gifting.

We see this in David's life.

He doesn't let his newfound status or significance go to his head. Immediately following the anointing by Samuel, we read:

329

"Saul sent messengers to Jesse and said, "Send me your son David, who is with the sheep." (1 Samuel 16: 19)

David has already returned to the wilderness, into obscurity, to faithfully look after his father's sheep.

Then again, in chapter 17, we read:

"David went back and forth from Saul to tend his father's sheep at Bethlehem." (17: 15)

Imagine knowing that one day you're going to be King. But right now, you have one of the lowest and most menial jobs there is.

Your current surroundings look nothing like the dream in your heart or the prophetic promises spoken over your life.

What you see and what God said appear to be miles apart.

And it's impossible, from a human standpoint, to see how God could bring His word to fulfillment.

What do you do in the meantime?

Be faithful with whatever God has placed in front of you.

Serve wherever He has placed you.

Even if it's not exciting or glamorous.

Even when no one sees or cares.

Daily faithfulness is key to being promoted by God.

Occasionally people ask me how I gained a large following on social media. They're hoping for some secret strategy or 'growth hack'.

I tell them the hard truth.

I have been posting prophetic content almost every day for six years. Even when very few people were reading it, I kept seeking to hear from God and sharing it.

Consistency and dependability are vastly underrated in our culture. Yet, **there are no shortcuts to promotion in the Kingdom of God.** As pastor and author Eugene Peterson said: *"Being a disciple of Jesus is a long obedience in the same direction."*

Be faithful where you are and allow God to promote you in His time.

3. RECOGNIZE OPPORTUNITIES WHEN THEY ARE PRESENTED.

David is sent to the battlefield to check on his brothers and bring them food. As he set out that morning, he couldn't have imagined that his life was about to change forever. He wasn't looking for his 'big break'. He was simply doing what his dad asked.

Upon his arrival, David is immediately greeted by the mocking taunts of Goliath. We read:

"David asked the men standing near him, "What will be done for the man who kills this Philistine and removes this disgrace from Israel? Who is this uncircumcised Philistine that he should defy the armies of the living God?" (1 Samuel 17: 26)

These are the first words we ever read from David in Scripture. They tell us a lot about this young man.

Up until this point in the story, nobody has even mentioned God. Everyone is completely consumed with fear of Goliath. Yet, it is inconceivable to David that anyone should be permitted to undermine Yahweh's reputation like this.

What everyone else accepted, he found intolerable.

That's a key for promotion in God's Kingdom.

Don't go with the flow. Refuse to accept the norm.

If something goes against the Word or the will of God, don't accept it or tolerate it.

Even if everyone else allows it - you have a higher standard. Your fear of the LORD is greater than your fear of any man.

The second thing I want you to notice is this - **David saw an opportunity.**

Look again at his question:

"What will be done for the man who kills this Philistine and removes this disgrace from Israel?" (v. 26)

While God's glory was utmost in his thinking, David also perceived that this was a moment where he might receive some reward or recognition.

Everyone else looked at Goliath as an opponent to be feared. David saw him as an opportunity for advancement.

Grasping for power and desperate self-promotion are nauseating. However, that doesn't mean that you shouldn't be ready to take full advantage of opportunities that God places before you.

Philippians 2:3-5 says:

"Do nothing out of selfish ambition or vain conceit. Rather, in humility value others above yourselves, not looking to your own interests but each of you to the interests of the others. In your relationships with one another, have the same mindset as Christ Jesus…

There's a vast difference between selfish ambition and Godly ambition.

- *God-created opportunities will have God at the center.*
- *Selfish ambition places self at the center.*
- *God-created opportunities will always be bigger than self.*
- *Selfish ambition is only about self.*

- *God-created opportunities keep truth foundational.*
- *Selfish ambition allows truth to become optional.*
- *God-created opportunities bring blessing to those around you.*
- *Selfish ambition uses those around you.*
- *God-created opportunities enlarge your world.*
- *Selfish ambition shrinks your world.*

Genuine humility is beautiful. It expresses the nature of Jesus who set aside His rights and took on flesh.

However false humility, shrinking down, dimming your light, denying your gifts, diminishing your potential, not fulfilling your destiny, and burying your talents - all rob God of the breathtaking glory that He wants to display through your life.

Imagine, for a moment, if David had not taken full advantage of this unique moment that God had placed before him. The history of God's people would look very different.

This was a set-up. While it would still be many years before David sat on the throne, this altercation in the Valley of Elah was a crucial step in advancing him towards his destiny.

David recognized an important opportunity when it was placed before him, and he seized it with both hands.

He didn't fight Goliath only to be promoted. But it was certainly a valuable incentive as he walked out on the field to face the giant.

It was risky to face this brute. That's why no one else was stepping forward to take on the challenge.

But the greater the risk, the greater the reward.

If you will do what no one else is willing to do, you can have what no one else has.

Are there any opportunities that God is placing before you that you're not taking full advantage of?

Maybe they don't seem to have any obvious connection to what you believe to be your primary calling. **Yet, it's amazing how God can use any event or situation to position us for His plans and purposes.**

That morning, David went to the Valley to bring supplies to his brothers.

But God had him there for a very different purpose – to take down a giant. The delivery boy would become the deliverer of a nation. And in the process, he would become front-page news.

If God is seeking to promote you, don't get in your own way. Recognize the opportunities that He is placing before you and seize them with both hands.

PROPHETIC ENCOURAGEMENT

YOU ARE BEING REPURPOSED FOR EXPANSION

You may experience that your calling has been reconfigured and reshaped - even reinvented - during this disruptive season.

It's not that your essence or core calling has changed.
But the way it is expressed or how it is worked out is going to look different in the days ahead.

The Father has been drawing you back to the very heart of your true identity - who you really are.
It's what you were wired for - what comes most naturally to you.
There's an ease and grace with it.
It carries unusual favor and enlargement.
It brings freedom, fulfillment, and life.

God has been slowly stripping away all the extraneous things that have been added over time that were never part of His desire or intention for you.
They were placed upon you through past experiences and wrong expectations from others.

This 'excess baggage' has become a distraction that has brought unnecessary stress, weariness, and overwhelm into your life.
It has diminished your joy in serving the LORD.
It's not the Father's desire or design for you.

Allow God to continue to strip away the things you don't need. They aren't compatible with where He is taking you.

You may feel vulnerable, insecure, and disorientated for a season.
You might not be sure where you 'fit'.

Soon you'll recover the passion you've lost and get back to the heart of who you really are.
Your God-given deepest desires will re-emerge.
You'll find your place.
You'll discover your people.
You'll get more deeply rooted and established in Christ.
You'll step into new levels of anointing and authority in your calling and assignment.
You'll come fully alive.

YOU ARE BEING REPURPOSED FOR EXPANSION.

DAY 33

GOD'S PROCESS OF PROMOTION | Part 2

BIBLE READING

When Eliab, David's oldest brother, heard him speaking with the men, he burned with anger at him and asked, "Why have you come down here? And with whom did you leave those few sheep in the wilderness? I know how conceited you are and how wicked your heart is; you came down only to watch the battle."

"Now what have I done?" said David. "Can't I even speak?" He then turned away to someone else and brought up the same matter, and the men answered him as before. What David said was overheard and reported to Saul, and Saul sent for him.

David said to Saul, "Let no one lose heart on account of this Philistine; your servant will go and fight him."

(1 Samuel 17: 28-32)

DEVOTIONAL

Throughout my life, I have had more jobs than I can count. I have worked for supermarkets, clothes shops, family businesses, multinational corporations, the postal service, and Coca-Cola.

For the past 20 years, I've been in full-time ministry, serving in various leadership roles at four different churches.

During all this time, I have watched many people get promoted and do a wonderful job in their new position.

I have also observed others who have been promoted way beyond their ability, capacity, or character. This rarely ends well for anyone.

More recently, I have been studying ministry leaders who thrive in their roles, grow healthy organizations, and go the distance. These men and women of integrity leave an inspirational legacy.

I have also reflected on other leaders who start out with great promise and potential. Their church or organization grows quickly, they're invited to speak at major conferences, and they write bestselling books. But tragically, things don't end well. They resign or they're forced to step down. Often, it's due to character flaws, moral failures, or other hidden, unresolved issues.

In some cases, they were promoted or given a large platform too soon. Their gifting took them further than their character could keep them.

In his book, *The Speed of Trust*, author Stephen Covey says:

*"There are no moral shortcuts in the game of business - or life. There are, basically, three kinds of people: the unsuccessful, the temporarily successful, and those who become and remain successful. **The difference is character.**"*

Character includes integrity, honesty, authenticity, and consistency. It's who you are when no one is looking.

Character builds trust. And trust is the bedrock of all long-term leadership success.

Yesterday, we started thinking about Kingdom promotion. We saw that **God promotes people**. Psalm 75:6-7 (KJV) says:

"For promotion cometh neither from the east, nor from the west, Nor from the south. But God is the judge: He putteth down one, and setteth up another."

We also learned that God promotes those:

- who seek Him first;
- who are faithful where they are; and,
- who recognize opportunities when they are presented.

Today, we will continue looking at David and examine two more key character qualities that God saw in this young man that led to his eventual promotion from the sheepfold to the royal throne.

1. TAKE RESPONSIBILITY.

At its core, leadership is taking responsibility. Leaders carry weight.

An employee can clock off the job, go home, and not give much thought to their work until the next day.

Leaders, on the other hand, rarely switch off completely. Especially senior leaders, business owners, founders of start-ups, etc. They constantly feel a burden of responsibility. The buck stops with them.

In his book, *Extreme Ownership*, former Navy Seal, Jocko Willink, writes:

"Leaders must own everything in their world. There is no one else to blame."

A lot of people want the title, prominence, and rewards of leadership. But they don't understand the level of responsibility that comes with it.

Leaders have sleepless nights. They usually have more difficult conversations than most people. There are constant problems to be solved, tensions to be managed, wages to be paid, and conflicts to be resolved.

Therefore, **God will only promote those who can handle responsibility well.** They take ownership. They can admit when they are wrong. They steward resources with diligence. They deal with difficult issues. They are willing to make tough decisions.

We see this exemplified in the life of David.

Initially, David was responsible with his father's sheep. When his dad asks him to check on his brothers, we read:

"Early in the morning David left the flock in the care of a shepherd, loaded up and set out, as Jesse had directed." (1 Samuel 17:20)

Firstly, notice that David left *early in the morning*. He didn't sleep in until lunchtime or hang around for a few days. He arose at dawn and set off. He took his assignment seriously.

Next, he ensured that the sheep were looked after while he was gone. He didn't just abandon his previous task when a new opportunity came his way. The sheep were his responsibility. It might not have been his dream job, but he did it wholeheartedly.

A few verses later, we read:

"David left his things with the keeper of supplies, ran to the battle lines and asked his brothers how they were." (v. 22)

Again, David took care of whatever had been entrusted to him. He was responsible and reliable in the small things.

My job as a leader is so much easier when my staff and volunteers take responsibility for the roles or tasks assigned to them. Previously, I have led congregations where I would frequently receive a message from a key volunteer late on Saturday night informing me that wouldn't be able to serve on Sunday. They had made other plans.

I probably should have been grateful that they told me in advance. Others simply wouldn't show up.

But here's what would have been so much better than merely notifying me of their absence - if they had found someone else to take their place.

That way, they're not just dumping their problem onto my lap. They're taking ownership and responsibility.

People who take responsibility are gold. They don't need to be micro-managed. They show up on time and stay at the task until it's finished. They're the kind of people I want to promote and keep on my team. I'm blessed to currently serve in a church filled with servant-hearted, dependable individuals like this.

Later, we learn that David took the responsibility of protecting his dad's sheep very seriously. Even if that meant risking his own life and fighting off wild beasts:

"David said to Saul, "Your servant has been keeping his father's sheep. When a lion or a bear came and carried off a sheep from the flock, I went after it, struck it and rescued the sheep from its mouth. When it turned on me, I seized it by its hair, struck it and killed it." (vv. 34-35)

Again, this demonstrates a sense of ownership, self-sacrifice, and a willingness to do whatever it takes to complete the task assigned to him.

Knowing all of this about David's character makes it less shocking when he steps forward and offers to fight Goliath:

"David said to Saul, 'Let no one lose heart on account of this Philistine; your servant will go and fight him.'" (1 Samuel 17:32)

There was a job that needed to be done. If no one else was willing to volunteer, David would take responsibility for dealing with this enemy of Israel.

Later, we read:

"As Saul watched David going out to meet the Philistine, he said to Abner, commander of the army, 'Abner, whose son is that young man?'" (v. 55)

When you are someone who takes responsibility, those above you pay attention. And God also notices.

It's only a matter of time before you get promoted.

Let me ask:

- *Are you responsible and reliable with what has been entrusted to you?*

- *Can others depend on you and take you at your word?*

- *If you're given a task, do you stick with it until it's finished?*

Don't underestimate the importance of taking responsibility. If other people can't trust you, it's unlikely that God will promote you.

2. DON'T BE DISTRACTED BY 'ALMOST'.

In my mid-20s, I went through a rigorous six-day interview process and was accepted to begin training for ministry. Upon being accepted, I deferred starting seminary for one year. I wanted to save some money to support myself during the three-year course.

At the time, I was working as a sales executive for a multinational company. It seemed unwise to tell my boss I'd be leaving in 12 months. I just kept working hard and planning for the future.

However, during that next year, my boss called me into his office and made me an almost irresistible offer:

"Craig, I want to retire at the end of this year. I've been talking to the top guys at headquarters, and we all think you should take my job leading the local division of the company."

It was a cushy job with a very good salary and great benefits. Plus, we dominated the market and had a stellar reputation.

In any other circumstance, I would have been elated. But this wasn't what God had called me to do. I smiled and politely declined my boss's kind offer.

However, he wasn't deterred that easily. A few months later, we had the same conversation.

I realized what was happening.

When God has prepared something for you, the enemy will almost always present you with an inferior offer. It is designed to distract and divert you from your true calling.

This 'alternative option' must be tempting, or you wouldn't even consider it. It will often appeal to desires within you that your primary calling can't fulfill – at least *not yet*.

This job offered me immediate wealth and status, something I wouldn't have if I attended seminary.

The 'alternative option' may even look 'almost' like what God has called you to do. You could easily justify considering it: *"Just think of the Kingdom impact I could have in that place."*

This isn't only about deciding between business or seminary. It could be in any area of life. **There's God's best...and then there's an 'almost'.**

It could be in a relationship, your career, education, ministry, buying a home, etc.

For example, if you're single and waiting for a Godly spouse, I can guarantee you that, at some stage, a person will express interest in you who is 'almost' what you've been longing for. They may have the looks and many of the personality traits that you find attractive. They will be your 'type'. But they aren't passionate about the things of God.

They're an 'almost' - designed to distract and draw you away from God's best.

A few years ago, I was offered a book deal by a major U.S. publisher. It was a generous offer. But I wasn't happy with several points in the contract. I politely declined.

I've never regretted my decision. It was an 'almost'.

Even Jesus was presented with an 'almost' in the wilderness:

"Again, the devil took him to a very high mountain and showed him all the kingdoms of the world and their splendor. "All this I will give you," he said, "if you will bow down and worship me." (Matthew 4: 8-9)

The enemy is sneaky. He's offering Jesus what will one day be His anyway. In Revelation 11 we read:

"...the kingdoms of this world have become the Kingdoms of our Lord and his Christ" (v. 15)

Here was the temptation. Jesus could have it *now* and avoid all the pain and suffering of the cross.

It was a shortcut, circumventing the most difficult parts of His assignment.

The enemy will do the same with you.

There's what God has promised. Then there is an 'almost'.

It will look good. It will be appealing. And it probably offers something that God will eventually give you. But it provides a quicker route to getting there.

It's a temptation and a distraction. It also tests your resolve to pursue what God has placed in your heart.

We see this many times throughout David's life.

When he is inside the palace, strumming his lyre to soothe Saul's demonic episodes, his life begins to look 'almost' like what Samuel had prophesied. He's not *on* the throne - but he is *beside* it.

After he fights Goliath, he becomes best friends with the King's son, marries Saul's daughter, and leads the Israelite troops to great victories in battle. Plus, in the streets, women are singing songs about his greatness. It looks 'almost' like the promise.

Even on the battlefield, when he steps up to fight Goliath, a distraction is immediately placed before him. David's eldest brother, Eliab begins to pick a fight with him. If David could win against Goliath, he could easily have taken down his brother. But this wasn't the battle God had called him to. It was a distraction and a deterrent. We read:

*"**He then turned away** to someone else and brought up the same matter, and the men answered him as before."* (v. 30)

In other words, **David remained focused on his primary calling from God.** It wasn't to battle his brother; it was to fight the real enemy.

- *In any area of your life, have you become distracted from what God has called you to do?*

- *Is there anywhere that you have settled for 'almost'?*

- *Have you gotten sidetracked from the 'promise' to pursue an inferior alternative?*

David was a man of focus and singular pursuit. As a worshiper and a warrior, He fixed his eyes on 'one thing':

"One thing I ask from the LORD,
this only do I seek:
that I may dwell in the house of the LORD
all the days of my life,
to gaze on the beauty of the LORD
and to seek him in his temple." (Psalm 27: 4)

God will promote those with a single-minded resolve to step fully into everything He has called them to.

They are willing to hold out for the fulfillment of all He has promised.

They refuse to settle for less than His best.

They won't say *yes* to inferior options.

They can't be distracted by 'almost'.

PROPHETIC ENCOURAGEMENT

THIS IS A TIME OF TURNING.

You are starting to sense a shift in your spirit.
Something is changing.

It's difficult at this stage to describe or define.
It's subtle.
But you know that something is stirring.
You can discern a change in seasons.
A move is imminent.

The blurriness will lift.
The fogginess will dissipate.
Blockages will be lifted.
Darkness will be illuminated.
You will begin to envision new possibilities.
A path will become clear before you.

Step into what the Spirit shows you.
Do what He says.
Even if it doesn't make sense.
Even if it seems impossible.
Even if you don't feel ready.

Your obedience will open doors.
Your faith will move God's heart and hand.
You will find favor and provision as you move into His good plans.

THIS IS A TIME OF TURNING.

DAY 34

GOD'S PROCESS OF PROMOTION | Part 3

BIBLE READING

When Eliab, David's oldest brother, heard him speaking with the men, he burned with anger at him and asked, "Why have you come down here? And with whom did you leave those few sheep in the wilderness? I know how conceited you are and how wicked your heart is; you came down only to watch the battle."

...David said to Saul, "Let no one lose heart on account of this Philistine; your servant will go and fight him."

Saul replied, "You are not able to go out against this Philistine and fight him; you are only a young man, and he has been a warrior from his youth."

(1 Samuel 17: 28; 32-33)

"The LORD rewards everyone for their righteousness and faithfulness. The LORD delivered you into my hands today, but I would not lay a hand on the LORD's anointed."

(1 Samuel 26: 23)

DEVOTIONAL

A January 2024 article in *Fortune* magazine carried the headline: 'Remote workers are promoted less than in-office colleagues'.

In this post-pandemic world, we know that many employees are finding it more convenient to work from home. However, studies are showing that the maxim *'out of sight, out of mind'* is apparently true for remote workers. When it comes to promotion, workers who go into the office are more likely to get a promotion or a pay rise from their boss.

The experts interviewed in the article suggest that even going into the office a few days a week is enough to ensure you aren't forgotten about. And when you're there, it's important to make sure you're noticed: *"The key is being intentional about getting those all-important in-person interactions while you are in the office."*

Is that what it takes to get promoted in God's Kingdom?

Do we show up now and again, and make sure we get noticed?

We've been thinking about the type of people God promotes. What qualities and character traits does God look for in those He raises into positions of Kingdom authority and influence?

So far, from the life of David, we've seen that God promotes those who:

- Seek Him first;
- Are faithful where they are;
- Recognize opportunities when they are presented;
- Take responsibility; and,
- Aren't distracted by 'almost'.

Today, we'll continue looking at David and explore two more important qualities that God looks for in those He promotes.

1.   HANDLE CRITICISM AND REJECTION.

Promotion generally brings some degree of increased visibility. And this wider exposure often attracts critics. As soon as you speak up, step up, or stand out, you draw attention and scrutiny from others.

The greater the level of promotion, the more of a target you become. Everyone will have an opinion about your abilities, appearance, performance, and motives.

Many people will be supportive and kind. But there is always a minority who will find fault in anything you do.

The negativity and criticism directed towards leaders can be brutal and debilitating. Therefore, if God is going to promote you, He will often first test how you handle criticism and rejection at your current level. In fact, it's been said that:

"God can only promote you to the level of your tolerance of pain."

I don't like that. I'd prefer to avoid pain.

However, as I examine the Scriptures and reflect on my own experience, I know it to be true. Pain precedes promotion. And promotion often brings more pain.

Criticism and rejection are a major portion of this pain that comes with promotion.

No matter how old you are, or how long you've been leading, you are never immune from feeling the sting of disapproval and negativity from others.

After two decades in leadership, I like to think I have a thick skin. However, a nasty email or snide comment can still pierce my heart and even make me question my calling.

I think of one email I received recently from a disgruntled former member of our church. They began by criticizing my preaching and then moved on to attacking my character and motives. They concluded their litany of grievances by informing me that our services had been so much better when I was on vacation and my assistant was in charge. Ouch.

John C. Maxwell is right when he says:

"The price of leadership is criticism."

David also experienced deep rejection and harsh criticism as God brought him to prominence.

First, when Samuel asks to see all of Jesse's sons, David isn't even invited to the dinner. His own father didn't consider him important enough to include him in this significant event.

Then, when he is considering stepping up to confront Goliath, his eldest brother launches a blistering attack:

"Why have you come down here? And with whom did you leave those few sheep in the wilderness? I know how conceited you are and how wicked your heart is; you came down only to watch the battle." (1 Samuel 17: 28)

When a stranger criticizes us, it can be difficult to take. When disapproval or negativity comes from those closest to us, the wounds cut especially deep.

First, Eliab scorns David's job. Then he moves on to attack David's character:

"I know how conceited you are and how wicked your heart is." (v. 28)

I want you to notice something.

What was it about David that God loved the most?

It was his heart. He was a man with a heart after God. (1 Samuel 13: 14).

The enemy will strategically focus his attacks on the areas of your life that make you the most effective for God's Kingdom. These are the character traits, abilities, and gifts that he perceives to be the greatest threat to his evil schemes. His goal is to have you shrink back and shut down in those areas.

He usually doesn't attack you directly. Instead, he uses people as proxies. He stirs up resentment, jealousy, suspicion, discord, bitterness, and division.

It is especially painful when family turns against you and those who were once close to you begin to question your motives. You either waste valuable time and energy defending yourself or you want to run away and escape the rejection.

David does neither when he comes under this verbal assault from Eliab. We read:

"He then turned away to someone else and brought up the same matter..." (v. 30)

He didn't retaliate. Nor does he crawl into a corner, overwhelmed by self-pity or discouragement.

He simply turned away and remained focused on the real enemy. His resilience was greater than his rejection. The mission before him was more important than the opinions of others.

How you respond to criticism and rejection can have a huge impact on your future.

Where the criticism and rejection are unfair and undeserved, do what David did: *turn away*.

Turning away can take different forms.

It can simply mean turning your back on the critic or leaving the room.

In other cases, when the negativity becomes especially nasty and destructive, that's when establishing boundaries comes into play again.

351

Several years ago, we went through a very painful rejection from a couple we loved and a relationship that we had poured so much into. What made it worse was that we did ministry together.

They attacked our characters, spread falsehoods, and sought to undermine us in every way possible.

For us, 'turning away' meant cutting off all contact and communication with them. We didn't disparage them or seek to hurt them in any way. But we knew that our calling was too important to get down into the dirt and allow them to continue to inflict hurt on our family or reputation.

While the pain took a long time to heal, I'm so thankful that we responded as we did. God has vindicated us and brought great recompense for all we walked through. Not long after that difficult season, I began to experience accelerated promotion in different areas of my life and ministry. I can see a clear correlation between God's increased favor and how we postured our hearts when we came under attack.

Reflecting on her own journey, author and speaker Joyce Meyer comments:

"I suffered tremendous rejection when I first began stepping out to follow God's call on my life. For a while, it was very hurtful and disappointing. However, I shudder to think how things would have turned out differently if I had decided to just give up - if I had allowed the fear of what others thought to stop me from moving forward."

If you can't bench press 100 pounds at the gym, trying to lift 250 pounds will crush you.

Similarly, if you can't handle criticism and rejection at the level you're currently at, God can't promote you to a place of greater visibility and responsibility. The weight of scrutiny and negativity would crush you.

2. DEMONSTRATE HONOR AND LOYALTY.

In the last decade, there has been a renewed focus within the Body of Christ on showing honor, especially towards those in authority.

Of course, honor has been abused or misused in some contexts. It has veered towards unhealthy worship of man or unquestioned obedience to leadership.

Still, I think an emphasis on honor is biblical, beneficial, and carries great blessing. **Honor is the protocol of God's Kingdom. Honor is the culture of Heaven.** A posture of honor should characterize our lives and our churches, and hopefully seep into our wider communities.

However, the challenge I've seen when it comes to honor is this – it's easy to demonstrate honor and show loyalty to someone when you agree with them. But what happens when they make a decision that you disagree with?

What if you expect them to promote you, but instead, they elevate someone else?

Or when you feel strongly about a position or cause, but they don't support you?

What about when your vision for where things should go clashes with the direction they think is best?

Do you remain loyal and show honor when those in authority say or do something that you find difficult to accept?

Again, we see honor and loyalty exemplified in David's life, especially in his relationship with King Saul.

We read:

"David said to Saul, "Let no one lose heart on account of this Philistine; your servant will go and fight him." (v. 32)

It's important to remember that David had already been anointed by this stage. He knew Saul's days were numbered and that he was God's chosen successor. If David hadn't confronted Goliath, Saul eventually would have had to step up. Saul's death in battle would only have expedited David's ascent to the throne.

Yet, David displayed unwavering loyalty and honor towards the King. He saw himself as Saul's servant. And he stepped up and took down the giant.

David's victory over Goliath solved a huge problem for the King.

However, his subsequent rise in popularity and obvious anointing from God aroused growing jealousy and resentment.

While David remained a loyal subject, it reached the point where Saul became intent on killing this perceived threat to his throne.

David spent much of the next decade as a fugitive on the run from a demented, but determined, King.

Yet, we see no hint that he ever showed dishonor or disrespect towards Saul. He never sought to undermine his authority or usurp his position. Even when he had the opportunity to kill Saul on several occasions, his response was:

"...I would not lay a hand on the LORD's anointed." (1 Samuel 26: 23)

David might not have agreed with Saul's behavior, but he still honored Saul's position. He refused to seize the throne, either by force or manipulation.

This is one of the main reasons why David's reign was so successful. He entered into it well. He remained loyal to Saul and chose, instead, to wait until God promoted him.

This is an area where many young leaders stumble.

I have watched individuals with great gifting and potential become over-ambitious and seek to elevate themselves into a position of leadership that is already occupied by someone else. They believe they can do a better job than the current leader.

Honor goes out the window, while jealousy, rivalry, resentment, and pride creep in.

354

They begin to speak negatively about the leader. They may even attempt to usurp their authority or split the church.

It can become incredibly messy and damaging for everyone involved. And it brings division and disrepute to the people of God.

Again, let me be clear. I'm not talking about blind loyalty where you ignore blatant sin or disregard heresy.

The congregation I currently lead was birthed out of a difficult church split. (This happened two years before I was appointed as their Pastor.) The separation happened because there was a fundamental disagreement on the person and work of the Holy Spirit.

One group was adamantly against any expression of spiritual gifts. They loved tradition and strongly opposed any minister who had ever sought to bring change.

The other group had experienced a significant encounter with the Holy Spirit. They had come alive to the things of God. And they wanted more.

After many contentious meetings, those in authority concluded that there was only one option – start a new congregation and let people choose to stay or leave.

And that's what happened.

There are times when we should go our separate ways.

I place a very high value on loyalty from friends and colleagues. However, loyalty doesn't mean that we should remain in relationships or alignments that are unhealthy, unbiblical, and unfruitful.

False loyalty will cause you to stay in places that God has told you to leave.

Blind loyalty allows the enemy to deceive you because you are unwilling to question things that you know in your spirit aren't quite right.

False loyalty will cause you to miss out on the new thing God is doing in your midst because you are unwilling to detach or disconnect from the old thing.

Loyalty to a person, group, denomination, or movement is good - but it is not as important as NOW obedience to God.

However, **even when there are 'irreconcilable differences', it is still possible to show honor and respect, even towards those who are treating you with dishonor and contempt.**

That's what happened with HOPE Church. The group who planted the new congregation sought to show honor and kindness towards those who were constantly criticizing and maligning them. They knew that the posture of their hearts was crucial in positioning them to receive blessing and favor from God. And our short history has shown that they were right.

Honor can be your standard, even if it's not other people's.

Pastor Bill Johnson says:

"Giving honor releases the life of God into a situation."

I agree. Again and again, I have witnessed God rewarding those who demonstrate honor and loyalty, especially when facing difficult criticism and rejection.

Honor shows you can be trusted.

Honor unlocks favor.

Honor positions you for promotion from God.

PROPHETIC ENCOURAGEMENT

THIS IS SPIRITUAL.
It's not just coincidence or chance.
There is an invisible, supernatural world all around you.
Spirits, some loyal to God. Others fighting for the enemy.
They are at war.

You, too, are a spiritual being.
You are part of this battle.
Good versus evil.
Light against darkness.
Truth versus lies.

You have divine authority.
Your prayers, your obedience, your worship, your declarations, your
boldness - they move and shift the trajectory of what happens around you.

Don't be a passive observer.
Don't accept how things are if you don't like them.
Fight with your spiritual weapons.
Demolish strongholds and tear down lies.
Expose deception and proclaim truth.

Don't shrink back.
Don't retreat.
Victory is assured.
Success has been secured.
The only way you don't win is if you don't show up.
THIS IS SPIRITUAL.

DAY 35

GOD'S PROCESS OF PROMOTION | Part 4

BIBLE READING

Then Saul dressed David in his own tunic. He put a coat of armor on him and a bronze helmet on his head. David fastened on his sword over the tunic and tried walking around, because he was not used to them.

"I cannot go in these," he said to Saul, "because I am not used to them." So he took them off. Then he took his staff in his hand, chose five smooth stones from the stream, put them in the pouch of his shepherd's bag and, with his sling in his hand, approached the Philistine.

…As the Philistine moved closer to attack him, David ran quickly toward the battle line to meet him. Reaching into his bag and taking out a stone, he slung it and struck the Philistine on the forehead. The stone sank into his forehead, and he fell facedown on the ground.

So David triumphed over the Philistine with a sling and a stone; without a sword in his hand he struck down the Philistine and killed him.

David ran and stood over him. He took hold of the Philistine's sword and drew it from the sheath. After he killed him, he cut off his head with the sword.

(1 Samuel 17: 38-40; 48-51)

DEVOTIONAL

Yesterday, I shared a little of the origin story of the church I've been leading since 2017.

In 2015, there was a painful separation in a small rural church between a group who wanted to go deeper in the things of the Spirit and others who preferred to hold onto religious traditions. Around 80 of the members who longed for renewal and revival moved on and HOPE Church was birthed.

What I didn't share is that the weekend before the split, Becky and I had ministered at this church for two days. A conference had been arranged almost a year in advance and we were the guest speakers. At the time, we were leading a church two hours away in the heart of Dublin city. While we were aware of some tensions, we had no idea we were walking into a community at breaking point.

As you can probably imagine, those who attended the Saturday conference were in the 'Holy Spirit camp'. They were a wonderful group, on fire for the Kingdom, and we felt an immediate bond.

At the time, I could never have imagined that, just a week later, there would be a permanent split in the congregation. Or that, two years later, I would become the pastor of this fledgling church called HOPE.

But God knew.

Our Sovereign King is so intentional in His planning and purposes. He sees the details and knows the future. He prepares and positions His people to be in the right place, at the right time.

Seven years on, HOPE has grown significantly, both spiritually and numerically. But still, there's no church anywhere that I would rather lead. It's far from perfect. But it's the right fit for me.

I share this story for two reasons.

Firstly, I want to remind you that **God is at work behind the scenes in your life.** Even when you can't see what He's doing, God is so specific and strategic in preparing you for the places and people that will be part of your future. When you get there, you'll look back and it will all make sense. As Paul Manwaring says, *"God wastes nothing, and He gets us ready."*

Secondly, **you won't fit everywhere, but you'll be perfect for somewhere.** While God is shaping you in this season, He has your next assignment and future alignments in mind. You are His best solution to a problem that doesn't yet exist.

Right now, you might feel like a misfit. Or a square peg in a round hole. But a time is coming soon when the pieces will all fit seamlessly together. You'll find your people and your place. You can completely be yourself because that's the only version of you they want.

That leads us back to David.

Today, we're continuing to think about what character qualities and attributes God is looking for in those He is seeking to promote and elevate.

1. BE YOURSELF.

As David prepares to confront Goliath, he is encouraged to wear Saul's armor:

"Then Saul dressed David in his own tunic. He put a coat of armor on him and a bronze helmet on his head." (1 Samuel 17: 38)

David is willing to try it on. But it's immediately obvious that wearing this gear will be more of a hindrance than a help. It will slow him down and trip him up. It doesn't fit because it was made for Saul, not David.

Sometimes, others will try to place things on your shoulders that God never intended for you to carry. It could be their way of doing things; their traditions and practices; their preferences and priorities; the weight of their expectations.

These people generally mean well. Saul was only trying to protect David. **But carrying something that isn't right for you will only exhaust you and make you ineffective.**

It's okay to try it. Walk around in it for a while.

But if it's not a good fit, **take it off.**

Don't become someone you're not to please other people. It will hinder your advancement and cause you to stumble.

You will be most effective when you are the best version of yourself, not a second-rate version of someone else.

It's also worth noting that **people who aren't willing to engage in the battle will try to tell you how to fight.**

Saul wasn't willing to confront Goliath, but he wanted to decide what David would wear.

Be wary of taking advice from those who would rather sit on the sidelines than engage in the action. They often have plenty of ideas and theories, without real-world experience and wisdom.

For example, I'm constantly amazed by the number of people on social media who express strong opinions about leadership and the changes that need to be made in the church. Yet, many of these 'experts' have never built or led anything of significance in their lives. I might even agree with some of what they are saying. But I'm not taking them seriously until they have spent some time on the front lines putting their ideas into practice. Show me your scars and I'll listen to your theories.

To accomplish his assignment, David had to recognize and be completely honest about what worked for him - and what didn't. That meant refusing to do things the way Saul would have preferred.

Sometimes it takes as much courage to say 'no' to someone on your side as it does to confront an enemy. You risk offending those who think they know what is best for you. But what else can you do? Just because something fits them doesn't mean it has to be worn by you.

Know who you are - and know who you aren't. Become comfortable in your own skin. God created you as a unique individual. You're not like anyone else. Nor are you supposed to be. Your assignment is perfectly tailored to fit only you.

David had no experience with armor and a sword. But he was very capable with a slingshot.

It might not have looked as impressive. But in times like this, experience and effectiveness matter more than appearance and the opinions of others.

2. GIVE IT EVERYTHING.

For 40 days, Israel's troops have watched and listened to Goliath mock them and their God. Yet, they have done nothing. They're frozen by fear and paralyzed into passivity.

Then David arrives on the scene and immediately things take a dramatic shift.

There's a stirring in the atmosphere. There's movement among the ranks. There's a sense that something significant is about to happen.

The stalemate has been disrupted by a shepherd boy who refuses to accept the status quo. God's reputation is at stake here. Doing nothing isn't an option.

Look at what we read:

"As the Philistine moved closer to attack him, David ran quickly toward the battle line to meet him." (v. 48)

Everyone was keeping as far from Goliath as possible. Not David. He runs directly towards the giant.

He's all in.

No half measures. No testing the water.

He's completely committed to the cause. His motto is *No retreat; No surrender.*

If He dies, so be it. But He cannot allow His God or Israel to be humiliated any longer.

Can you imagine the excitement in Heaven that day?

Picture the angels watching with anticipation as this boy with a slingshot runs towards this behemoth carrying a sword and spear.

They already knew how this would end. **Because when you fully commit to what matters most to God, God will fully commit to your success and victory.**

All of Heaven backs you up. You cannot fail because He has already determined the outcome.

Your unreserved passion and God's supernatural power converge to make the impossible become inevitable. **Giants have to fall face down before a man or woman after God's own heart.**

In these turbulent days of shaking and warfare in the physical and spiritual realms, there will be many giants to confront.

Sadly, much of the church is like the army of Israel. **They're wearing the uniform but avoiding the battle.** They might look good from the outside, but up close, they're fearful and unwilling to fight for what matters most.

However, a remnant is rising. Men and women who have a heart like David. A heart after God's own heart.

They are more concerned for God's reputation than their self-preservation.

They are a people burning with passion who will make things happen.

They've been prepared in the wilderness and proven faithful in the hidden places.

Now God is calling them out of obscurity and onto the front lines.

They've fought the lion and the bear. They have the scars to prove it. Now it's time to confront the giants in the land.

They see what everyone else sees. But they see it through a different lens. A lens of *God can*, not *we can't*.

They are more consumed with the glory of God than the opinions of people.

They're not seeking a platform. They're ready for a battle.

They are fierce in their devotion, unbridled in their worship, and relentless in their pursuit.

They are the untamed ones. Even a little bit crazy.

But times like this require those who don't conform to the norms and who are considered extreme by those who only want to blend in.

They are emerging. One here, another there. Slowly, without any fanfare or show.

And they are being strategically positioned by the Spirit of God to stand up and step out when the moment is right.

You can sense the shift. You can hear the sound. You can feel the change in the atmosphere.

And as this remnant begins to arise, giants will start to fall.

Their scoffing will be silenced.
Their mocking will be muted.
Their deception will be displayed.

Justice and righteousness will once again rule in the land.

There will be vindication and victory for the faithful.

The glory of God will be revealed.

3. FINISH WHAT YOU START.

We all know the story. David knocks the giant down with just a sling and a stone. He could have turned around and basked in the glory of the moment. But the job wasn't finished:

"David ran and stood over him. He took hold of the Philistine's sword and drew it from the sheath. After he killed him, he cut off his head with the sword." (v. 51)

Goliath was already dead. Why cut off his head?

David wanted to make it clear to everyone watching that this enemy was finished. The giant that had taunted them for so long wasn't going to recover and make a comeback. He was gone.

In our own battles, sometimes we knock the giant down, but we don't cut off his head.

You claim a victory in some area, but it's not long before that destructive habit, that stubborn sin, that limiting belief, reappears and attacks again with great force.

You think you've dealt with a person who has been opposing you or a situation that has draining you. But a month later, you're confronted with the problem again.

Stop playing nice. There are some things that you can't be anything less than ruthless with.

Cut off the head.

This isn't a game. The devil is on a mission: to steal your passion, kill your faith, and destroy your destiny.

You must do whatever it takes to get totally free from the taunts, bonds, and intimidation of the enemy. There can be no half-measures.

Cut off the head.

You can't afford to live in these cycles of oppression any longer.

You can't continue to circle the same mountain again and again.

You must be resolute and determined to finally walk free.

Cut off the head.

Your future is at stake here. But so too is the future of those whom God has called you to impact.

This is personal. And it's also generational.

If you don't defeat this, your children will be forced to confront it.

You have an assignment from God.

Don't settle for a partial victory.

Be decisive. Finish the job.

Don't just knock the giant down. Cut off his head, once and for all.

PROPHETIC ENCOURAGEMENT

I AM BRINGING YOU OUT OF 'BLAH'.
I am breaking you out bland and barren.
You are coming out of containment and constriction.
I am removing false restrictions and religious restraints.
I am lifting lids and smashing ceilings.
I am cutting chains of people-pleasing and severing cords of control.
I am freeing you from false expectations and the fear of man.

For too long, you have been circling around and around, but not advancing.
There has been little sense of joy, purpose, or vision.
You have felt stuck, deadlocked, and drained.

Life is "fine". You are "fine".
But you're desperately longing for more than "fine".
You were initially happy for a rest - but life has grown stagnant and stale.
Boredom is setting in.
You are now ready for a change, but nothing is shifting.

You have stayed here long enough.
It's time to move on.
I am taking you from monotonous to movement and then to momentum.
I am going to:
Shake things up.
Stir the waters.
Shift your schedule.
Disrupt your routine.
Alter your plans.
Reorient your direction.
Remove some of the crutches you have been leaning on.
Make the difficult decisions.
Change is here. Don't look back.

It will be unsettling and unnerving.
You will be tempted to settle for less.
To retreat back to safety and certainty.
But you were created for more and you are called to so much more.

This will not just be a season of "recovery", but of advancement and progress.
You will take territory and displace devils.
You will receive fresh vision and revelation, and experience tangible encounters.
I am drawing you deeper and taking you further than you have ever been.

For some, there will be a major plot twist.
The unplanned and the unexpected.
There is unfinished business that I want to fulfill in your life.
I am going to tie up loose ends and bring assignments to completion.
Say 'yes' - even if nothing makes sense.

I am giving you back your edge.
I am pouring in fresh passion and purpose.

No more stuck and stagnant.
No more boredom and humdrum.
I am calling you higher, further, deeper - beyond your boundaries.
Let go of how you think things should be.
Enter and embrace where I am taking you.

I AM BRINGING YOU OUT OF 'BLAH'.

DAY 36

GIVE IT TIME

BIBLE READING

Another parable He put forth to them, saying: "The kingdom of heaven is like a man who sowed good seed in his field; but while men slept, his enemy came and sowed tares among the wheat and went his way. But when the grain had sprouted and produced a crop, then the tares also appeared.

So the servants of the owner came and said to him, 'Sir, did you not sow good seed in your field? How then does it have tares?'

He said to them, 'An enemy has done this.'

The servants said to him, 'Do you want us then to go and gather them up?'

But he said, 'No, lest while you gather up the tares you also uproot the wheat with them. Let both grow together until the harvest, and at the time of harvest I will say to the reapers, "First gather together the tares and bind them in bundles to burn them, but gather the wheat into my barn."

(Matthew 13: 24-30)

DEVOTIONAL

One of the best pieces of leadership advice I've ever received is:

"Recognize the difference between a problem to be solved and a tension to be managed".

As a 'fixer', I want to solve everything. Yet, I've discovered that not every problem is solvable. At least not in the short term.

For example, if you have two people on a team who have very different personalities, there's likely to be some difference of opinion. Even the occasional clash of views.

You can't really solve that problem without removing one of them.

And you probably shouldn't solve it.

Both bring different perspectives and ideas that make the whole thing more interesting and fruitful.

Instead, you must find a way to manage the tension.

But I don't like tension. It makes me uncomfortable. I want to resolve it immediately. Fix it. Deal with it. Get rid of it.

I've discovered that if I try to deal with a tension prematurely, it can be counterproductive.

It can make the situation worse.
It can damage relationships.
It can block an opportunity.
It can stunt development and growth.

Therefore, it's better to hold off and give it time. See what it can become. Gain clarity on what's really happening.

In the parable of the wheat and the tares, Jesus is talking about living with tension.

THE INFILTRATION OF THE ENEMY

The farmer in the story was very intentional in only sowing good seeds into his field. This represents God the Father sowing good things and Kingdom people into this world.

However, even planting good seeds doesn't prevent the infiltration of the enemy:

"...but while men slept, his enemy came and sowed tares among the wheat and went his way." (v. 25)

Notice how subtle the enemy is. He came at night while everyone was asleep. And he sowed seeds that looked very much like the seeds sown by the servants.

Pay attention to the order of events.

The enemy never sowed any weeds until the wheat had been planted.

Nor did he plant in a random field.

It was in precisely the same field where the servants had planted.

The point is - **the enemy only goes after the good in our lives. He focuses on the fields with the most potential for harvest.**

He sees the people who might be most effective for the Kingdom, and he intentionally targets them.

He sees the ministries that will grow and disrupt his evil schemes and he concentrates his forces on destroying them.

So, if it feels as though the enemy's attacks have been relentless and exhausting, take heart. It likely means he has discerned your future. And you are a threat to his kingdom!

Here is where we get to the tension that I talked about at the beginning:

You want to do something great for the Kingdom of God.

So, you step out in faith, serve, give, share the Gospel.

Very soon you face opposition, criticism, problems, or challenges.

Instinctively you conclude that it must not have been the right thing to do.

You want to solve the problem. You're tempted to retreat. To quit. Or dial things down.

No! It's likely that the attack isn't happening because you were wrong. It's because you were right.

The activity of the enemy is a sign that God is at work there. And so, Satan wants to stop you before the work grows and becomes a real threat. The spiritual warfare is a tension that you must manage as you continue to advance and take new ground.

GREAT FAVOR WILL BE GREATLY OPPOSED

Through the years, I've discovered that great favor often comes with great challenge.

God's blessing is frequently accompanied by some type of burden.

Promotion usually comes with people's criticism or jealousy.

We see this in the Gospels.

As the ministry of Jesus increased, so did the opposition from the religious leaders. As more and more people encountered the Kingdom, Jesus encountered the fiercest criticism.

Jesus didn't avoid confrontation or destroy the religious elite. He could have. Rather, he lived with the tension and continued to preach and demonstrate the Kingdom.

In the parable, notice that the enemy didn't dig up the good seed. Rather, he sought to corrupt the good environment in which the seed was planted.

372

The enemy can't destroy the seed inside you – the Word and work of God in your life.

But he can surround you by weeds so that you become distracted and don't develop what God has placed within you.

He will bring adversity, temptation, opposition, sickness, criticism, negativity, offense, hurt, or distraction.

He will seek to plant other things in your life, heart, environment, and circumstances.

The goal is to sabotage the work of God by bringing mixture into your life. That way he can restrict the harvest or, at least, devalue the harvest.

WAIT AND SEE

When the crop starts to grow, the servants realize what has happened. They see the tares or weeds mixed in with the wheat.

Instinctively, they want to uproot everything. That's the obvious and most immediate solution – pull up anything and everything that looks remotely like a weed.

And that's usually what I want to do when I face tension.

I find it difficult to handle the presence of weeds. It stresses me.

I think I need to do something immediately.
I need to say something.
I need to sort this out.
I don't like the uncertainty.
I like everything neat and tidy.
I don't like looking at the weeds.
I can't relax while the weeds are there.

However, sometimes we want to deal with things too quickly. We want to separate things too early. We want to resolve everything prematurely. We want to solve the problem, so we don't have to manage the tension.

Look at the master's response:

"But he said, 'No, lest while you gather up the tares you also uproot the wheat with them. Let both grow together until the harvest..." (vv. 29-30)

He essentially says: *"Don't tear up the weeds just yet. Let them grow together for a while. We will deal with the problem - but just not yet."*

At certain times, **we must learn to manage tension instead of immediately trying to resolve every issue.**

There is wisdom is waiting. If you try to fix it too soon, you'll make it worse.

So, for now, leave it alone.

It's not that you're wrong, or that the weeds aren't bad. **It's just that the timing isn't right.**

At other times, it can be hard to tell the difference, at least for a while.

We can mistake what looks like a weed and tear it up only to discover that, if we'd just left it, it would have produced a harvest of wheat.

Some things take time.

Our impatience, perfectionism, and desire to tie up all loose ends can cause us to prematurely uproot and tear down some good things that God is growing.

We panic and rush to bring resolution.

But if we'd only waited, we'd have been able to avoid much heartache and hurt.

All our friends are getting married, so we commit too quickly to someone who might not be worthy of our affection.

Give it time.

House prices are rising sharply, so we pay too much to climb onto the property ladder.

Give it time.

We get anxious that something (or someone) is slipping away, so we cling too hard and sabotage it.

Give it time.

I've discovered that **if I try to get rid of every weed in my life, I'll also destroy a lot of the wheat.**

This isn't an excuse for sin. I'm not suggesting that we should blindly ignore everything. Some things are obviously evil and are going to do real harm. They need to be rooted out immediately. Some things can't wait. They need to be dealt with quickly. So please don't see this as an excuse for avoiding issues or allowing sin to go unrepented in our lives.

But when it's not so black and white, or if you're not sure what to do, often the best plan is - wait and see.

If it's a weed, you can always deal with it later. **Keep sowing good seed and give it time.**

For example, when I'm writing a book, I want every chapter to be immediately perfect. But if I spend all day looking for errors and typos, I'll become paralyzed by perfectionism, and it will never get completed. So, I write now and edit later. I'll allow the wheat and the weeds to grow together.

In some areas of life, you need to just give it time.

How it appears right now is not the final product. It's simply one necessary stage of the process. But if you get fixated on perfecting or resolving everything too early, it will never grow and become all it could have been.

The seed never looks like the final crop, but you don't immediately discard it.

You must give it time.

And don't forget that wheat can still grow even when it's surrounded by weeds. The work of God can still flourish in the presence of evil and sin. Because *"Greater is the One who is inside you than the one that is in the world"* (1 John 4: 4).

So, stop waiting for the perfect environment, the perfect time, or all the resources you think you need before you begin what God is calling you to do.

Start where you are, with what you have.
And give it time.

Don't keep putting off moving forward until your life is more perfect and holy and mature.

Start where you are, with what you have.
And give it time.

Stop obsessing over the work of the enemy so much that you become overly focused on every sin in your life.

Start where you are, with what you have.
And give it time.

Focus on the work of God, not the activity of the enemy. Look for what's good in a situation, instead of getting fixated on what's bad.

In your relationships or marriage, your focus on wheat or weeds will determine how much that connection will flourish.

I have many weeds in my life. I am fully aware of them. My wife is also aware of them. But she chooses to focus on and speak about the wheat that she sees growing. That makes for a healthy marriage.

What will you focus on?

Some of us are experts in weeds. We obsess over every weed and ignore the wheat. We focus on what's wrong and miss everything that's right.

I can choose to be grateful for the wheat even in the presence of the weeds.

I can praise God for His goodness and blessings even when my circumstances aren't all I'd like them to be.

What is your primary purpose, role, and calling?
To grow wheat?
Or to hunt weeds?

Don't become so focused on pulling weeds that you stop sowing and nourishing the wheat.

Some things are still taking root. You don't know how they're going to turn out.

So, wait and see. Live with the tension.

Give it time.

PROPHETIC ENCOURAGEMENT

THIS IS A CATALYZING MOMENT.

Amid the swirl and instability, a seismic shift is happening.
In you.
Around you.
In the heavenly realms.
Everything is moving, turning, resetting, realigning.

It is unsettling.
You can sense something bubbling, rising, stirring, emerging.
It can feel difficult to find a secure footing.

A monumental shift is happening.
The Kingdom is advancing.

But the opposition is fierce.
The Spirit has been brooding and hovering over the nations.
The prophetic decrees and prayers of the saints have been heard.
The Father is creating something new.

It's unclear and not defined yet.
It may not be how you expected it to look.
But it's coming. It's accelerating and gaining momentum.
It's getting closer and clearer.

You won't have to push it too hard or force it to happen.
But also don't become passive and complacent.

Perceive what it can become through the eyes of faith.
Lean into it. Take hold of it. Steward it. Tend to it.

In the Kingdom, things are often slow, slow, slow…then swift.

We wait, we wait, we wait…then suddenly it appears.

That is how this is going to happen.

God is moving!
The dam is breaking.
The war in the heavenlies is raging.
The nations are shaking.
The angelic host are winning.
The people are praying.
The ekklesia is rising.
The slumbering are awakening.
The tide is turning.
The glory is coming.
The fire is spreading.

The ground is so dry, one spark is all it will take.
He will send the fire. You - fuel and fan the flames.

After a long and testing season, the Father is coming to refresh and reignite
His people.

Signs will begin manifesting all around you.
You will see demonstrations of the Spirit's power.

God is moving outside of the 'ordinary'. You can't even conceive what He has in store.
Many will be taken on a new trajectory that they have never imagined.

This is not a time to replicate or duplicate what is already there or what has been.

It is a time to initiate and innovate, reform and reimagine, create and pioneer, dream and design.

Draw new maps. Explore the land.
Reinvent. Redefine. Reshape.

It will require courage to step into the new. Major adjustments may be required.

The stage is being reset.
You are being positioned into place.
This is a window of opportunity to make a bold and brave move.

THIS IS A CATALYZING MOMENT.

DAY 37

DON'T THROW AWAY YOUR BIRTHRIGHT

BIBLE READING

Isaac prayed to the Lord on behalf of his wife, because she was childless. The Lord answered his prayer, and his wife Rebekah became pregnant. The babies jostled each other within her, and she said, "Why is this happening to me?" So she went to inquire of the Lord.

The Lord said to her,
"Two nations are in your womb,
and two peoples from within you will be separated;
one people will be stronger than the other,
and the older will serve the younger."

When the time came for her to give birth, there were twin boys in her womb. The first to come out was red, and his whole body was like a hairy garment; so they named him Esau. After this, his brother came out, with his hand grasping Esau's heel; so he was named Jacob. Isaac was sixty years old when Rebekah gave birth to them...

...Once when Jacob was cooking some stew, Esau came in from the open country, famished. He said to Jacob, "Quick, let me have some of that red stew! I'm famished!" (That is why he was also called Edom.)
Jacob replied, "First sell me your birthright."
"Look, I am about to die," Esau said. "What good is the birthright to me?"
But Jacob said, "Swear to me first." So he swore an oath to him, selling his birthright to Jacob.
Then Jacob gave Esau some bread and some lentil stew. He ate and drank, and then got up and left.
So Esau despised his birthright.

(Genesis 25: 21-34)

DEVOTIONAL

Have you discovered *Facetune* yet? It's a phone app that allows you to smooth out wrinkles, whiten your teeth, and remove any imperfections from your photos.

Of course, I haven't tried it. But I know people who obviously use it on every photo they post on social media. There are usually tell-tale signs. Their face is just *too* smooth and their teeth *too* white. It's unnatural. Nobody can look *that* good at their age!

I love that the Bible doesn't filter its leading characters. God lets us see the wrinkles, spots, warts, and other blemishes of the men and women He has used throughout history. I'm glad. It makes them more relatable. Because I can't connect with perfect. But I can relate to broken.

In the book of Genesis, Isaac and Rebekah desperately longed to have children. However, it just wasn't happening. Their emptiness brought great frustration. Yet, they never gave up. For 20 years they prayed and cried out to the LORD. And He answered their prayer, giving them not one, but two babies.

Even before they were born, in Rebekah's womb, these babies were battling for dominance. A wrestle and struggle that would continue throughout their lives.

The story goes that one day Esau came in from hunting. He was famished. His younger brother, Jacob, just happened to be cooking some stew. Esau smelled the food and implored Jacob: *"I have to have some of that stew. Gimme some right now."*

To which Jacob replied: *"Okay. But first, sell me your birthright."*

As the oldest son, Esau had all the privileges. They received the birthright meaning that they got a double share of the family inheritance, and they also had a special blessing from their father. They were the next in line to carry on the family name.

Jacob is offering a ridiculous exchange. A bowl of his stew for Esau's birthright. I mean, seriously. It was lentil stew. It wasn't even made from chicken or beef!

But even more incredible is that Esau accepted the terms of the agreement. He says: *"I'm so hungry that I'm going to die. So, what's the point in having a birthright anyway?"*

And he signs over the privileges of his birthright for a bowl of vegetable stew.

It would be like me saying: *"Give me your home and your car. In exchange, I'll give you a ham and cheese sandwich."*

There are a few lessons for us here.

The first is this:

1. NEVER MAKE A PERMANENT DECISION ABOUT A TEMPORARY CONDITION.

Was Esau literally going to starve to death?

No.

It was a temporary condition of hunger.

He could have walked into the kitchen and made himself some food. He could have gone outside and hunted something.

But at that moment, his temporary experience of hunger *felt* much more important than his birthright.

Throughout the years, sadly I have watched many people make impulsive decisions to satisfy a temporary need or desire. Often those decisions have had long-term, even permanent, consequences.

Several years ago, I spent a day with the leader of a thriving, growing church. I was so impressed by him and the ministry. But I could also see he was exhausted. So, I counseled him to get some rest. He shrugged off my advice. The church 'needed' him too much.

Six months later he had resigned, and the sordid story was headline news in our local press. In his weariness and loneliness, he had initiated an affair with a much younger female in his congregation. Eventually, they were caught, bringing devastation to his family and the church.

Like Esau giving up his birthright, some decisions can't be undone.

Of course, God's grace can cover all our sins. But it doesn't erase the consequences of our actions.

Some things are priceless. Do not give them away for less than they're worth because there is a need that you want satisfied.

Never make a permanent decision about a temporary condition.

Secondly, and along the same lines:

2. DON'T SACRIFICE WHAT YOU WANT *MOST* FOR WHAT YOU WANT *NOW*.

We live in a culture of instant gratification. We expect to have our wants, needs, and desires immediately satisfied.

We don't like waiting.

And so, we get ourselves into all sorts of bother because we sacrifice long-term gain for short-term pleasure.

Let's use money as an example. Maybe you'd like financial security in the form of savings, life insurance, etc. But you also want designer clothes, a bigger house, a nicer car. So you sacrifice the long-term goal of financial security for the short-term satisfaction of impressing people with your 'stuff'.

We see it in relationships. People desire to settle down, they want a good husband or wife, they long for the stability of a long-term relationship. But they sacrifice that because they move from one short-term relationship to another, then another. Then they wonder where all the good guys and girls have gone.

Even in our health and appearance, we want to be healthy or slimmer, but we're not willing to sacrifice the short-term pleasure of eating junk food for the goal that we ultimately want to achieve.

We want immediate gratification.
We want satisfaction now.
We don't like discipline and waiting and self-restraint.

The problem is, *when you're too hungry for something, you will always pay too much for it.*

My wife, Becky, will often ask what I would like for dinner. The problem is that she tends to ask me right after I've eaten lunch. I find it difficult to answer because I'm already full.

When you're fully satisfied, some things don't hold the same appeal as they do when you're starving.

If I have been fasting for a few days, I will literally eat almost anything. I will even eat vegetables. (I hate vegetables!). But I just crave to have that hunger satisfied.

Don't make decisions when you're too hungry for something.

I'm not just talking about food here.

When you're starving for attention or affection, you will give yourself to people that you normally wouldn't go near.

When you're starving for more money, you will do things to attain that money that you wouldn't do otherwise.

When you're starving for some excitement in your life, you don't tend to make wise decisions.

Esau completely underestimated how much he was giving up because he could only feel his intense hunger in that moment.

Apply that to your own life.

Where are you paying too much to satisfy a temporary hunger?

Where are you sacrificing what you want in the long term to fulfill a need or desire that you have right now?

And one final thought, again connected to the previous two points:

3. BE CAREFUL WHO YOU TALK TO AND SPEND TIME WITH WHEN YOU'RE IN A SUSCEPTIBLE STATE.

When you're feeling weak and vulnerable, be cautious about who you spend time with. Because sadly, there are some people, like Jacob, who will take advantage of your momentary weakness.

There are people who you shouldn't text late at night.

There are people who you shouldn't hang out with when you're feeling lonely.

There are people that you shouldn't go onto their social media accounts at certain times.

Because if you do, you will potentially end up in a situation that you will later regret.

Notice that we are simply told that *"Esau ate the stew and then he got up and left."*

It doesn't even mention if he enjoyed the food. It doesn't tell us if it was good stew. It doesn't let us know if he was satisfied. He ate it, got up and left. In a few hours, he would be hungry again.

Don't give up what you want most for what you want now. Don't sell your birthright for a bowl of beans.

385

In Christ, you have an inheritance:

*"I pray that the eyes of your heart may be enlightened in order that you may know the hope to which he has called you, **the riches of his glorious inheritance in his holy people**…"* (Ephesians 1: 18)

God has incredible plans and purposes for your life. He desires to do so much in you and through you.

The devil can't take those plans and purposes away.

But we can give them up.

We can sacrifice our inheritance for something else that we think will satisfy us. We can trade it for temporary pleasures.

Throughout the years, I have met people who are way more gifted than I am and who could go much further than I could ever go. But sadly, they have thrown it away because they couldn't hold off on satisfying their hunger.

I have seen too many people marry the wrong people because they were too hungry to get married.

I have watched people shipwreck their lives because they were too hungry for success.

I have seen people devastate their families because they were too hungry for physical pleasure.

It grieves me to see so much wasted potential.

But these men and women are also a cautionary tale. I don't want to make the same mistakes.

God gave us appetites and desires. They are good. They're part of being human.

But we are responsible for how we use and direct them.

386

The writer of Hebrews later reflects on this sad and sordid story:

"Make every effort to live in peace with everyone and to be holy; without holiness no one will see the Lord. See to it that no one falls short of the grace of God and that no bitter root grows up to cause trouble and defile many. See that no one is sexually immoral, or is godless like Esau, who for a single meal sold his inheritance rights as the oldest son. Afterward, as you know, when he wanted to inherit this blessing, he was rejected. Even though he sought the blessing with tears, he could not change what he had done." (Hebrews 12: 14-17)

God's Word shares these tragic stories as examples to protect, preserve, and prosper our lives. Let's learn the lessons:

Never make a permanent decision about a temporary condition.

Don't sacrifice what you want most for what you want now.

Be careful who you talk to and spend time with when you're in a susceptible state.

PROPHETIC ENCOURAGEMENT

I WILL UNBURDEN YOU

The Lord wants to unburden you from situations and relationships that have been weighing you down.

You have taken on responsibilities that He never intended for you to carry.

Or you were to carry them for a season, but you have held onto them.

Now they are wearying and draining you.

You are diligent and dependable and have sought to meet the expectations of others and yourself.

387

But, along the way, you have lost a bit of yourself.

Your joy has dissipated.

Your passion has waned.

The fire has dimmed.

Life has become predictable and routine.

Fatigue, frustration, and even boredom have become the norm.

You're tired of trying to please everyone.

Yet inside you sense a subtle stirring. A voice calling you to more.

It's like a gentle wind rekindling the embers of a fire that once burned so brightly.

God is going to restore the passion and joy that were stolen from you in this last season.

He is going to re-ignite the zeal that disappointments and setbacks have robbed from you.

Where you have constantly had to contend and battle, a new freedom and ease is coming in your walk with the Lord.

The pressure to perform is being lifted off from you.

You will begin to express who you truly are - without fear or hindrance.

You will share your thoughts without concern about what others think.

You will walk with purpose and poise.

Your spark is coming back.

You are coming alive again.

The LORD will show you that His yoke is easy and His burden is light.

I WILL UNBURDEN YOU.

DAY 38

TRANSITION AND IDENTITY

BIBLE READING

They came back to Moses and Aaron and the whole Israelite community at Kadesh in the Desert of Paran. There they reported to them and to the whole assembly and showed them the fruit of the land. They gave Moses this account: 'We went into the land to which you sent us, and it does flow with milk and honey! Here is its fruit. But the people who live there are powerful, and the cities are fortified and very large. We even saw descendants of Anak there. The Amalekites live in the Negev; the Hittites, Jebusites and Amorites live in the hill country; and the Canaanites live near the sea and along the Jordan.'

Then Caleb silenced the people before Moses and said, 'We should go up and take possession of the land, for we can certainly do it.'

But the men who had gone up with him said, 'We can't attack those people; they are stronger than we are.' And they spread among the Israelites a bad report about the land they had explored. They said, 'The land we explored devours those living in it. All the people we saw there are of great size. We saw the Nephilim there (the descendants of Anak come from the Nephilim). We seemed like grasshoppers in our own eyes, and we looked the same to them.'

(Numbers 13: 26-33)

DEVOTIONAL

One of the most unusual jobs I ever had was acting as a "filler" or "extra" in police lineups (or identity parades as we call them in the U.K.).

At the time, I was a college student and desperate for cash. One of my roommates discovered that you could apply for this 'position' at our local police station by simply filling out a form describing your physical appearance. Then, a few times a week, you received a call to come along and stand in line with a bunch of other guys in front of a one-way mirror while the witness on the other side attempted to identify the perpetrator of a crime.

It was easy money. And because I'm average height and build, I was called quite often. My ginger-haired mate who was 6-foot 4 inches tall wasn't in high demand.

However, there was a downside. For some reason, I always got stressed that I would get picked out by the witness and be accused of a crime I didn't commit.

I know it's ridiculous, but I became nervous standing there knowing there was potentially a criminal standing next to me. My palms would get sweaty, and I would do a weird facial expression. The more anxious I became, the more suspicious I looked.

My identity might have been 'innocent' but I felt like I was 'guilty'. **My mentality didn't match the reality.**

The same could be said for many of us. Our sense of identity is misaligned with our reality. Or, to put it another way – **what you think about yourself is different than what God says about you.**

In Numbers 13, it's been two years since the Israelites fled the cruel slavery of Egypt. They might no longer be oppressed physically, but in their heads and hearts, they are still in the grip of bondage.

Moses sends 12 spies to scout out the Promised Land. The reconnaissance mission was designed to motivate everyone else to cross over into the land and take what God had told them was already theirs:

*"Send some men to explore the land of Canaan, **which I am giving to the Israelites.**"* (v. 2)

When they return, their report starts positively:

"We went into the land to which you sent us, and it does flow with milk and honey! Here is its fruit." (v. 27)

In other words, the land is exactly like God told us it would be - a place of plenty and abundance.

However, things quickly go downhill from here:

"We can't attack those people; they are stronger than we are.' And they spread among the Israelites a bad report about the land they had explored. They said, 'The land we explored devours those living in it. All the people we saw there are of great size. We saw the Nephilim there (the descendants of Anak come from the Nephilim). We seemed like grasshoppers in our own eyes, and we looked the same to them.'" (vv. 31-33)

Look at their words:

"We can't..."

"...they are stronger than we are..."

"The land...devours..."

And here's the final nail in the coffin:

"We seemed like grasshoppers in our own eyes, and we looked the same to them."

These men had been liberated from slavery for two years. God had done incredible things. They had a front-row seat as He sent ten plagues on the

Egyptians, parted the Red Sea, provided water from a rock when they were thirsty, sent quail and manna when they were hungry, and led them by a pillar of cloud and fire through the desert.

Again and again, Yahweh demonstrated that He was a good, faithful, and powerful God who deserved complete trust from His people.

But, in their hearts, they were still weak, powerless, frightened slaves who had a mentality of poverty, lack, and survival.

They saw themselves as grasshoppers – small, weak, vulnerable, inferior, common, and fearful.

Their identity hadn't caught up with their reality.

NEW YOU, OLD IDENTITY

Recently, on a podcast, I heard author Mark Manson say this:

"Identity lags reality by one to two years. There is a lot of psychological fallout from a rapid change in status."

I've thought a lot about that in relation to transition.

Change is the outer shift that takes place. Transition is the inner journey of navigating that change.

The external change can sometimes happen quickly.

You receive a promotion. You inherit a large sum of money. You retire from your job. You lose a loved one suddenly.

Overnight, your outer world has changed. But emotionally and psychologically, it usually takes much longer to adjust to the new reality.

Even when the change doesn't happen quite so quickly, it still takes time for you to embody it internally.

392

For example, imagine you've lost 100 lbs of weight over an 18-month period. The world might see you as a thinner person. But inside, you still 'feel' like a fat person.

Or you've risen to the top of your field in business or sport in a relatively short space of time. You can still feel intimidated and out of place when you're around other successful people in those areas.

How the world sees you and how you see yourself can be very different.

Everyone expects you to turn up as this newly ascended version of you. Yet, your insecurities, fears, doubts, and inclinations haven't changed that much.

It takes time for your inner world to catch up to the outer one.

In the six stages of transition that I teach, I call this 'disorientation'.

You've left where you were – a place, a relationship, a role, a ministry. You know who you're not. But you're not yet sure who you are.

Your old identity has ended. But your new identity has yet to be formed. And so, you're experiencing the tension of transition.

YOUR INTERNAL THERMOSTAT

It's been said that we all have an internal thermostat. This is your self-identity, and it encompasses the thoughts, beliefs, ideas, systems, and concepts that you hold to be true about yourself.

In many ways, this thermostat is the governor of your life. It seeks to keep you at a certain 'temperature', let's say 20 degrees.

Any significant change in your life moves the temperature up or down. Immediately your internal thermostat recognizes the discomfort of this shift and attempts to regulate you back to 20 degrees.

This thermostat becomes like a barrier to change, keeping you confined and constricted in a situation that is no longer helpful or healthy.

393

That's why every time life became difficult in the wilderness, the Israelites immediately wanted to return to Egypt. Their internal thermostat had been set in slavery. So familiar bondage was more appealing than uncomfortable freedom.

It's also why a large percentage of lottery winners end up going broke after a few years. Their bank balance may have changed but their identity around money has remained the same.

When you step into the 'new', it will always take time to acclimate and 'grow into' your new environment.

Acknowledge and accept that. For a season, it will be hard. There will be an internal pull to go back to your old identity.

It's completely normal to feel that way. Everyone experiences this when they go through a change.

If you don't grasp that, one of the following might happen.

You'll think you made the wrong decision to leave the old. You might even assume the discomfort is God telling you that you've made a mistake. After all, if this was God's will, wouldn't it be easier? And wouldn't you have complete peace?

Or you will begin to self-sabotage in your new role. Because you feel uncomfortable or inadequate, you'll start to behave in destructive ways that thwart your progress in your new place, position, or relationship. Unconsciously, you're trying to fail so you'll be forced to return to what is familiar.

I know several women who have spent years in harmful and abusive relationships. Finally, they meet a kind, stable, caring man. Things usually start well. But as soon as the relationship begins to get serious, the woman sabotages it. She might start provoking irrational arguments, cheat, or break up with her partner for no reason. Often, she goes back to a relationship with an abusive partner.

394

It's hard to understand. But her internal thermostat is telling her that she's not worthy of a man like this. By self-sabotaging, she is trying to protect herself from getting hurt again.

I know a church leader who was doing a great job leading a church of 100 people. Then, he was appointed to a role as Senior Pastor of a church with over 1000 members. For a while, everything seemed to go well. But soon he began to make restructuring decisions deliberately designed to make the church smaller. He essentially wanted to dismantle this flagship congregation into smaller churches of...you've probably guessed it...around 100 people. That's where his thermostat was set. Eventually, he had to move on.

SIZE UP

So, how do you grow into your new identity?

How can you navigate change without self-sabotaging and returning to the old version of you?

As I've already said, part of adapting to change is simply acknowledging that the discomfort is normal and giving yourself time to acclimate to the new environment.

When I hire a new staff member, I always assume that it will take six months for them to settle into the role. Because in almost every job I've had, that's how long it took me.

But there's also another way to shift your inner identity even before your outer reality changes.

Begin to 'size up' in advance.

Our son Elijah loves clothes and trainers. And unfortunately, his favorite brands aren't cheap!

Because he's 11 years old and growing quickly, when I purchase clothes or shoes for him, I always size up. I'm fully aware that they'll be a little too big for a while. But he'll soon grow into them, and they'll fit perfectly.

In the same way, we can size up our identity. **We can intentionally 'try on' something bigger and wear it for a while until it begins to fit more comfortably.**

Let me share how this happened in my life.

I grew up in a household where we had just enough. My parents worked hard, and I never lacked anything. But I knew money was tight and we couldn't afford anything considered 'luxury'.

This 'just enough' identity manifested in different ways throughout my life.

As a kid, I always thought my friends lived in nicer houses and their parents drove better cars than ours. I don't know if it was true, but in my mind, it was a fact. I felt inferior because everyone had more than us.

In my 20s, I got into a huge amount of credit card debt. This little piece of plastic allowed me to have all the things that I felt I'd missed out on in childhood. So, I spent money frivolously on things that I didn't need. It took me years to pay off that debt.

I also struggled with giving and tithing for much of my Christian journey. I knew I should be generous. But I was scared if I gave money away, I wouldn't have enough.

I always bought old vehicles and drove them until they literally fell apart.

We never had any savings. Every penny that came in was quickly spent.

When a former church housed our family in rat-infested, damp, smelly accommodation, I accepted it. It was 'enough'.

And when it came to family trips and vacations, we would almost always stay in budget accommodation. Honestly, some of the places we slept... I wouldn't allow our dog to stay there!

I could go on, but you can see the pattern.

I had a poverty mentality. My internal thermostat was set at 'just enough and no more'.

Around seven years ago, God really began to challenge me in this area.

He spoke to me and said: *'It's time to size up and prepare for 'more''*".

I had no idea what that meant. But over time, some changes slowly started taking place.

Firstly, He began to place me around people who were on a higher level than me in different areas of life. Wealthy business owners, entrepreneurs, pastors of large churches, published authors, influential online coaches, significant prophetic voices, and other successful leaders in different spheres.

In most cases, I wasn't trying to meet them or befriend them. For various reasons, they happened to come into my world.

I watched them and learned from them. I enjoyed their company. I absorbed their wisdom.

But more than that, I began to understand their mindset.

They thought differently to me.

Where I saw lack, they saw abundance.

Where I was preoccupied with obstacles, they perceived opportunities.

Where I could only see problems, they were looking for potential.

Where I had settled for certain standards, theirs were much higher.

Where I saw money as a scarce resource to be hoarded, they used it as a tool to be invested and increased.

Slowly, something began to shift inside me. I wasn't even fully aware of it until recently.

I began to give away money to the point where I now love expressing generosity.

I started to take hold of opportunities that I previously wouldn't have had the confidence to attempt.

I cleared my debt and even began to grow my savings. We now have a down payment ready if we find a house we like. That would have been inconceivable just five years ago.

We started eating in nicer restaurants and buying clothes that weren't always on sale.

I purchased a car that I actually enjoy driving. And I surprised my wife with the black Mini that she'd wanted for years.

We slowly began to stay in better hotels when we went on vacation. In each upgrade, initially, I felt like an imposter. But soon, the next level became normal.

The identity change didn't happen overnight. And I'm still a work in progress.

But God has been breaking the poverty mentality that kept me confined for four decades of my life. It's been incredibly liberating. And I am so thankful. (So are Becky and Elijah!)

Where is God calling you to upgrade your identity to align with a new reality?

It could be a reality that you're already experiencing but not fully enjoying. Your thermostat is constantly trying to pull you back to an old, more comfortable version of yourself.

Or it could be a reality that God is leading you into. He wants to take you further and higher, but that will require an upgrade in your identity. Your mindset must shift. The temperature on the thermometer needs to move.

As we'll see tomorrow, that's how God prepared people for significant promotion. He slowly exposed them to the next level before they arrived there.

Beginning today, you can start making small changes to size up.

It could mean trying something new or different that is slightly outside your comfort zone.
It might mean forming connections with people who are at a higher level in your sphere of work.

It could involve saying 'yes' to an opportunity that you feel unqualified for.

It might be as simple as buying a nicer pair of shoes or eating at a fancier restaurant. Or booking a better standard of hotel next time you go on vacation.

I know there's a cost - monetary and psychological.

But what is it costing you to stay where you are?

Refusal to embrace their new identity cost Israel 40 years of wandering in the wilderness.

Only two of the original spies - Joshua and Caleb - crossed over into the Promised Land. Because they saw themselves as God saw them.

Tragically, the others never entered what God wanted to give them. They saw themselves as grasshoppers and consequently spent their lives living small and fruitless lives.

That's not going to happen to you.

You are not a grasshopper. You are a called, chosen, loved, and anointed son or daughter of the King.

Don't settle for anything less than God says you are.

PROPHETIC ENCOURAGEMENT

IT IS COMING. BUT PROBABLY NOT HOW YOU EXPECT IT.

Don't disregard it or dismiss what God is doing in your life because it's not what you thought it would look like.

God is going to show up in unique, different, and surprising ways in this season.
What you have prayed for, longed for, waited for - what He has promised - it will come.

But it won't be packaged how you thought it would be.

Or it will come through someone you could never have imagined.

Or from somewhere completely off your radar.

Be very careful that you don't miss God's provision because it arrives in an unusual parcel.

Don't reject it because it's not how you thought it would appear.

Israel expected a military Messiah; God sent them a vulnerable baby.

They expected a powerful deliverer; God sent them a suffering servant.

Yet, through His frailty and suffering, He brought a greater deliverance than they could ever have imagined.

Similarly, God is going to fulfill His promises and prophetic words in your life in unusual and uncommon ways.

Don't miss the moment of His visitation.
Watch for what you've been waiting for.

IT IS COMING. BUT PROBABLY NOT HOW YOU EXPECT IT.

DAY 39

A PREVIEW OF YOUR FUTURE

BIBLE READING

So Samuel took the horn of oil and anointed him in the presence of his brothers, and from that day on the Spirit of the LORD came powerfully upon David. Samuel then went to Ramah.

…Saul said to his attendants, 'Find someone who plays well and bring him to me.'

One of the servants answered, 'I have seen a son of Jesse of Bethlehem who knows how to play the lyre. He is a brave man and a warrior. He speaks well and is a fine-looking man. And the LORD is with him.'

…David came to Saul and entered his service. Saul liked him very much, and David became one of his armour-bearers. Then Saul sent word to Jesse, saying, 'Allow David to remain in my service, for I am pleased with him.'

Whenever the spirit from God came on Saul, David would take up his lyre and play. Then relief would come to Saul; he would feel better, and the evil spirit would leave him.

(1 Samuel 16: 13-23)

DEVOTIONAL

Several years ago, my friend took over as CEO of his family's food service business. Over several decades, his father had built it into a successful company. However, business had begun to plateau in recent years. My friend, who was in his mid-30s, knew that there was significant potential for growth. But he was struggling to get a clear picture of what that might look like or what steps he should take to move forward. His dad's ways of running the business were all he'd ever known.

Then, while attending an international conference, he met a top executive from a major US company in the same industry. Within a few months, he flew his entire management team from the company in Ireland to spend several weeks with the company in the States. They were given complete access to all their systems, processes, and procedures.

Just a few years after returning from that trip, my friend had grown his company to four times the size it had been before. **Seeing what the next level looked like made it much easier to get there.**

Yesterday, we began thinking about transition and identity. Often God wants to move us forward or promote us to another level, but we struggle to step into the new. Our internal thermostat pulls us back to the comfortable and familiar. Our identity lags behind our new reality.

One of the ways God begins to upgrade our identity is by exposing us to glimpses of our future reality before we fully step into it.

Like my friend with his family business, we get to see beyond the narrow confines and limited experiences that we have become accustomed to. We are inspired, our vision is enlarged, and we begin to see the potential of what could be.

While we don't yet inhabit the next level, we have visited it and taken mental snapshots that help motivate us to persevere until we get there. **We sometimes have to see it before we can be it.**

PROXIMITY TO THE PALACE

One way God exposes us to our future is by placing us in proximity to those who are already there. We get around people who are living the kind of life we want to live or fulfilling the calling that God is leading us toward.

We see this happen in David's life.

At the time when he was anointed as the future king of Israel, David's life had been largely limited to his father's house and the sheep field. However, immediately after Samuel departs from Bethlehem, we read that David is summoned to the royal palace.

"One of the servants answered, "I have seen a son of Jesse of Bethlehem who knows how to play the lyre. He is a brave man and a warrior. He speaks well and is a fine-looking man. And the Lord is with him. Then Saul sent messengers to Jesse and said, 'Send me your son David...'"
(1 Samuel 16: 18-19)

What are the chances of that happening?

David has been hidden out in the field, surrounded only by sheep and wild animals. Yet, a servant of Saul just happened to know that the young shepherd was also gifted in playing music.

Later, David would write:

"The steps of a good man are ordered by the LORD, And He delights in his way." (37: 23)

He was clearly speaking from personal experience.

God was strategically positioning David in exactly the right place to expose him to a preview of his future. He might have been called to the palace to play the harp. But he also got to see up close what it was like to be a king.

As David strummed, he was able to observe royal behavior and palace protocol. His world was enlarged, and he also formed a vital relationship with Saul's son, Jonathan. This season provided the best possible preparation for David's future as Saul's successor.

I described yesterday how, when God began to call me to think bigger, He started to surround me with people who were excelling in different areas. Their words of wisdom and the example of their lives helped shift me out of a poverty mindset into believing for more. My internal thermostat was raised.

Sometimes these people will appear in your life by God's providence. Other times, you will need to be intentional in finding them.

Each year I sign up to be part of a mentorship community. I think of an area where I want to grow and find someone with greater expertise and experience in that field. Some of these are in-person and some are online.

For example, this year I'm part of Dr Sharon Stone's *School of the Prophets*. There's a financial cost involved, but it's a very worthwhile investment. Mentorship has accelerated my growth and helped me avoid costly mistakes that others have learned from their own bitter experiences.

Consider these questions:

- As you think about your future, where might God be leading you?

- What could the next level look like?

- Are there two or three areas where you need to grow/develop if you're going to get there?

- Who is ahead of you in those areas that could mentor you or help you get there faster?

Proximity is one of God's greatest tools in your season of preparation.

He will direct you to people and places that will play a part in forming you for the future.

Recognize them when they enter your world and take full advantage of the opportunities they offer you.

SNAPSHOTS OF LIFE'S COMING ATTRACTIONS

As well as exposing you to people and places that are aligned with your future, God often begins to give you glimpses and snapshots of what He is preparing for you.

This can take different forms. We see some of them exemplified in Joseph's life.

As a teenager, Joseph had two dreams in which sheaves of corn and then the sun, moon, and eleven stars bowed down before him (Genesis 37). At the time, these night visions were probably quite confusing. But later, when his father and brothers came to Egypt to buy grain during a famine, suddenly everything 'clicked' and they made perfect sense.

You too may begin to have visions or dreams of where God is leading you. They don't always make sense that the time because what you're seeing is unfamiliar. You might not even pay much attention to them. But years later, when you enter a new environment, the pieces fall into place. You realize, *this was that*!

Or you find yourself having déjà vu moments. It feels like you've been in a place or met someone before. In one sense you have. God has already shown you it in your spirit or in your imagination.

You might start to be drawn to certain things that you'd previously little interest in. Or you begin to randomly meet people from a particular place and you sense that God has brought them across your path for a reason.

For example, in the two years before we moved to Dublin, I strangely began to find myself drawn to Irish movies and TV shows that were set in that city. Prior to this, I'd never had any inclination to live there. But in this season, God began to reorient my heart and desires in that direction.

Then, just as we began to consider a move to Dublin, one evening Becky and I were out for a dinner date in Belfast.

Over the course of the meal, we began to make conversation with the people sitting at the table next to us. I asked one man what he did for a living. He replied: "I'm actually the priest of a church called Saint

Catherine's in Dublin." It was the neighboring Catholic Parish to the church we would soon be leading. And our future church also met in old building that was formerly known as Saint Catherine's!

When we eventually moved to the city, this man was instrumental in opening doors for us in an area that had traditionally been very hostile to our expression of church. God granted me favor with him, in advance, through a 'chance' meeting.

Sometimes it's almost as if God gives you a trailer or movie preview about your future. It's enough to get you interested, but not so detailed that it spoils the newness and excitement when you actually arrive there.

Again, we see something similar in Joseph's life. Long before he was promoted to the second highest position in the land of Egypt, Joseph began to 'find favor' with Pharoah's officials:

"Joseph found favour in his eyes and became his attendant. Potiphar put him in charge of his household, and he entrusted to his care everything he owned. From the time he put him in charge of his household and of all that he owned, the LORD blessed the household of the Egyptian because of Joseph." (Genesis 39: 4-5)

It wasn't the position God had ultimately destined for Jospeh. But it was another step in his preparation to getting there.

God will even use the most negative and challenging circumstances to prepare us for our future.

Later, Joseph was falsely accused of rape and thrown into prison. It probably seemed that his dreams had been shattered. But even in prison, he made a crucial connection with Pharoah's chief cupbearer. This relationship with later be instrumental in elevating him to a position of great power and responsibility.

People and circumstances come into our lives that, at the time, appear to have little relationship with our destiny or calling. Some of them might even bring difficulty or pain. But later, we look back and join the dots. We realize: *if it wasn't for all of **that**, we wouldn't be doing **this***.

A member of our former church, Adrienne, gave birth to a baby boy with a rare genetic condition. Little Hugh never left the hospital during his nine months of life. I don't think I'll ever forget the day I officiated this precious child's funeral. The small wicker casket at the front of the packed church was heartbreaking to look at.

Yet, amid the most tragic of moments, God began to birth something beautiful.

During those nine months that Hugh was in hospital, Adrienne noticed that that there were many other parents, like herself, who spent every day at their children's bedside. But unlike her, they didn't live close by. While Adrienne went home to her own bed each night, these parents slept in chairs or on the floor of the hospital room in some sort of makeshift bed.

Even during the final months of Hugh's short life, God began to place a vision in Adrienne's heart.

I didn't mention that Adrienne is also a gifted entrepreneur who owns a chain of over 20 pharmacies.

After Hugh's death, she used her finances and business acumen to purchase two large buildings directly opposite the children's hospital. These were transformed into 'Hugh's House' which provides free accommodation and food, 365 days a year, to families of children who are in hospital.

Adrienne's exposure to the plight of other families in need has been used by God to bring life and light into the most painful of circumstances. It's also given Adrienne a national platform to share her story.

NOTHING IS WASTED

Back to David. When he was summoned to the palace to play the lyre for Saul, it's unlikely that he immediately made the connection between this musical job and his calling to be the future king. As he was strumming, he wasn't looking at Saul thinking: "I'm going to sit on your throne one day soon." He was simply using one of his gifts as it was required. On the surface, the two things - kingship and music - didn't seem to be related.

It's the same with you.

There are stages in our lives when God puts us in places or circumstances that may not seem to make sense for accomplishing our calling.

Yet these places are an important part of God's plan. They expose us to a future that we might not otherwise be able to envision. They give us proximity to individuals who are living the kind of life that we might one day step into. And we form relationships that become pivotal in providing companionship, wisdom, and resources during a later stage in our journey.

As I reflect on my own life, I'm amazed by how situations and meetings that seemed insignificant at the time became strategic in shaping my future.

Some might call this serendipity or coincidence or happenstance. I believe it is God's providence.

Perhaps you look at your life and your current surroundings and circumstances, there appears to be a massive misalignment between what you see, and the dreams God has placed in your heart.

But He is positioning people and situations around you that are subtle signposts to where He is leading you.

He is stirring your heart and gently drawing you in a new direction.

He is giving you glimpses or snapshots of the future He has prepared for you.

I've said it before: *God wastes nothing, and He gets us ready.*

PROPHETIC ENCOURAGEMENT

YOU'RE MAKING A COMEBACK

As I was driving, I was especially drawn to the trees.

Blown about by the strong wind and beaten by the cold rain, they looked completely stripped and bare in this winter season.

Yet, I felt reminded by the Lord that this is only a temporary state.

They would not remain like this forever.

The season will soon change, and they will grow new leaves and flourish. They will return to their former fullness, color, and beauty.

Perhaps you feel as if you have been stripped back in this past season.

The storms have shaken you, the season has been very severe.

You feel vulnerable, exposed, and almost naked like you've nothing left to lose or give.

The LORD would say: **You will return. This is not how things will always be. It's not over. And you're not finished.**

As sure as the trees will grow new leaves and color shall come back, so your season is changing. New life is being restored.

You're making a comeback.

Your roots have deepened, and you have developed resilience and strength through the winter and the storms.

You will once again bud and bloom, more beautiful and bold than ever.

Take heart. Stay strong. The winter is almost over.

YOU'RE MAKING A COMEBACK.

DAY 40

GRIEVING YOUR LOSSES

BIBLE READING

And Moses the servant of the LORD died there in Moab, as the LORD had said. He buried him in Moab, in the valley opposite Beth Peor, but to this day no one knows where his grave is. Moses was a hundred and twenty years old when he died, yet his eyes were not weak nor his strength gone. The Israelites grieved for Moses in the plains of Moab thirty days, until the time of weeping and mourning was over.

Now Joshua son of Nun was filled with the spirit of wisdom because Moses had laid his hands on him. So the Israelites listened to him and did what the LORD had commanded Moses.

(Deuteronomy 34: 5-19)

After the death of Moses the servant of the LORD, the LORD said to Joshua son of Nun, Moses' assistant: 'Moses my servant is dead. Now then, you and all these people, get ready to cross the River Jordan into the land I am about to give to them – to the Israelites.

(Joshua 1: 1-2)

DEVOTIONAL

As I write this devotional, our family is experiencing a season of sorrow and grief. Recently, Becky's mom passed from this life to be with Jesus.

Of course, we don't grieve as those without hope. We know that she is with her precious Savior, her suffering has finally ended, and we take great comfort in the certainty of Christ's return and resurrected life in the new creation.

But still, we mourn. Because loss is painful. Especially the loss of those we love.

When I initially finished the first draft of my book *The Tension of Transition*, it felt incomplete. I had dealt with endings, different types of transitions, navigating through the 'messy middle', and entering and embracing the new.

But I knew something was missing.

Over time, I realized that I had failed to adequately address the deep sense of grief, loss, sadness, and regret that you often experience as you walk through a season of transition.

Transition, by its very nature, involves change.

And change brings loss.

Even if you know that God has initiated the transition and is leading you through the change, you still feel the pain of letting go of something or someone who has been an intricate and important part of your life.

You have to relearn how to live life without them.

For a while, you may forget that they are no longer around.

You instinctively pick up the phone to call or message them.

You talk about them as if they're still here. Our son, Elijah, yesterday talked about visiting his "Granny and Grandpa's house" - even though his "Granny" is no longer there.

So many small things can trigger memories of how things used to be. And while life must go on, we come to terms with the reality that some things will never be the same again. We now have to reconstruct a life without the person, place, or thing that was a part of our identity.

MOURNING AND MOVING

We see God's people experience this deep sense of loss following the death of Moses. We are told:

"The Israelites grieved for Moses in the plains of Moab thirty days, until the time of weeping and mourning was over." (Deuteronomy 34: 8)

The normal mourning period in Jewish culture was seven days. But here, the people mourned for thirty days. This scripture doesn't indicate whether the LORD instituted this additional three weeks of grieving, or if it was something the children of Israel came up with on their own. But it's clear that the death of Moses impacted them very deeply.

Because, while every loss brings some degree of pain, not all losses are equal.

Some losses can be processed and moved through in a matter of days.

Others take much longer before we begin to find our bearings or feel like we can face the world again.

Nor should we imagine that on day 31 the Israelites suddenly got "over it" and life for the community returned to normal.

Grieving isn't like that. It can't be turned off and on like a faucet. It comes in intermittent and often unpredictable waves.

We might think we're doing fine. Then something happens and we realize that the wound in our soul is still very tender. We've still some way to go towards the healing we need.

Perhaps that's why in Joshua 1, we read:

"After the death of Moses the servant of the LORD, the LORD said to Joshua son of Nun, Moses' assistant: 'Moses my servant is dead. Now then, you and all these people, get ready to cross the River Jordan into the land..." (vv. 1-2)

Moses' death was not news to Joshua at this point. He's been lamenting this loss with his people for 30 days.

So why is God stating the obvious?

I think it's because God knows that Joshua is in danger of getting stuck in this place of mourning. He's overwhelmed by sorrow. He's immobilized by grief. He's struggling to see any sort of future without the leader he has faithfully served for 40 years. He feels inadequate to lead the people like Moses had.

It's as if God says to him:

"Joshua, it's time to get up and press forward into the next stage of the journey.

I know you don't feel ready. That's alright. You'll never feel fully ready. Don't let that stop you.

You can still mourn, but you must begin to move.

You will continue to grieve, but you have to get going.

Moses is dead. Accept that he's not coming back. Honor His memory and legacy by finishing the work He started.

As I was with Moses, I am with you.

He might be gone, but My promises still stand.

Now, get ready to cross over into the land I am giving you."

THERE ARE MANY TYPES OF LOSS

I have discovered that grief isn't something we only experience when a person whom we love dies. There can be many other losses in our lives that aren't as obvious but are still incredibly painful. These include:

- Separation or divorce.

- Disability or a serious illness.

- The death of a faithful pet.

- A miscarriage, infertility, or inability to have children through age.

- The shattering of a lifelong dream.

- Retirement from a long career.

- Someone you love and trust betrays you.

Then there are more natural losses:

- Loss of youthfulness as you get older, and your skin begins to wrinkle and age.

- You relocate to a new area and lose some close friendships.

- Relationships that don't work out the way you hoped.

- Your children become less and less dependent on you as they get older.

- You lose a position, role, or responsibility.

We will all experience loss in different areas of our lives, and we will walk through the 'valley of the shadow' many times throughout our lives.

Therefore, **we must understand and accept that grief will be an unavoidable part of our journey.**

When our family left the church we had poured so much into, I significantly underestimated the sense of loss and grief I would experience.

Upon our departure, we took a sabbatical rest, beginning with two months in the States. The first few weeks were great. It felt like I was finally taking the long overdue vacation I needed.

However, it wasn't long before I began to feel emotionally flat and numb.

I found it difficult to understand or express what was going on inside me. We were living in an amazing beachfront house in LA, waking up each morning with nothing to do but watch the surfers and spend time together as a family. I should have been on a high. So why was I feeling negative emotions?

As I began to examine my soul and process what was going on, it became clear that I was experiencing grief over the various losses that had just taken place in my life.

It took me a while to accept this. I thought grief only happened when a person we loved died. But over time, I began to identify other losses that my soul was mourning:

I had lost my position and identity as the leader of a thriving, growing church.

I had lost a very close friend through a relationship breakdown during our final month.

I had lost the connection to the many other friends we had made during our five years in that city.

I had lost the members of a wonderful congregation who I had pastored and grown to love and care for deeply.

I had lost doing the thing that I loved most in ministry – preaching God's Word each Sunday.

I had lost the house our family had been living in.

I had lost my sense of stability that came from getting paid a salary every month.

I had lost security and certainty about the future. I had no idea what lay ahead for me or my family.

I could go on. But you get the idea.

I had relinquished so much more than I anticipated when I resigned from my role.

I wasn't just leaving a job. I was leaving a life behind.

And now, I was walking through all the stages of grief that psychologists say we experience. I felt a mixture of sadness, anger, regret, confusion, guilt, and acceptance. It would take a while before I reached the final stage - hope.

I'm fully aware that my experience was very minor compared to the pain and grief you may have had to endure.

But the point remains. **Whenever you walk through any significant transition, it's difficult to anticipate and prepare for all the losses it will bring.**

Some of them will surprise you. You didn't think you were so attached to that person, place, or thing. Yet, you feel its absence profoundly.

Others will be easier than you anticipated. You thought you would miss them more than you do.

Either way, be aware that acknowledging, grieving, and processing your losses will be part of the journey toward your next season or assignment. Healthy endings usually lead to better new beginnings.

PROCESSING YOUR LOSSES

I'm not someone who talks a lot about my emotions, so I pushed them down, expecting that they would go away. As you can probably guess, that didn't work.

Eventually, I had to start facing up to my grief and loss.

I began processing each one individually, allowing myself to feel whatever it was I was feeling, however uncomfortable that was. For example, if I felt anger, I asked myself: "Who or what is this anger directed towards?" Was it an individual? The situation? Myself? All three?

I also asked myself some hard questions. I needed to take responsibility for areas where I had regrets about some of the things I had said or done, especially during those final months. There were conversations that I could have handled differently and decisions I made that were hurtful to people I cared about.

It's common to experience regrets or guilt when we experience transition. When emotions are running high or life is filled with uncertainty, we don't always show the best version of ourselves. We have a tendency to say or do things we later wish we could change. Sometimes, we will be able to apologize and make amends. In other cases, for whatever reason, we can only move on and learn the lessons, so we do better next time.

I had to accept the lack of closure we experienced as we moved on from that place. Because of the breakdown in some relationships, it felt like everything happened too quickly. Both the church and our family had little time to prepare for or process the massive change we were experiencing. Goodbyes were rushed. There was misunderstanding and confusion about why we were leaving. Some people felt like we had simply abandoned them.

I will talk more about closure later in this book, but **sometimes things come to an end without the resolution or sense of conclusion that you would have liked.**

Maybe someone exited your life much quicker than you had anticipated or expected.

Perhaps you didn't get to say a proper goodbye or express how you really felt about them.

Or maybe things finished in a fractured state with loose ends that may never be neatly tied up.

Whatever it is, **sometimes seasons will end in what seems like an unfinished way.** Part of your grieving process will involve dealing with unresolved issues, remorse, regrets, and the things you could or should have said or done. **But you cannot wait for closure before you move on.** Trust the LORD with pieces that can't be fixed.

Overall, I just felt sadness that people who had been so central to our lives were no longer there. I missed them. We had been close. And now we weren't.

It took the two months we spent in California for me to grieve properly. Most mornings, I went for long runs or walks on the beach by myself, replaying events in my head and bringing them before the LORD in prayer.

As time moved on, I began to turn a corner. The heaviness lifted, joy returned, and made peace with all that had happened.

I've found that a good sign that you have started to move through grief is when you can talk about the people or events without experiencing strong internal or external emotions. That's when you know that you are speaking from a healed scar, not a seeping, open wound. If you break down in tears or seethe with anger every time you mention what you went through, more time for healing is required.

GOD'S CALL IS GREATER THAN YOUR LOSS

The bottom line is this: **the call of God is greater than any loss, hurt, pain, betrayal, or rejection that we might endure.**

God again acknowledges the loss of Moses. But then He instructs Joshua:

"Now then, you and all these people, get ready to cross the River Jordan into the land I am about to give to them – to the Israelites...

As I was with Moses, so I will be with you." (vv. 2; 5)

Those two words are important: *"Now, then..."*

There always comes a point where we have to make a decision:

Will I move into what God wants me to do *now*, or will I remain stuck in *then*?

Moses was wonderful. He had a special and unique relationship with God. He was the only leader the people had ever known. He would be sorely missed. But that was *then*.

Now is what matters. Joshua is reminded that the mission of God is bigger than any individual, no matter how great they were. Moses might be gone, but God's presence and promises remain.

It's good for us to remember that the purposes of God are greater than any individual person.

In church, we get attached to people, especially leaders who have impacted our lives. And when, for whatever reason, they move on, we are sometimes left feeling bereft and abandoned. We can't imagine the ministry continuing without the leader.

And, while things might look different, God's purposes are never dependent on any one person.

People play their part. They fulfill their assignment. They complete their calling. And when they move on, we grieve and mourn their loss.

But then we get back up, wash our face, take off our funeral clothes, and press on with the purposes of God.

He is still at work and will raise up others to build upon and advance all that has gone before.

WALK THROUGH THE VALLEY

If you're grieving a loss today, allow yourself to feel it as deeply as you need to. Confront it head-on. Deal with it as honestly as you can. Don't hide from your hurt or bury your pain.

Grieving is good, normal, natural, and healthy.

But don't allow yourself to get stuck there.

The Bible says that we *"**walk through** the valley of the shadow of death."* (Psalm 23: 4)

It does not say that we camp there or build a house there.

No matter what we lose or have taken from us - we keep moving forward.

Sometimes it will be with tear-filled eyes and a broken heart.

But it should also be with a deep assurance that God is able to take all the broken pieces and put them back together to create a beautiful future for us.

It might not look like how we hoped, planned, or imagined it. But it can still be filled with meaning, purpose, love, and joy.

PROPHETIC ENCOURAGEMENT

YOU ARE FIGHTING FOR YOUR FUTURE.

Some of you right now are experiencing spiritual attacks and opposition which is intense, relentless, and almost overwhelming.

Your weaknesses and vulnerabilities have been exposed and the enemy is taking full advantage of every opportunity to assault and undermine you.

The temptation is to give in and give up.

But YOU MUST FIGHT!

Understand just how much is at stake.

The enemy is not so much going after who you are now as he is seeking to kill and destroy the destiny that the LORD is opening up before you.

He has perceived who you can become, and he is seeking to stop it before you get there.

This is not just about you personally – it is about the people you will reach and the impact your life will have.
You cannot be passive, you cannot lie down, you cannot give up.

YOU MUST FIGHT!

You are not alone.
The LORD goes before you.
The heavenly host surrounds you.
But this does not excuse you from the battle.

YOU MUST FIGHT!

Refix your focus.
Shake off passively.

Rise up and take your stand against the enemy.

The LORD has given you the victory.

But YOU MUST FIGHT!

DAY 41

INCOMPATIBLE

BIBLE READING

Now John's disciples and the Pharisees were fasting. Some people came and asked Jesus, "How is it that John's disciples and the disciples of the Pharisees are fasting, but yours are not?"

Jesus answered, "How can the guests of the bridegroom fast while he is with them? They cannot, so long as they have him with them. But the time will come when the bridegroom will be taken from them, and on that day they will fast.

"No one sews a patch of unshrunk cloth on an old garment. Otherwise, the new piece will pull away from the old, making the tear worse. And no one pours new wine into old wineskins. Otherwise, the wine will burst the skins, and both the wine and the wineskins will be ruined. No, they pour new wine into new wineskins."

(Mark 2: 18-22)

Therefore, if anyone is in Christ, the new creation has come: The old has gone, the new is here!

(2 Corinthians 5: 17)

DEVOTIONAL

I typically only watch two types of programs on TV – crime dramas and property shows.

In the second genre, one of my favorites is called *Love It or List It*.

In *Love It or List It* the hosts help homeowners decide if they should stay in a house that no longer fits their lifestyle. While their current home is being renovated, they are shown completely new properties within their budget. At the end of the show, they must decide if they'll stick with their old fixed-up house or move.

It always amazes me how often the participants *love It* rather than *list It*. An extension and a new kitchen are enough to convince them to hold onto a property that has so many obvious downsides. At the same time, they are turning down the opportunity to live in a bright, spacious, new property that meets all their needs.

The show illustrates a common trait among humans. **Given the choice, most people would rather patch up the old which is familiar than risk stepping into something completely new.**

We would rather renovate than replace.

In Mark 2, Jesus tells two short parables about patches and wineskins.

While both are essentially illustrating the same point, usually we focus on the wine and wineskins. However, I believe there are important lessons to learn from the cloth and the patch.

FASTING AND FRICTION

The context of this story is that Jesus appears to be enjoying himself way too much with the wrong sorts of people. He's feasting while all the religious people of his day are fasting. And they're not impressed by his disregard for their self-imposed rules and restrictions:

"While Jesus was having dinner at Levi's house, many tax collectors and sinners were eating with him and his disciples, for there were many who followed him.

...Now John's disciples and the Pharisees were fasting. Some people came and asked Jesus, "How is it that John's disciples and the disciples of the Pharisees are fasting, but yours are not?" (vv. 15; 18)

It's interesting that the disciples of John the Baptist and the Pharisees are upset with Jesus' disciples. Everywhere else, these two groups had very little in common.

John was a prophetic voice preparing the way for the promised Messiah.

The Pharisees were deeply committed to the old order of things.

Yet here they join together around a mutual grievance. They are bonded by what they are against. They are united by their criticism.

We sometimes see the same happen today. Two groups who would otherwise not get along find common ground when faced with a mutual enemy or cause. For example, during a war, nations that usually have little comradeship may form an alliance against an aggressor.

We also see it in the church. During COVID, many (including myself) who would strongly disagree with John MacArthur when it comes to his theology of the Holy Spirit supported His stand against government overreach.

Currently, within my own denomination, groups that differ in many areas of theology and practice are uniting around issues of human sexuality and their opposition to same-sex marriage.

Of course, we want to promote unity and it is important to take a stand together against certain issues. There can be strength in numbers.

However, we should also recognize that a unity built solely around a particular grievance or cause is a very tenuous bond. Unless one group has a genuine change of heart about the other, it's only a matter of time before the union fractures or disintegrates.

Back to Mark chapter 2. John's disciples and the Pharisees are bothered that Jesus' disciples are feasting instead of fasting. Have they a right to be annoyed?

According to the Old Testament Law, there was only one day a year that fasting was mandatory for Jews – the Day of Atonement. However, over time, a practice had developed of fasting two days a week – on Mondays and Thursdays. While it wasn't a Biblical requirement, fasting soon became seen as a badge of superior spirituality and holiness. Your level of devotion to God was measured by how rigorously you adhered to these man-made rules.

Jesus is having none of it. He will not be bound by human regulations or the fear of man.

And so, this growing tension is developing between his disciples who are enjoying food and those who are fasting. Much like my wife, when she hasn't eaten for a few hours, they are 'hangry'.

Understanding this context sheds some light on Jesus' little parable:

"No one sews a patch of unshrunk cloth on an old garment. Otherwise, the new piece will pull away from the old, making the tear worse." (v. 21)

In essence, Jesus is saying that those who are fasting are attempting to 'patch up' Judaism. However, the old garment of corrupt religion cannot be fixed with a few additional religious acts or pious rituals. That might work for a while, but it's only a temporary solution. It's too damaged at its core to simply undergo an external makeover. Instead, it needs to be replaced with something completely new.

That 'new' thing is a person. And he's standing in front of them.

The Messiah, Jesus, didn't come to patch up the old religion. He came to fulfill the Law and replace it with himself.

Religion can never make us right with God. Instead, faith in Christ alone gives us access to the Father.

Fasting in itself isn't wrong. In other places, Jesus promoted it. However, you completely miss the point if fasting becomes a religious duty or badge of spirituality.

Fasting, or any other religious activity, doesn't have the power to deal with the root issue of humanity – the sinfulness of the heart. Only the blood of Jesus can make us a "new creation" (2 Corinthians 5: 17). Anything else is a cosmetic and superficial change that brings no lasting change.

To get back to my housing analogy at the start, they're attempting to renovate a home that is no longer fit for purpose. They need to leave it behind and move into an entirely new property.

TENSION AND TEARING

Let's apply Jesus' analogy of the patch and the garment to some other areas of our lives where we try to renovate rather than replace.

If you're on the younger side, this story may make little sense to you. Today, people buy jeans that are already ripped at the knees. When I was a kid, that wasn't considered cool. Holes in your clothes meant you were poor.

I grew up in a home where we didn't have an abundance of money. When I got new pants (or *trousers* as we call them here), my mom normally purchased a pair that was at least a size too large (and too long). Therefore, she would turn up the hem at the bottom and sew them into place. As I grew taller, she would then gradually 'let down' the hem. The problem was that there was often a distinct line permanently impressed into the fabric, showing everyone that you had started wearing these pants when you were four inches shorter.

As if that wasn't embarrassing enough for a kid, whenever I would fall (which was often) and get a hole in the knee of my pants, my mom would cut a patch from an old pair in the wardrobe and sew it over the tear. Even though it was evident to everyone that the two materials didn't match, it was more cost-effective than buying a new pair.

Evidently, there's nothing new under the sun. Back in Jesus' day, people did something very similar. When a garment got ripped or torn, a patch would be sewn over the hole to cover it up.

However, because the patch was made from new, unshrunken cloth, the two materials were incompatible. They may have initially looked fine together. However, when the garment was washed, the patch would shrink causing a tear even greater than the original damage.

In meditating on this story, I asked myself:

Why would a garment tear in the first place?

(i)   IT'S OLD AND WORN OUT.

The garment was once good and new and fit for purpose. However, over time, because of constant use, the material has worn thin. Eventually, the threads simply have no more strength. They break, creating a tear.

Similarly, there are things in our lives that were once good, healthy, and beneficial. They served us well in that season.

However, over time, they haven't become bad. They've just become old. There's no 'give' left in them. We can try to keep it in our life but increasingly it's falling apart. It's no longer fit for purpose.

I can immediately think of certain church practices and structures that fall into this category. There are ways of doing things that served us well in the last season, but they aren't strong or robust enough to carry the weight of growth and change in the next season.

Even with particular worship songs - we may have sung something six months ago and it was infused with life. However, when we sing it again now, it feels flat and empty. It's not bad. But the anointing was for the last season. It's worn thin. The grace on it has lifted.

(ii)   THERE WAS AN EVENT THAT CAUSED A SPLIT.

Perhaps the material appeared perfectly good. It might even have been fairly new. But the person wearing the garment fell over. Or the material got caught on a nail. Some accident or event has caused a tear.

The same can happen in our own lives and relationships. On the surface, everything might have appeared good. However, a sudden rupture is caused by an unexpected argument. Or a split happens because of an isolated incident.

You didn't see it coming. But it's caused damage that can't be undone.

That happened in one of my close relationships. It had always appeared strong and solid. Then, one day, out of the blue, there was a disagreement. Words were exchanged and the friendship was irreparably damaged.

(iii)   YOU HAVE GROWN OR CHANGED.

Sometimes, as a kid, I wouldn't only grow taller - I also got wider. More than once, I experienced that painfully embarrassing moment when I bent over or reached down and heard a tear at the back of my pants.

I had grown. But my clothes remained the same size. There was nothing wrong with them. They were just now too small.

That also happens in life. We grow, enlarge, increase, or change in some areas while our environment remains the same.

Over time, this can cause an increasing tension to develop between us and our surroundings.

They may not be outdated, bad, or broken. They just no longer fit who we've become.

We feel contained and claustrophobic. Something has got to give.

If we don't step into a new, larger environment eventually there will be a split. The only alternative is that we shrink back down to our old size.

This can happen in friendships. You become more intentional about growing in some area, for example, in your relationship with God or personal development. Your friend is happy with how they (and you) are. As you change, it becomes clear that you have less and less in common than before. You're not on the same level or wavelength. Eventually, your relationship is ruptured by a disagreement, or you quietly become more distant and removed from each other.

Maybe you've been part of a church for years. However, more recently, you've become unsettled. Perhaps you're struggling to find real spiritual nourishment there. Or you need closer, deeper relationships. You find yourself becoming easily irritated and annoyed by certain things (or people) there. It's probably time to think about finding a new environment that can help you continue to grow.

I've been in ordained ministry within the Church of Ireland for almost 20 years. While I've never fit the mold, since 2020, it's become more and more difficult to remain within my denomination. I have changed while it has remained the same. While there are many good, Godly people there, realistically, it feels like it's only a matter of time before we go our separate ways.

RENOVATE OR REPLACE?

What's holding me back from making a break from my denomination today?

Probably the same thing that's keeping you in relationships and places that you've outgrown.

It feels more costly to replace than it is to renovate.

Not financially, necessarily. But emotionally and relationally.

The price of discarding the old feels too high.

Friendships might get fractured.

People will misunderstand your motives.

You have too much invested already.

You're not sure where else you would go.

You have no viable alternative.

There's security and predictability in your current situation.

You're waiting for something major to happen and then you'll walk away.

Until then, you'll keep patching things over and trying to make it work.

You hope that a temporary solution can cover a permanent problem.

But, deep down, you know that you're only postponing the inevitable.

It's only a matter of time before a greater tearing and separation happens.

As we finish up today, let's apply this to a few areas.

Perhaps you're exhausted. You have been for a while. You need a significant change in your schedule or an extended break, like a sabbatical. Instead, you keep taking a few days off here and there. They provide some temporary relief. But they don't sort out the root of the problem. You're trying to patch what needs to be replaced.

Maybe you're dating someone and they're a decent person. But deep down, you know they're not right for you. Eventually, you plan to break up. But right now, there are few other options. And you don't want to be alone. So, you tell yourself that something might eventually shift in your current relationship. You're trying to patch what needs to be replaced.

Perhaps there are issues in your family that no one is willing to confront. Every time they're brought up, things are swept under the carpet. Or promises are made that aren't kept. You know things can't stay this way. But you're also scared of what might happen if you push the issue too hard. So, you live with behavior that's damaging and destructive. You're trying to patch what needs to be replaced.

Take some time aside today to prayerfully and honestly answer the following questions:

- *What in your life needs replaced but you're attempting to repair it?*
- *Where needs a complete overhaul but you're trying to do a makeover?*
- *What is no longer working but you're unwilling to let it go?*
- *What have you outgrown to the point that it's become restrictive and draining?*
- *Where is there constant tension and friction in your life? Why is it not going away? What needs to change?*
- *What area of your life are you continually frustrated because there's temporary behavior modification without real heart change?*
- *What are you hiding, covering over, or avoiding dealing with? What would your life look like if you ripped off the patch and addressed the root of the issue?*

The sad truth is that some things can't be patched, repaired, mended, or fixed.

They must be replaced.

You can try your best. But too much damage has already been done.

433

Or they just no longer work, at least not for you.

They're incompatible with where God is taking you.

You can feel the resistance and tension. It's like you're being pulled in different directions.

Something's going to give eventually.

The split can be accidental or intentional. Right now, you still get to choose.

You can replace the old. Or you can wait for it to fall apart.

I know it's costly to make the change that's required. But think about the price you're paying if things stay the same.

Jesus came to bring you into a completely new life, not to patch up your old life.

He came to replace religion as the way to God, not to fix or modify it.

He doesn't make bad things better. He makes all things new.

Stop patching over the old. God has a brand new garment waiting for you.

PROPHETIC ENCOURAGEMENT

A WORD FOR THOSE WHO HAVE BEEN WOUNDED BY THE CHURCH

My child, I know you have been wounded by My people.
They looked like sheep but acted like wolves.
You were betrayed, rejected, misunderstood.
It has left you feeling so empty, vulnerable, and insecure.
You doubt yourself.
You doubt your judgment about other people.

You doubt your ability to ever trust like that again.

They took something from you and you're not sure if you're ever going to get it back.
Let me tell you, My child, you will return.
I will restore the years the locusts have eaten.
I will repay you for your faithfulness and I will give you recompense for your pain.

Thank you for how you have postured your heart throughout this.
You have not allowed offense to take root.
Yes, there have been times of bitterness and anger, but you have not wallowed in it or permitted it to consume you.
There will still be difficult days ahead. But I will take you through them as I have taken you through this.

I promise you that one day you will look back at this time and be thankful that it happened.
I know that's hard to even imagine now but I love to take broken pieces and make something beautiful out of them.
It brings Me glory.

Please know that I love you, My child.
I am so sorry for how My people have wounded you.
I understand.
I was wounded by My own people.
I was rejected. I was betrayed.
I know how you feel.

This is not the end for you.
Don't allow this to define you.
I have used it to refine you for greater things.

Lean into Me. Rest on My shoulder.
Don't fret about those who seem to get away with inflicting so much hurt.
Trust Me with them.

My righteousness and justice are perfect.
Keep close to Me.
I am your shield and strength.
I will heal you and restore you.

I have so much more for you.
If you only knew...

Don't get stuck here.
Keep going.
Press through.

Well done - My precious, chosen, called, anointed child.
I love you.

DAY 42

SECOND CHOICE WORLD

BIBLE READING

In the third year of the reign of Jehoiakim king of Judah,
Nebuchadnezzar king of Babylon came to Jerusalem and besieged it. And
the Lord delivered Jehoiakim king of Judah into his hand, along with some
of the articles from the temple of God. These he carried off to the temple
of his god in Babylonia and put in the treasure house of his god.

Then the king ordered Ashpenaz, chief of his court officials, to bring into
the king's service some of the Israelites from the royal family and the
nobility - young men without any physical defect, handsome, showing
aptitude for every kind of learning, well informed, quick to understand,
and qualified to serve in the king's palace. He was to teach them the
language and literature of the Babylonians. The king assigned them a daily
amount of food and wine from the king's table. They were to be trained for
three years, and after that they were to enter the king's service.

Among those who were chosen were some from Judah: Daniel, Hananiah,
Mishael and Azariah. The chief official gave them new names: to Daniel,
the name Belteshazzar; to Hananiah, Shadrach; to Mishael, Meshach; and
to Azariah, Abednego.

But Daniel resolved not to defile himself with the royal food and wine, and
he asked the chief official for permission not to defile himself this way.

(Daniel 1: 1-8)

DEVOTIONAL

Recently, we placed an online order with our local supermarket. When the delivery arrived, the driver informed us that they had made some 'substitutes'. Certain items we'd ordered weren't in stock, so they'd exchanged them for what they considered to be similar goods. We then had to decide if we would accept the substitutes or send them back to the store.

'Similar', it seems, is a word that's open to a broad interpretation. We ordered apples and they sent pears. In place of our favorite brand of ice cream, we received their own generic brand.

Although we sent them back, at least ours was better than other 'substitutions' that I read about online recently.

In one case, someone ordered lemons but was sent citrus washing-up liquid.

Someone else ordered toothpaste but received curry paste.

Another customer ordered toilet roll and was offered scouring pads. Ouch!

Chicken burgers were substituted for vegetarian burgers. Not. Even. Close.

In life, we like to get our first choice in most things. Especially when it's something important, we don't want to settle for a substitute or second best.

Yet sometimes we find ourselves living in what I call a 'second-choice world'.

Things don't always go how we planned or expected.

Our dreams and desires aren't fulfilled.

What we hoped for doesn't happen.

We get blindsided and find ourselves in a situation that we could never have imagined.

The self-help gurus and even some preachers might tell us that we can live our 'best life' every day.

But that's simply not true.

In a sinful, broken world sometimes things fall apart.

And no matter how hard we try - they can't be fixed. To tell you otherwise is to set you up for a life of disappointment and frustration.

We have our first-choice world, where everything goes as planned.

But somewhere along the way, it gets substituted for a second-choice world.

It might not be awful. But it's a long way from what we wanted.

Yet, the Bible shows us that we can still flourish and thrive in a second-choice world.

Our surroundings and circumstances might not always be good. But God is just as faithful and can empower us to experience joy, make an impact, and prosper in a place much less than perfect.

WHEN YOU FIND YOURSELF IN BABYLON

In 605 BC, the Babylonians invaded Judah. As well as ransacking the silver and gold in The Temple, they also carried off the brightest and best young men of Judah. We read:

"Among those who were chosen were some from Judah: Daniel, Hananiah, Mishael and Azariah." (v. 6)

So, Daniel and three other fellas, probably still in their teenage years, are among those who are brought to Babylon.

Suddenly they find themselves plucked out of a privileged existence and brought to a foreign land, with people who don't care who they are. There's a different language, customs, food, morals, and pagan gods.

Think about this for a moment.

Imagine you're 16. You're intelligent and attractive, from a wealthy, well-known family. You've lived a safe, comfortable, existence your whole life. Everything is going in the right direction for you. The future is bright. (This is hypothetical. Stick with me.)

Now imagine that China invades your country. Millions of Chinese troops flood across the land and no one can stop them. Eventually, they get to your city or town. One day, there's a knock on your door. Someone interprets what the soldiers are saying. A decision has been made to bring you and a few of your friends back to China.

After a long journey, you arrive in Beijing. You look and dress differently from everyone else. You don't understand a word anyone is saying. There are no Christians anywhere. You don't know how long you're going to be here. (And Bruce Willis or Liam Neeson aren't coming to rescue you.)

What would you do?

You didn't want this; you would never have chosen it.

Yet here you are, in your second-choice world. Actually, this probably wouldn't have been your second, third, or hundredth choice.

How do you handle it?

Okay, I know this example seems completely unbelievable.

So, let's bring it closer to home.

All your life, you've dreamt of becoming a wife and mother. You have loved and served God for as long as you can remember. At high school and college, while all your friends were partying and hooking up with guys, you remained pure and stayed faithful to Jesus. You dated one guy for three years. You were sure he was the one. Then the relationship fell apart. That was six years ago, and you haven't met anyone suitable since. All your friends are married and starting families. And you're genuinely happy for them. But deep inside, there's a growing ache. You wonder if it will ever happen for you. You don't know what else to do other than continue to pray. Until things change, you're living in a second-choice world.

As a young man, you were told that if you worked hard and went to college, you'd be able to live the good life. So, that's the path you took. Now, years later, you're stuck in a job that drains the life out of you. But it's secure and you have a family to provide for. You live in a constant state of mild depression, longing for some excitement and adventure in your life. Sometimes you imagine starting your own business. Or even a new life. But you love your wife and kids. You don't want to be foolish or reckless. So, perhaps this is just how things are going to be from now on. You're living in a second-choice world.

Life was going great for you. You had everything you wanted – a successful career, a wonderful spouse, kids at college. You were looking forward to retiring early and traveling as a couple. Then, during routine medical tests, a tumor was discovered. More scans showed that cancer had spread throughout your body. Even with the option of aggressive treatment, the prognosis isn't good. You're living in a second-choice world.

Could you relate to any of the above?

If not personally, you probably know someone with a similar story. Because unfortunately, no matter how much advertisers and marketers promise you the existence of your dreams - if you will just buy this, go here, or do that - life often doesn't work out that way.

The reality is, life can be good, but this side of heaven, it will never be perfect.

As someone once said, life is what happens while you were expecting something else.

A lot of life may be spent in a second-choice world.

So, what do you do?

Do you resign yourself to a miserable life?

Do you hide away and avoid anything that might cause pain or heartache?

Do you accept everything that happens assuming it must be the will of God?

No. I believe that, with God, you don't have to just settle or survive a second-choice world. You can also be empowered to flourish and thrive there.

That's what we see in the life of Daniel.

SINGING IN A STRANGE LAND

Daniel and his three friends find themselves dislocated and disorientated in a foreign and pagan culture. And this isn't an overnight visit. They're going to spend the rest of their lives in this place. They will face immense pressure to conform and compromise their beliefs, values, and behavior.

In some sense, as believers in the 21st century, we're living in Babylon. We're people who belong to the Kingdom of God but we're living in a culture that is increasingly hostile to Christian values and Biblical truth.

In many societies, Christians were once celebrated. People appreciated our moral values and the blessings they brought from God on our land.

Then Christians became tolerated. People put up with us as long as we didn't force our beliefs upon them.

Nowadays, Biblical Christianity is viciously opposed in many sectors of society. We are deemed a threat to the extreme liberal agenda.

I believe we are going to see widespread persecution intensify in the coming days. There will be powerful forces pressurizing the church to compromise and conform. In the words of 1 Peter 2:11, increasingly we have become "foreigners and exiles" in our own land.

On a more personal level, we each have our own problems, pain, challenges, and brokenness. In our families, workplaces, relationships, and health, we find ourselves in situations that we wouldn't have chosen. We long for Jerusalem but are exiled in Babylon.

How can you flourish in a second-choice world?

Let me share three principles that I see in the first chapter of Daniel.

(i)   FOCUS ON WHAT YOU CAN CHANGE.

"The chief official gave them new names: to Daniel, the name Belteshazzar; to Hananiah, Shadrach; to Mishael, Meshach; and to Azariah, Abednego." (v. 7)

Upon their arrival in Babylon, Daniel and his friends were immediately assigned new names. In Biblical times, names were incredibly important. Your name represented your identity and your character. They were also prophetic, revealing something of your destiny.

Daniel, Hananiah, Mishael, and Azariah were all Hebrew names. They all referred to Yahweh or Elohim – the one true God. So, every time they introduced themselves, they were talking about the God of Israel.

However, the new names given to them are all connected to various Babylonian gods such as Aku and Nebo.

In many ways, it was an insignificant change. But it was the Babylonian method of slowly and subtly eroding their identity as Hebrews who worshipped Yahweh.

So, what did they do?

Did they protest or put up a fight?

Or perhaps make huge badges with their Hebrew names visible for everyone to see?

No. They did nothing.

They may not have liked names, but they weren't going to lose their lives over them.

There are battles they would fight and lines they wouldn't cross. But this wasn't one of them.

They understood that they couldn't choose what names people called them or control the labels that were placed on them.

People could call them anything they liked. But they didn't have to live according to the labels and the identities that were placed on them.

They may not have liked it, but they went along with the name change.

Now, look at verse 5:

"The king assigned them a daily amount of food and wine from the king's table..." (vv. 5)

On the surface, this sounds great. They were offered the finest Michelin star food every night.

I would have liked that. A lot. Not Daniel:

"But Daniel resolved not to defile himself with the royal food and wine, and he asked the chief official for permission not to defile himself in this way." (v. 8)

What's going on here?

They were happy to be called by different names but weren't willing to eat the King's cuisine.

For Daniel and his friends, there was something about this food and wine that they simply couldn't accept. Notice it says that they would not "defile" themselves. Eating this food would make them spiritually unclean.

Some people think it was because the food was sacrificed to Pagan gods or idols.

We don't know for sure. But to eat the royal cuisine would mean compromising their walk with God.

So, this is where they decided to draw the line and refuse to conform to the Babylonian culture.

People could change their names. They had no control over what others called them.

But they could choose what food they put in their mouths each day.

They focused on the things they could change, not the things they couldn't.

It's the same for you in your second-choice world.

You can spend your life angry, frustrated, or depressed about things that are outside of your control.

Or you can focus your time and energy on the things that you're able to do something about.

For example, you may not be able to choose where you live or work right now. But you can choose how you show up there each day.

Perhaps you're single and struggling to meet a potential partner. You can't force someone to fall in love with you. But you can choose to get out and socialize and get involved in different groups and events where you increase your chances of meeting someone.

445

Plus, we can all improve our appearance and how we present ourselves in some way. I know that God looks at the heart, but man usually starts with the externals. Do the best you can with what you have.

You might be stuck in a job you hate right now and see no way out. But could you take a part-time course and learn a new skill that would equip you to apply for something different in a year? Or could you start a side hustle as an alternative source of income and fulfillment?

Maybe life hasn't turned out how you planned. You've been through betrayal and divorce and feel discarded and alone. You can't change what has happened. But you can take your difficult experiences and help other people who are going through similar situations. Turn your wounds into your work.

Stop obsessing over things you can do nothing about.

And stop stressing about what other people might think or say about you.

Instead, shift your focus onto the changes you can make and apply your time and energy there.

Improving those areas of your life may not take you out of your second-choice world, but it will make your time there much more fruitful and fulfilling.

(ii) DON'T COMPROMISE YOUR CONVICTIONS.

Daniel and his friends didn't care much what names they were called. But they didn't want to eat the defiled food. That was a step too far. So, they drew and line there and said *no*.

When you find yourself in a second-choice world, decide what your values and standards are going to be.

What are willing to do to make your situation better there? And what are you not prepared to do?

446

What price are you willing to pay to keep your convictions, maintain your morals, and remain devoted to Christ?

For example, if you're single and desire to be married, decide up front what kind of people you'll date and who you'll turn down.

I can't tell you the number of people I know who wanted to marry a believer but dated and married someone who didn't share their commitment to Jesus. In many cases, it started when they wavered on their convictions early on and chose to go on a date with a non-Christian.

Decide on your relationship non-negotiables in advance - and stick to them.

In work, determine what you're willing to do to get promoted and what you'll say *no* to. Even if it means less money or disapproval from your boss, what are the lines that you will not cross?

God honors those who honor Him. You may not experience the blessings or benefits of putting God first immediately, but I promise, they will come.

In 2020, for many people around the world, COVID plunged us into a second-choice world. Lockdowns and social distancing weren't what we'd planned for or expected. Many things were outside our control.

But there were also a lot of things that we could choose to say *yes* or *no* to. Too many people gave up their rights completely and didn't challenge anything they were told, even if it wasn't legal.

During the first three months, I developed certain convictions about what I was willing and unwilling to do as a church leader. Some of these had a cost attached. I was reported to the police three times. (On each occasion, they found no reason to proceed with the case.) My position brought me into sharp disagreement with the church authorities in my denomination. I lost some friends and a few church members left.

No matter how much pressure was applied, I couldn't compromise my convictions. Even if that meant being fired or having to resign. There were some lines I couldn't cross.

447

I don't expect everyone to agree with me. But I do believe we all need to have some convictions. Otherwise, when we find ourselves in a second-choice world, we'll be tossed around all over the place by every opinion and pressure that comes our way.

(iii)   BE A SOLUTIONIST

Notice that Daniel and his friends didn't refuse to eat the king's food in a rude or obnoxious way. They were polite, and respectful, and offered an alternative solution to their superior:

"Daniel then said to the guard whom the chief official had appointed over Daniel, Hananiah, Mishael and Azariah, "Please test your servants for ten days: Give us nothing but vegetables to eat and water to drink. Then compare our appearance with that of the young men who eat the royal food, and treat your servants in accordance with what you see." So he agreed to this and tested them for ten days." (vv. 11-14)

Don't forget that Daniel and his friends are experiencing a nightmare situation. This is everything they didn't want. Yet, rather than sulking, self-pitying, or being difficult, they are seeking ways to make the most of their time in this second-choice world.

They try to work with their boss and make his life better, as well as their own. Daniel says: "Try our idea for ten days. Then, if it's not working for you, we can discuss other options."

At the end of this time, they had demonstrated that they could avoid the king's food and actually look healthier than everyone else.

It takes no wisdom or creativity to find problems or things to complain about. There's so much wrong with the world around us that often the temptation is to point the finger and criticize rather than offer alternative solutions.

In these difficult days we are coming into, governments and rulers will need wisdom from Heaven to survive and succeed. As a believer, like Daniel, you have access to divine solutions to every problem. We read:

"In every matter of wisdom and understanding about which the king questioned them, he found them ten times better than all the magicians and enchanters in his whole kingdom." (v. 20)

Don't hide your light. Speak up. Offer a new perspective and Godly wisdom into the challenges we are facing. But do it with kindness, honor, and respect.

In your second-choice world, God can give you wisdom, insights, and creativity that will enable you to advance and have significant influence.

BETTER, NOT PERFECT

There is no perfect life. Nor is there any perfect place, marriage, spouse, job, church, or family.

But there is a faithful and loving God.

He might not make everything perfect today. But He will partner with you to make them better. And He will also make you better in the process.

Whatever you're facing, never forget: **God is with you. God is for you. God has not abandoned you.**

Some things in your life might not be how you want them to be. Make every effort to change what you can.

But in those areas that are outside of your control, God will work with you there. **You can experience His presence, power, provision, and protection in a way that you might never have in your 'perfect' world.**

Stay faithful, press in, and trust Him in the midst of the mess.

Like Daniel, you can bloom in winter, shine in the darkness, and have a powerful influence on the people around you in your second-choice world.

PROPHETIC ENCOURAGEMENT

DON'T SHORTCUT THE PROCESS. THE SHIFT IS COMING.

For a long time, it has felt like everything is a little bit blurred and foggy.

You've been battling distraction, struggling to focus or get a clear vision for the future.

You know that a shift is coming - yet nothing is changing.

You sense it inside you, even around you - yet everything looks the same. It feels like it's taking much too long.

Delay has brought discouragement. You're so weary from waiting.

You're even beginning to doubt some of what God has spoken to you.

You're longing to step into the next assignment He has for you.

You are so ready for something to change. But nothing is shifting.

The LORD would say:

This long season of dislocation has not been punishment.

It has been pruning and preparation, proving and testing, dismantling and equipping, realigning and repositioning.

The shift is coming. Things are turning.

The heaviness is lifting. The delay is breaking.

The "new" is emerging.

You will have unexpected conversations and significant connections.

Doors will open and opportunities will be presented.

You will begin to discern the voice of the LORD with increased sharpness and sensitivity.

450

He will give you fresh vision and focus for the future.

The way forward will become clear. He will show you the next steps.

In the meantime, don't allow discouragement or despondency to influence your decisions.

Don't birth an 'Ishmael' through frustration and haste.

Don't try to find shortcuts or manipulate things.

Don't force what God hasn't endorsed.

Those who wait for the LORD will renew their strength.

Those who trust in the LORD will experience His goodness and favor.

Those who obey the LORD will walk in His blessing.

It won't be long now. You will see.

Things are moving. You are ready to be released.

THE SHIFT IS COMING.

DAY 43

BUILDING IN BABYLON

BIBLE READING

This is what the Lord Almighty, the God of Israel, says to all those I carried into exile from Jerusalem to Babylon: "Build houses and settle down; plant gardens and eat what they produce. Marry and have sons and daughters; find wives for your sons and give your daughters in marriage, so that they too may have sons and daughters. Increase in number there; do not decrease. Also, seek the peace and prosperity of the city to which I have carried you into exile. Pray to the Lord for it, because if it prospers, you too will prosper." Yes, this is what the Lord Almighty, the God of Israel, says: "Do not let the prophets and diviners among you deceive you. Do not listen to the dreams you encourage them to have. They are prophesying lies to you in my name. I have not sent them," declares the Lord.

This is what the Lord says: "When seventy years are completed for Babylon, I will come to you and fulfill my good promise to bring you back to this place. For I know the plans I have for you," declares the Lord, "plans to prosper you and not to harm you, plans to give you hope and a future."

(Jeremiah 29: 4-11)

DEVOTIONAL

Have you ever overheard part of a conversation and jumped to conclusions based on the snippet that you heard? Perhaps you even overreacted? However, when you discover the full story, you realize you misunderstood what was being said.

Context is important.

We live in a world of soundbites. We are given snippets and little chunks of information from which we draw conclusions.

We see a post on social media and make all sorts of assumptions about somebody's life or circumstances. But we have no context around what we have seen. It's simply a snapshot, not the entire story.

And context matters.

It's the same when we come to the Bible. There is a danger of taking verses out of context because we like them as they stand on their own.

Verses like Psalm 37:4 where God says: *"I will give you the desires of your heart."*

We love verses like that. We think, "Whatever I want, God will give it to me."

I call them *fortune cookie verses*. You know, the little piece of paper that tells you something trite and general like, *"You will find happiness and success."*

We want to believe it's true because it's positive or it makes us feel good.

We do the same with Deuteronomy 28: 13 which says: *"The LORD will make you the head, not the tail."*

These are great verses. And they're all true.

But it's important to read them in their original context. Otherwise, we can find a verse in the Bible to support anything we want it to say.

One of the verses that I have been guilty of doing this with in the past has been Jeremiah 29:11:

"For I know the plans I have for you," declares the Lord, "plans to prosper you and not to harm you, plans to give you hope and a future."

Christians love that verse. God has good plans to prosper us and give us a wonderful future.

Who wouldn't like a verse like that?

And yet, most believers have never read that verse in the context of the other verses surrounding it. Or the circumstances and situation that it was speaking into.

I believe there are some things in Jeremiah 29 that God wants to say to you today.

I want to share three simple truths from this chapter of Scripture.

1. JUST BECAUSE YOU DON'T LIKE IT DOESN'T MEAN GOD ISN'T IN IT.

"This is the text of the letter that the prophet Jeremiah sent from Jerusalem to the surviving elders among the exiles and to the priests, the prophets and all the other people Nebuchadnezzar had carried into exile from Jerusalem to Babylon." (Jeremiah 29:1)

The events surrounding this chapter are the same as we saw in yesterday's devotional – the Babylonian exile.

Because of their immorality, idolatry, and injustice, God removed His hand of protection from His people and allowed them to be carried off to Babylon.

He had sent several prophets to warn them and to call the people back to Him. Jeremiah was one of these prophets.

For 20 years, he had admonished the people of God in Jerusalem to repent or things would not go well for them.

However, they hardened their hearts and ignored the mercy of God.

Eventually, the Jews are taken into exile in 597 BC. King Nebuchadnezzar carried off the best and the brightest boys from Jerusalem to Babylon which was about 1000 miles away.

But look at verse 4:

"This is what the Lord Almighty, the God of Israel, says to all those I carried into exile from Jerusalem to Babylon..."

Verse 1 tells us that Nebuchadnezzar carried them off to Babylon.

But in verse 4 God says, *"I carried them into exile."*

Which one was it? Was it Nebuchadnezzar or God?

It was both at the same time.

In His absolute sovereignty, God used a pagan king to fulfill His purposes in His people.

They didn't want to go to Babylon. They didn't choose it. It's 1000 miles away from family and friends. It's a foreign, pagan culture where they don't understand the language, religion, or customs.

This is their second-choice world.

But God says:

"I brought you here. I know it looks like Nebuchadnezzar was responsible. But it was Me. He just paid for the journey. He was doing my bidding. You might not like it. You may not want to be here. But I brought you here because I have a purpose for you in being here."

It is so important to understand that **God will do whatever it takes to get you wherever He wants you to be.**

He will use people and circumstances that you like. And He will even use your enemies and challenging events.

Because God's highest priority is not your preference, comfort, or convenience. His highest priority is His sovereign plan.

Nebuchadnezzar was an evil man. While the Bible makes it clear that our God cannot sin or do evil, He will, if necessary, even use the schemes of evil people to accomplish His greater purposes.

God does not micromanage our lives. But there are certain plans that He has ordained and decreed that must happen.

And sometimes the process of making those things happen, He will bring us into places or situations that we would rather avoid.

But just because we don't like it doesn't mean God isn't in it.

The temptation for us as 21st-century Christians who think that God exists primarily for our comfort and convenience is that when we find ourselves in uncomfortable situations, we assume that God doesn't want us there.

So, we want to run away. We try to back out. We attempt to escape the discomfort as quickly as possible, without realizing that we might be there for a purpose, for a time, for a season, so that God can do something in us and through us that couldn't happen if we weren't there.

Joseph understood this. When his brothers came to Egypt to buy food from him, he told them:

"…you intended it for evil but God meant it for good."

He's not saying that what they did was okay. He's clear that their behavior was evil. But even in the evil that they intended, God intended to work it for good.

God used their sin to accomplish a greater purpose. It looked like his brothers sent Joseph to Egypt. And they did. But God also took him there.

456

Here, in Jeremiah, we read that it was God who took His people to Babylon. It looked like Nebuchadnezzar. But it was also the sovereign hand of the LORD.

So, let me ask you:

Where has God taken you right now?

Do you like where you are in life?

Is this everything you dreamt it would be?

We all find ourselves in places and circumstances that we want to get out of.

And I'm not saying that we should always stay there.

What I am saying is this: *Just because it's uncomfortable doesn't mean God isn't in it.*

As I look at the global shaking that we are currently experiencing, none of it is comfortable.

COVID wasn't comfortable.

This wars in Ukraine and Gaza - there's nothing comfortable about them. Iran attacking Israel and the likely escalation. It's not comfortable.

But just because we don't like it doesn't mean that God isn't at work in it and through it to accomplish a greater purpose.

To paraphrase Joseph: *Human leaders may intend it for evil, but God intends it for good.*

I often hear people say: "My God wouldn't do that."

Who are we to say what God would and would not do?

Often that's simply our preferences speaking.

And God is so much greater than our preferences and personal desires.

God's eternal purposes are so much more expansive than this uncomfortable moment that we are currently living through.

He is the God almighty, the Lord of Heaven and Earth.

He rules over all of history and humanity.

He is the creator of the cosmos and the sustainer of the universe.

He is God, and I am not.

Who am I to dare to tell Him what He can and can't do?

He does not submit to my will. I submit to His will.
Even if I don't always like it. Or it's uncomfortable. Or it's not my preference.

Just because I don't like it doesn't mean God isn't in it.

2. GOD WANTS YOU TO BUILD IN YOUR SECOND CHOICE WORLD.

"Yes, this is what the Lord Almighty, the God of Israel, says: "Do not let the prophets and diviners among you deceive you. Do not listen to the dreams you encourage them to have. They are prophesying lies to you in my name. I have not sent them," declares the Lord." (vv. 8-9)

At the time of Jeremiah, some prophets in Babylon were telling the people that this would be a very temporary exile. They prophesied that God would have the people back in Jerusalem within two years. The people loved this message. This was what they wanted to hear.

Consequently, they started to live as if they wouldn't be staying there for very long. They settled on the outskirts of the city. They didn't unpack their suitcases. They avoided getting involved in life in Babylon.

Because, as far as they were concerned, this was all just a short stopover before God brought them home again.

It's amazing how quickly we will accept preaching and prophetic words that confirm what we already want to hear.

It happened 2500 years ago, and it happens today.

We don't like preaching that challenges us. We want everything to make us feel good.

We don't like prophetic words that aren't in line with our personal desires: *'God, just tell me that I'm going to be rich, happy, and healthy. Amen!'*

When I released my prophetic word about 2020, it was out of line with what many other prophetic voices were sharing. They were declaring it to be the year of 'double blessing' and '2020 vision'. And then I came along with a word about shaking and division and disorder.

When I initially sent it to those on my email list, many people unsubscribed. They thought the word was too negative. Some told me that it wasn't what they wanted to hear. It didn't match up with what all the other prophetic voices were saying.

Then four or five months later they emailed me back, apologizing. Everything that I had shared was happening.

The role of the prophetic is not to tell you what you want to hear. It is to declare the word of the LORD - the written word of God and what God is speaking in this season.

Often, that will be comforting and encouraging. However, at other times, it will be confronting, uncomfortable, and challenging.

The apostle Paul wrote this to Timothy:

"For the time will come when people will not put up with sound doctrine. Instead, to suit their own desires, they will gather around them a great number of teachers to say what their itching ears want to hear."
(2 Timothy 4:3)

The people of God need the Word of the LORD! Whether it's positive or negative. Whether we like it or don't.

We need the truth of God to be able to stand firm when everything around us is being shaken. That's what Jeremiah brings. Look at what he says in verse 10:

"This is what the Lord says: "When seventy years are completed for Babylon, I will come to you and fulfill my good promise to bring you back to this place."

You can imagine their reaction when they heard this:

"Seventy years! Bring the other prophets back. We like their message better. Two years we can handle. Seventy years is much too long."

Jeremiah was speaking uncomfortable truth. But people would rather believe comfortable lies than to face the reality of uncomfortable truth.

And yet, look closely at what Jeremiah was telling the people:

"Build houses and settle down; plant gardens and eat what they produce. Marry and have sons and daughters; find wives for your sons and give your daughters in marriage, so that they too may have sons and daughters. Increase in number there; do not decrease." (Jeremiah 29:5-6)

When there is shaking and instability all around you, it's very difficult to plan for the future. You go into survival mode, just trying to make it through today rather than thinking about six months, a year, or five years from now.

Especially if you think that your negative circumstances are temporary. You batten down the hatches and wait until the difficulty has passed. And then you'll get on with your life, building and doing the things that you want to do.

But God says this to His people:

"Amid all the uncertainty, I want you to build.

In the shaking, I want you to settle.

Even though life is unpredictable, I want you to plant.

When you are surrounded by chaos, I want you to live with confidence.

With all the intensity around you, I want you to increase.

Don't put off building for your future because your circumstances right now aren't ideal.

In the middle of this place that you don't want to be, I want to establish you – build houses, plant gardens, get married, raise a family.

You're going to be here for 70 years, whether you like it or not. So, you may as well make the most of it."

And I believe that is a word for us today.

Stop waiting for perfect conditions or circumstances or surroundings before you do the things that you know God wants you to do.

Stop allowing the unpredictability around you to lead to passivity inside you.

Stop putting off or procrastinating because everything isn't exactly how you would want it to be.

Stop permitting uncertainty to keep you stuck in your comfort zone.

Ecclesiastes 11:4 says:

"Whoever watches the wind will not plant; whoever looks at the clouds will not reap."

In other words, if you're always looking out the window for perfect weather conditions before you plant seeds, you won't do it. Therefore, you will never reap anything. You'll not be productive.

The truth is – your life will never be perfect.

461

Your circumstances will never be perfect.

Your job will never be perfect.

Your church will never be perfect.

Your marriage will never be perfect.

Your finances will never be perfect.

Your relationships and your health will never be perfect.

So, stop putting your life on hold, waiting for some perfect future that's never going to happen.

Don't trade your destiny for a fantasy.

In all of the shaking, instability, uncertainty, and unpredictability, God wants you to build. If you do your part, He will bless and establish you.

God then tells them to pray for their second-choice world. To pray for the prosperity of the city - this place that they don't want to be. Pray His blessing upon it, because if He blesses the city, that blessing will spill over into their lives.

And that is His desire for you.

Seek His blessing over your second-choice world. Wherever you are, bring His goodness, speak His favor, carry His light, share His hope. Don't curse the darkness around you. Shine your light and ask Him to bring transformation.

3. GOD WILL BLESS YOU IN PLACES WHERE YOU DON'T THINK YOU CAN BE BLESSED.

Finally, we come to the famous verse 11:

"For I know the plans I have for you," declares the Lord, "plans to prosper you and not to harm you, plans to give you hope and a future."

God tells His people – and I believe He would say to you today:

"You might be somewhere you don't want to be. And you may have been here for a long time.

But here's the thing you need to be assured of: I know the plans I have for you.

You don't know My plans yet. But I know them. I have good plans for you.

Even in these uncertain times and in this uncomfortable place - I have good plans for you.

All of this is not by accident. This is not bad luck or happenstance or coincidence or circumstance. This is my Divine providence. I have good plans for you.

My plans for you are not limited to the place where you would prefer to be.

I have plans for you in this place that you want to escape from. And those plans for you are good.

I want to prosper you in your second-choice world.

I want to bless you in the place where you feel like an outsider.

I want to give you hope and a future in what looks like a hopeless place.

I want you to flourish in what looks like the most unfavorable conditions.

You are here because of My purposes. And while you are here - I have good plans for you."

And I love that His 'plans' are plural.

God doesn't only have one plan for your life. He has multiple plans.

You cannot thwart God's plans through one wrong turn or a single bad decision.

He has a plan A.

And if you mess that up, He has a plan B.

If you take a wrong turn there, He has a plan C.

His plans are flexible, not set in stone. He takes account of the multitude of choices you can make.

Yes, you can delay your progress or take a detour. Obedience matters.

But if the desire of your heart is to please Him, you can always return and be restored.

God knows the plans He has for you.

He wants to prosper you today.

Do you believe that?

Not only financially. The Hebrew word for *prosper* does include financial blessing. But is so much greater than that. It means *wholeness, peace, nothing missing, nothing broken, flourishing, increasing, expansion, blessing.*

God says: "I have good plans for you even in surroundings that don't seem good."

I have also discovered that God's blessing is determined by my surroundings or circumstances. God has prospered me in places I didn't want to be.

We also see that in the life of Joseph. In the pit, the prison, or the palace – God blessed and prospered him.

Why? Because God had good plans for him.

And God has good plans for you. Plans to bless and prosper you. Even in your second-choice world. Even if the place where you find yourself today isn't where you want to be.

His plans for you are so, so good.

Even if what's in front of you looks nothing like your first-choice world - work hard, act with integrity, give it your all, honor those above you, make wise choices, and be faithful in the small things.

Just because you don't like it doesn't mean God is not in it.

God wants you to build and flourish amid the shaking.

God will bless you where you don't think you can be blessed.

PROPHETIC ENCOURAGEMENT

YOUR SPIRITUAL SENSES ARE BEING SHARPENED

The Father is amplifying your spiritual perception.
In the coming days, you will find that you have greater discernment and heightened sensitivity of what is happening 'behind the scenes.'

You will see beyond the visible and physical.
You will hear more than that which is audible.
It's as if the static has been removed and you are able to tune precisely into Heaven's frequency.

In recent months, your spiritual sensitivity has been dulled by interference from the enemy.
He has sought to confuse and confound God's people, bringing a dullness, lethargy, and listlessness into our lives. The Lord's presence hasn't been so manifest or tangible.

Things are now changing.
Press in once again. Push through. Re-engage.

The spiritual dullness is being dispersed.

You will once again hear the Holy Spirit speak with fresh clarity.
Your prayers will increase in potency and power.
You will sense and see what the Father is doing around you.
You will speak with increased prophetic authority.

YOUR SPIRITUAL SENSES ARE BEING SHARPENED.

DAY 44

PIONEERS AND SETTLERS | Part 1

BIBLE READING

Terah became the father of Abram, Nahor and Haran. And Haran became the father of Lot. While his father Terah was still alive, Haran died in Ur of the Chaldeans, in the land of his birth. Abram and Nahor both married. The name of Abram's wife was Sarai..Now Sarai was childless because she was not able to conceive.

Terah took his son Abram, his grandson Lot son of Haran, and his daughter-in-law Sarai, the wife of his son Abram, and together they set out from Ur of the Chaldeans to go to Canaan. But when they came to Harran, they settled there.

Terah lived 205 years, and he died in Harran.

(Genesis 11: 27-32)

"The LORD had said to Abram, 'Go from your country, your people and your father's household to the land I will show you.

...So Abram went, as the LORD had told him; and Lot went with him. Abram was seventy-five years old when he set out from Harran."

(Genesis 12: 1; 4)

DEVOTIONAL

When God called us to lead HOPE Church, I returned to live in my hometown that I'd left 25 years ago when I went off to college. Honestly, I really didn't think I'd ever be back here. Hadn't Jesus said something about a prophet having no honor in his own town and among his own people (Matthew 13: 57)?

Yet, God had clearly called us here, and, after years of moving around and recovering from burnout, there was something comforting about the familiarity of it all. I didn't need GPS to find my way around. I understood the people and the culture. My family was known in the area, so we had an immediate level of trust. My parents, as well as some old friends from high school, started coming along to our church.

It made the transition smoother and more seamless than our life had been for many years. Becky found a good job in her field of work. Elijah quickly settled into a wonderful elementary school. And the church immediately began to grow with new people showing up each week.

Yet, for the first five years, I found it difficult to settle and put down roots. We loved the people and the place, but often it felt like a temporary stopover while we waited for further instructions. We didn't even hang pictures on the walls of our house. That felt too permanent.

Having conversations with old friends whom I hadn't seen in almost three decades also disturbed me. I discovered that many of them had never left this place. Some still lived in the same part of town where they had grown up. Other than perhaps a week of summer vacation in Spain, their entire existence was largely confined to a five-mile radius. They were genuine, kind, salt-of-the-earth people. But I couldn't imagine a life like that.

Almost seven years on, I'm much more at peace here. If God calls us to move on, we won't hesitate. But we've come to truly value some stability in our family life and the quality of the people in this community. We've even hung a few pictures around the house.

I've also realized something: **there are two groups of people – *pioneers* and *settlers*.**

And, perhaps my more profound recent revelation has been this: **we need both. One is not better than the other.**

This latter understanding is important because **sometimes pioneers tend to look down upon settlers.** They can be seen as unadventurous, safe, predictable, overly cautious, and even boring.

Pioneers, on the other hand, are the ones taking all the risks, blazing trails, pushing boundaries, taking hard knocks, and living life on the edge.

And while some of the above may be an accurate description, **one group cannot survive without the other.**

If everyone were a pioneer, life would be chaos. And if everyone was a settler, nothing would ever change.

We need each other.

Pioneers are not better than settlers. They're just wired differently. And as we'll see, in His infinite wisdom, God intended it that way.

Which are you – a pioneer or settler?

Maybe you're a combination of both, depending on the season.

Or – and here's where things might get uncomfortable – perhaps you're a pioneer who has settled. And God wants to get you moving again.

THE ORIGINAL PIONEERS AND SETTLERS

In early times in undiscovered countries, there were those who went on ahead into the wilderness to explore new territories. They took chances, often risking their lives to explore the unknown so they could return and share the experiences of their journey with others who were to follow later.

These explorers were often referred to as *pioneers*.

They were skilled at crossing unbridged rivers and trailblazing through thick forests. Their most important assets were courage and the ability to fend off a hungry predator.

They were willing to face danger to ensure it would be safer for others to follow and expand into uncharted territories.

Settlers were those who received the information and maps from the pioneers and later followed the path that was laid out for them.

Their intention was to establish a new community and allow many more who would want to follow to do so safely. Their job was surveying the land, expanding on the crude buildings put up by the pioneers, and establishing trade. Their skills were more refined than the pioneers'. They were craftsmen, blacksmiths, farmers, and bankers.

Settlers were important as they brought order to a new beginning. It is critical to establish norms, processes, and procedures, as well as laws. These would make life easier for those who would later become part of the new community.

Settlers had no desire to go out and place themselves in harm's way. They didn't want to explore the next valley or climb the next peak. They were more interested in safety and security than in adventure and excitement.

However, once the settlers arrived, life for the pioneer changed. Their skills were in less demand. They felt crowded in the streets. Their days became slow and lacked challenge.

Eventually, it was time for them to move on. They knew they'd be happier under the stars, charting out the location of the next frontier town, and creating a legacy for other men and women to follow.

21ST CENTURY PIONEERS AND SETTLERS

Most of our planet has already been discovered and explored. Therefore, in one sense, now we're all pretty much settlers. We're occupying lands that have already been pioneered.

However, pioneering and settling is more a mentality or mindset than an exploration of uncharted lands. It's a way of viewing life, progress, and change.

Pioneers are still the pathfinders, initiators, and trailblazers in every sector and industry.

They are always asking, *"What's next?"* Change is their normal. They venture freely into the unknown because they are not tied to the known.

Pioneers love to explore new countries or areas. They prefer to rent apartments rather than buy houses – at least until they know if they're going to be staying around for long. They can move quickly because they are not tied to long-term commitments.

Settlers buy houses. They put down roots. They go day to day and live fully in the present. There is a consistent and predictable rhythm and pace to their life. They tend to vacation in the same spots each year rather than explore new destinations. Predictability is preferable to uncertainty.

While pioneers often fly solo and take risks, settlers are more concerned about their families and their responsibilities. They tend to move when it's safe and when others are willing to come along with them.

Pioneers see the big picture and are always rethinking and re-imagining how things *could* be. Innovation and experimentation lead to many failures but also occasional massive breakthroughs.

Settlers have a more limited perspective on life and think more about incremental improvements rather than major overhauls. Their motto is more likely to be: *If it ain't broke, don't fix it.*

Pioneers will have lots of acquaintances – people they've met on their travels to far-flung places. But these connections won't have much depth.

Settlers know fewer people - but are likely to have much deeper relationships.

In the business world, pioneers are most often the entrepreneurs and founders of companies. They often use their hobbies, dreams, and aspirations to provide a new product or service and start a new business. Think Steve Jobs or Elon Musk.

Settlers are more likely to be intrapreneurs and employees. They work within those new business organizations, focusing on improving processes and procedures.

PIONEER AND SETTLER CHURCHES

The difference between the pioneer and settler mentality can also be seen in many areas of church life.

When it comes to ministry, for example, the settler church tends to be more self-centered, focused primarily on the wants and desires of those in the church family.

The ministry of the pioneer church, on the other hand, is centered on changing the world. They want to reach the lost, feed the hungry, and impact the city and nations.

When it comes to the unchurched, the settler church says: "Everyone knows we are here. They can come and join us if they want to."

The pioneer church, however, is very intentional in connecting with the lost and offering an invitation to be part of the Kingdom.

The settler church views its members as a group of hurting people who need continual strokes of support and encouragement.

Conversely, the pioneer church sees its members as an army of people who need to be mobilized and equipped to bring transformation to the world around them.

The settler church sees the pastor as a chaplain whose primary job is to visit members to make sure they feel good about the church.

The pioneer church sees the pastor as an apostolic leader whose primary job is to equip the saints for ministry and impact.

In settler churches, change is almost always resisted.

In pioneer churches, change is pursued.

WHEN PIONEERS ARE TEMPTED TO SETTLE...

Earlier, I said that pioneers aren't better than settlers. They're just wired differently. However, that disposition towards safety, security, and predictability doesn't excuse any of us from pursuing the call of God wherever He may lead.

In one sense, every Christian is a pioneer. We follow Jesus, *"the pioneer and perfector of our faith"* (Hebrews 12: 2)

If Christ is Lord of our lives, we must be willing to obey and follow His leading, even when it's uncomfortable, painful, or the future is uncertain.

We simply can't settle for less than God has made available for us.

In Genesis 11 we read:

"Terah took his son Abram, his grandson Lot son of Haran, and his daughter-in-law Sarai, the wife of his son Abram, and together they set out from Ur of the Chaldeans to go to Canaan. But when they came to Harran, they settled there.

Terah lived 205 years, and he died in Harran." (vv. 31-32)

Tereh was Abram's father. We are told that he set out with his family from Ur of the Chaldeans and was headed for Canaan, the Promised Land. It was a 1000-mile journey.

However, it says that *"when they came to Harran, they settled there"* (v. 32).

Tereh started as a pioneer. He set out with a destination in mind. But something happened along the journey, and he stopped short, just past the halfway mark in the journey.

He gave up too soon and settled for less than God's best. We're told that he died where he settled.

What happened? How did Tereh go from pioneer to settler?

We can't be sure. But I think the text gives us some clues:

*"While his father Terah was still alive, **Haran** died..."* (v. 28)

*"But when they came to **Harran**, they settled there."* (v. 31)

Tereh's youngest son, Haran, tragically died at an early age. And where did Tereh later settle? In a place called Harran.

The names are almost identical.

Perhaps Tereh got to a place that reminded him of the son that he had lost, and he just couldn't move on.

He got stuck in grief.

He settled because of his sorrow.

He stopped because of past hurt.

He couldn't move beyond his losses.

That happens, doesn't it?

In the mid-19th century, 300,000 pioneers migrated from the mid-west of America, heading south and west along what would become known as the Santa Fe Trail, heading for Santa Fe, New Mexico, in search of gold and souls and cattle.

Along the way, they would stop for a rest at a place that was nicknamed 'Blue Camp 20.' 'Blue' after the nearby Blue River, 'Camp' because, well, that's all it was: a temporary settlement on the edge of the wilderness. And '20' because it was conveniently situated twenty miles - a day's walk - from the town of Independence, where the Santa Fe Trail began.

Blue Camp 20 was the first stop on the way from somewhere to somewhere else. It was a transitory place, a dividing line on the journey separating the known from the unknown, the familiar from the unfamiliar, it was the point of no return.

Once you left Blue Camp 20 the journey would be 700 miles to Santa Fe, through arid plains, deserts, and mountains, going through dangerous Native American territory.

But what would happen to many of the pioneers is that they would reach Blue Camp 20, pause on their journey for a night to get some sleep, and prepare themselves mentally and practically for the next stage of their journey.

The next morning, they would wake up and think, "Just one more day here – then I'll set out in pursuit of the dream."

Another day would pass, and another one, and eventually many of the former pioneers got comfortable and simply settled and made their home at Blue Camp 20.

They decided that, while it wasn't where they had originally intended to go, it was better than the prospect of traveling another 700 miles on foot, dodging rattlesnakes, and risking their lives.

So, they settled down and built themselves businesses serving the passing trade: alcohol and provisions, girls and religion, shoeing horses and fixing wagons for the steady stream of fur traders, gold speculators, mercenaries, and missionaries striking out from here for Santa Fe.

Over time the campsite became a settlement, and the settlement became some kind of shantytown. They had lost sight of their original vision and settled for a smaller version of what they had once hoped for.

And they renamed it: Little Santa Fe.

This new name allowed the settlers the illusion of thinking they had actually arrived. Plus, it was safer than taking the chance to get to the real thing.

But it was only a copy; a smaller, less grand version of the actual destination.

We'll explore this further tomorrow, but in our own pioneering journey, sometimes we start out brave and bold but somewhere along the way we lose our confidence and courage.

We face loneliness, rejection, and setbacks.

Things don't work out how we planned or it's much more difficult than we expected. So, we begin to wonder if we made the right decision to leave in the first place.

We fail in some area and decide to play it safe, so we don't have to go through that humiliation again.

We get distracted by something or someone that draws us away from our primary calling.

Someone betrays us and we struggle to trust anyone again.

We carry wounds and pain and shame.

And the road ahead looks daunting, difficult, and uncertain.

It could be many things.

We're weary and we need to rest. That's understandable.

So, we stop.

Initially, we're just planning to rest for a bit, catch our breath, and heal from some wounds.

However, soon we settle. We slowly put down roots.

We build a house in a place where we had originally planned to pitch a tent as we passed through.

The stopover has become the destination.

We finished up in a place that's not the real Santa Fe.

If God has placed a dream or vision in your heart, don't settle for a miniature, reduced replica of the real thing.

You might be safe, but you'll never be fully satisfied.

PROPHETIC ENCOURAGEMENT

THIS IS A FINISHING SEASON

This is a time of endings and new beginnings. Not just in the natural – but also in the spiritual.

The LORD is bringing many of the last season's assignments to a conclusion.

You may experience some tension because you know that your time in this particular area is coming to a close.

Yet, it may not feel as if you have completed it or that everything has gone as you hoped/planned.

But the Lord would still say: "Well done."

You faithfully stewarded what He gave you.

You did everything you could with the resources and time that you had.

Hear that again: "Well done!"

Don't overstay in an attempt to tie up every loose end.

Some issues may feel unresolved and some tasks undone.

You may not get complete closure. That's OK.

When God clearly opens the exit door…walk through it.

Trust Him if you can't see the way forward. Something new is beginning to emerge on the other side.

This is a finishing season.

So, finish well. And hear Him say: "Well done."

DAY 45

PIONEERS AND SETTLERS | Part 2

BIBLE READING

But you will receive power when the Holy Spirit comes on you; and you will be my witnesses in Jerusalem, and in all Judea and Samaria, and to the ends of the earth."

(Acts 1: 8)

...I have trailblazed a preaching of the Message of Jesus all the way from Jerusalem far into northwestern Greece. This has all been pioneer work, bringing the Message only into those places where Jesus was not yet known and worshiped. My text has been,

Those who were never told of him - they'll see him!
Those who've never heard of him - they'll get the message!

And that's why it has taken me so long to finally get around to coming to you. But now that there is no more pioneering work to be done in these parts, and since I have looked forward to seeing you for many years, I'm planning my visit.

(Romans 15: 20-23 MSG)

DEVOTIONAL

The nights we spoke with tongues of fire,
The days we walked out on the wire,
We were young and we were not afraid...

(John Mark McMillan, 'Tongues of Fire')

I've previously mentioned that the church I currently lead, HOPE, started in mid-2015 when a group of people in a traditional rural church radically encountered the power and presence of the Holy Spirit. They were met with fierce resistance from those who wanted to maintain the status quo of religious tradition and a more formal style of worship. So, eventually, with the blessing of our overseers, they launched out into the unknown and gathered as a new community.

Apart from occasionally visiting as a guest preacher, I wasn't around for the first two years during the inception of HOPE. But I know they moved from place to place, meeting everywhere from bars to barns. They pressed through opposition and obstacles, as well as dealing with constant misunderstanding and misrepresentation. These 60-70 faithful followers of Jesus weren't sure if they would make it and ever become a 'real' church. But they were a pioneering people, willing to do whatever it took to follow Jesus wherever He led them.

During their second year, they finally moved into a building they could call home. It was (and still is) ugly, difficult to locate, and has woeful parking. (I often joke that you need a prophetic word of knowledge just to find us!). But it was in their preferred geographical area and had more than enough space to accommodate their needs.

Just when they thought they'd finally found some stability, their founding pastor announced that he was moving on. Hence, in October 2017, I became their new pastor.

When I arrived at HOPE, I discovered a wonderful, warm group of people, committed to Jesus and one another.

But I also soon realized something else. **Some of the people there had gone as far as they could go.** They had been willing to make sacrifices and endure the discomfort of change to get to where they were. But now, they wished to stay there. **The pioneers wanted to settle.**

When the church began to grow quite quickly, there were mixed emotions. They were grateful that newcomers wanted to be part of their fledgling community. But they also struggled with no longer feeling like the "family" they once were. Previously, they'd known everyone's name. Many of them were related! Now, increasingly they looked around the room and didn't recognize a significant proportion of the faces.

I also made some structural and leadership changes to accommodate the growth. What had worked with 70 people proved to be unsuitable for 200. These shifts meant that some key leaders lost their positions, prominence, and influence. They were graceful, but I could tell they missed how things used to be.

Then COVID arrived in 2020. I took a difficult stand in keeping our church doors open after the first few months of the pandemic whilst most churches remained solely online. I was by no means reckless, but still, I was attacked, misunderstood, and vilified by some within and outside the church. However, I felt an unwavering conviction that God's people should not be controlled by the fear that was so pervasive all around us.

During this period, we began to attract many new people from a wider area who wanted to be part of a church that was willing to push back against the draconian and unreasonable restrictions.

Some of the original, founding members of the church took a more cautious approach to COVID and stayed away for almost 18 months. I had no problem with their stance. Each person was encouraged to prayerfully come to their own position.

However, when they finally did return to 'in-person' gatherings, they stepped into a completely new congregation. The original members were now a minority. In their absence, new people had filled leadership and volunteer roles.

Also, some ministries that had been 'successful' prior to 2020, were shut down. I refused to restart them. They felt like an old wineskin. And new initiatives had begun to flourish. The heart and DNA of the church remained the same, but it looked and felt very different.

Over the next six months, a proportion of these original 'pioneers' moved on from HOPE. They left honorably and were released with our blessing. **But it underlined for me that some people can only accept so much change. They are able to pioneer so far, but no further.** When things become too uncomfortable and unfamiliar, they long to retreat back to something more settled and predictable.

Pastor and prophet, Jeremiah Johnson, is accurate in his observation:

"You can try to explain to settlers all day long the process of how you got to where you are and it will never be good enough for them, and that's okay. You have to understand that being led by the Holy Spirit looks erratic and is quite frankly tiring to them. The new challenges and financial needs that pioneers find exhilarating to tackle and can't wait to see how God comes through become a major burden and fear for settlers. When you are most excited, they are most likely terrified. Pioneers and settlers are just wired differently. Period."

Now, three years on, again we're in one of those periods of significant change in HOPE. We've long outgrown our current building and have recently employed several new staff members. We are pressing deeper into God's presence than ever before and removing the residue of religiosity that is so pervasive in our land.

We sense we're at a tipping point as a church. And while many are excited by what the Spirit is doing, I can also feel rising apprehension and unsettledness among a few of our members and leaders. **They want to embrace the new thing. But change is hard because it also means letting go of the old thing.**

THE CERTAINTY OF CHANGE

The story of HOPE Church is a parable or picture of how you and I typically adapt to change and transition.

Many of us feel the call to pioneer. We have no time for religious traditions, man-centered formulas, or outdated methods. We long to be on the cutting edge of whatever the Spirit is doing in our generation. We see ourselves as the radical remnant, willing to do whatever it takes to extend God's Kingdom and reach the lost. We are the trailblazers and forerunners who are forging a new path into uncharted territory.

However, we all have our limits. **There is a threshold of change at which even the most adventurous among us begin to feel uncomfortable.**

We too want the new. But we are also attached to the old. We wonder if it might be possible to hold onto both.

We see the need for new structures and a shift in the way we do church and ministry. We just don't want it to interfere with the things that I cherish most.

We want to see new leaders raised up and released into their giftings and callings. But not at the expense of losing my position, prominence, or platform.

We desperately long to reach the lost and make disciples of people from every background and demographic. But why should I have to sacrifice my preferences to accommodate them? Certainly, it's their job to fit into our existing system and culture.

We pray for a powerful move of the Holy Spirit among us. So long as it looks like previous revivals and doesn't bring embarrassment or disrepute to our church community.

We desire to be radically sold out for the Kingdom of God and to go wherever the Spirit leads. But in our minds, we have preconceptions of what that might look like. And our mental picture rarely involves rejection, criticism, misunderstanding, loneliness, or hiddenness.

You get where I'm going with this.

In the words of the prophet Meat Loaf, our response to the pioneering call can sometimes be: *"I will do anything for love, but I won't do that."*

This is a challenge for me right now. I've said before that I didn't want to lead a large church. Yet, in just the past three months, our church has grown by another 25-30%. And I know if we acquire the larger building we are looking at, we will likely double in the next few years. Part of me loves the excitement of it. And yet, another part of me wants to run away! God is pushing me beyond my threshold.

Also, we're currently making changes in our family life that will bring about a significant reduction in household income. We've sensed God leading us in this direction for a while but kept putting it off because of the discomfort and cost. Now, as we prepare to finally 'pull the trigger', we're experiencing a mixture of apprehension and excitement.

Pete Greig, founder of the 24/7 Prayer Movement writes from experiencing these pivotal moments of significant change:

"At transitional moments in life, God tests our hearts…

Why?

Because he knows that the choices we make at the crossroads determine our future direction and destiny. The priorities we establish in the gear-change moments of life set our trajectory for years to come."

Where can you relate to this?

- Is there any area where God has been speaking to you about making a decision but you're putting it off because of fear, discomfort, or the potential cost?
- What is God messing with that you cherish and don't want to change?

- Where have you found yourself anxious, apprehensive, annoyed, or even offended recently? Might this be pointing to an area where God wants you to stretch and grow?

In this new era, constant change is about the only thing we can be certain of. The words Joshua 3: 4 have never been more appropriate than they are today:

"...you have never been this way before..."

It used to be that staying the same and avoiding too much change was the safest option.

However, in this Divine reset, an unwillingness to push beyond where you have previously been is a certain precursor to stagnation, irrelevance, decline, and death.

The problem is that we don't have a roadmap for where we're going. We know that many of the old ways no longer work. We're increasingly sensing a shift. God is leading His people into something new. But, right now, we don't know what that looks like. Everything feels blurry and indistinct. It's disorientating and confusing.

The temptation, as always, will be to retreat to what we know. To regress to the comfortable and familiar. To go back to tried and tested formulas.

But there's no life there. The grace has lifted. Those activities and pursuits are empty, hollow, and void.

I believe that we're being invited, like the Israelites in their period of the 'in-between', to follow the cloud through the wilderness.

We move wherever God moves.

We pause whenever the cloud stops.

We never get too settled or comfortable because at any moment we might need to pack our bags and step into the next stage of the journey.

While we might not have a roadmap, we do have a Guide.

As we daily keep in step with the Holy Spirit and immerse our minds in God's Word, He will lead us through this uncharted territory towards the Promised Land.

As my friend and fellow traveler, Nate Johnson says:

"Blueprints that our forefathers built with simply can't be borrowed, copied, and pasted in our day. We need an ear for hearing the word of the Lord, eyes for seeing the plans and purposes of God, and a mouth that can declare with accuracy and unction what God is saying as it regards the advancing of His kingdom in the earth."

PROPHETIC ENCOURAGEMENT

GET READY. IT'S TIME.

I know you've been waiting for so long.
It feels as if you have been walking in circles forever.
Stuck in cycles of false hope and disappointment.
Always sensing you're close, but never seeing the fulfillment.

The wilderness has brought weariness.
I know you're confused and frustrated.
It's been such a long and lonely path.
But you've kept going. Pressing through. And now you're stepping up to the threshold. It's time to move.
Get ready.

You will begin to glimpse the other side.
Where you've been struggling to sense what's ahead, I am imparting fresh vision and spiritual sight.
Your eyes will be opened.
Your spirit will be stirred.
You'll start to imagine possibilities and potential.
It will reignite something inside you.

A fire that has almost gone out.
A passion that has faded.
A joy that has dissipated.
Dreams that are nearly dead.

I'm breathing afresh on you, bringing dry bones back to life.
You will rise again with vigor.
Get ready.

You're coming to the crossing point.
But first, you must finish getting ready.
I know you think you're ready.
But there are still some things that are not in order.
In your walk with Me, in your relationships, and in other areas of your life.

You've been avoiding difficult conversations. You've been putting off necessary decisions. You've been holding back from what you know you need to do.
You've been clinging to things I have told you to release and relinquish.
You can't bring them with you. They will hinder your progress.
You know that already. Let them go.
Get ready.

There will be a clear sign that it's time to move. But there will also be a short window of opportunity.
So, you cannot be passive or hesitant.
Move quickly. Bravely. Boldly.
Step in, keep moving, cross over.

Fully enter, embrace the new, and get established.
Don't stop short or settle for 'almost there'. Leave the grave clothes of the last season behind.
Things you have lost, those who have left you.

You've waited too long to miss this moment. You have been sifted, pruned, pressed, and prepared.
Now prepare to step into the promise.

GET READY. IT'S TIME.

DAY 46

PIONEERS AND SETTLERS | Part 3

BIBLE READING

Then Jesus came to them and said, 'All authority in heaven and on earth has been given to me. Therefore go and make disciples of all nations, baptizing them in the name of the Father and of the Son and of the Holy Spirit, and teaching them to obey everything I have commanded you. And surely I am with you always, to the very end of the age.'

(Matthew 28: 18-20)

We put no stumbling block in anyone's path, so that our ministry will not be discredited. Rather, as servants of God we commend ourselves in every way: in great endurance; in troubles, hardships and distresses; in beatings, imprisonments and riots; in hard work, sleepless nights and hunger; in purity, understanding, patience and kindness; in the Holy Spirit and in sincere love; in truthful speech and in the power of God; with weapons of righteousness in the right hand and in the left; through glory and dishonor, bad report and good report; genuine, yet regarded as impostors; known, yet regarded as unknown; dying, and yet we live on; beaten, and yet not killed; sorrowful, yet always rejoicing; poor, yet making many rich; having nothing, and yet possessing everything.

(2 Corinthians 6: 3-10)

DEVOTIONAL

Pioneer. Trailblazer. Forerunner. Reformer.

All these terms have been used to describe those who are forging uncharted paths and finding fresh language to express what God is doing in this new era of the church.

But what exactly do they mean? And can they be used to describe you and me?

I've been asking myself that question over these past few days.

Am I a pioneer?

The dictionary defines a *pioneer* as:

- *One who ventures into unknown or unclaimed territory to settle.*
- *One who opens up new areas of thought, research, or development.*

It was also a military term that was used to describe a smaller unit that would be sent ahead of the main force tasked with making roads, digging entrenchments, and clearing the way in preparation for the arrival of the rest of the troops.

So, where does that leave me (and you)?

While I have launched several ministries, I've never planted a church from scratch.

I lead a church that, on the surface, would appear fairly conventional.

Theologically, I am very conservative and charismatic. I'm not planning on deconstructing my faith any time soon.

I don't consider myself especially radical, creative, or innovative.

I have little desire to sail off into the sunset in search of unreached tribes or to sell everything I own and go live among the margins of society.

And I'm guessing, you might not be too dissimilar to me.

Yet, there's something within me that is dissatisfied with much of what we call 'the church'.

It's difficult to pinpoint precisely what it is, but there has been a growing unease for some time with how we do things.

More and more, I've been struggling to know exactly where I 'fit' in the Christian world.

I find parts of it too wacky and excessive, whilst other parts are way too tame and lifeless.

I'm too reformed for the liberals, but too charismatic for the reformed crowd.

I long to encounter the power and presence of the Holy Spirit but have no time for hype or excessive emotionalism.

I love much of our modern worship movement but also find many of the songs bland, repetitive, and self-focused.

I want to war against the kingdom of darkness but have little desire to go demon hunting.

I am passionate about the prophetic but don't want to churn out candy-coated words that have no depth or substance.

I believe in spiritual authority and giving appropriate honor but am wary of exalting human leaders and I can't tolerate spiritual abuse or manipulation.

I want to have influence and impact in the world but find the self-promotion, platform-building, and competitive spirit in our corner of Christendom nauseating.

I want to be known as someone who boldly stands for holiness, righteousness, and truth. But I want my life to be exemplified by grace, compassion, and kindness.

I could go on, but I can already see you nodding in agreement with many of the above statements.

We don't really fit into the current 'model' of church, but we don't want to throw the proverbial baby out with the bathwater and abandon all expressions of modern Christianity.

We're longing for the real thing, without pretense or hypocrisy.

Committed community marked by authenticity, transparency, love, generosity, and service.

Biblical teaching, saturated with theological substance and Holy Spirit revelation.

God-centered, Christ-exalting worship that isn't playlist, formulaic, or written to appease music industry executives.

Genuine spiritual power and authority that is clearly backed by heaven and makes hell nervous.

Verifiable healings, miracles, signs, and wonders without the white suits, big hair, weirdness, or hype.

Abundance and financial provision without greed or Christian pyramid schemes.

Real unity and oneness among believers without watering down the truth to the lowest common denominator or faking 'niceness'.

Sometimes, it feels easier to describe what we *don't* want than it is to articulate or express what we know is slowly gestating inside us.

We know that the 'old thing' no longer works for us. But the 'new thing' hasn't yet taken definition or shape.

And so, we must continue to live in that tension as we journey through this pivotal transition into the next era.

That's okay.

We could all probably quote Isaiah 43: 18-19:

"Forget the former things;
do not dwell on the past.
See, I am doing a new thing!
Now it springs up; do you not perceive it?"

But do you notice - **God doesn't attempt to name or define the 'new thing' He is doing?** It was 'springing up' in front of the people, yet they weren't yet able to fully perceive it.

We too must allow time to pass before we rush to label or explain what God is doing in our day. The details and definition will emerge as we walk in daily, faithful obedience.

So, back to our original question.

Are you a pioneer? Am I?

Truthfully, I think for most of us, it's too early to say. Only time will tell.

As the 'new thing' continues to emerge, will we be willing to embrace something that isn't polished or fully finished?

Can we live with the messiness and mistakes that inevitably accompany any new move of God?

Will we be discerning enough to separate the genuine and real from the fake and deceptive?

Are we prepared to break from old, familiar alignments to walk unknown paths with those who are also carrying this 'new thing' in their hearts?

Are we willing to set aside deeply ingrained methods and mindsets to pursue heaven's blueprints and the new wineskin for the church?

Are we prepared to pay the price that will inevitably be required from those who question the established order and upset the status quo?

This last question is perhaps the most important.

Because I think we romanticize pioneering and reforming. Social media, online communities, and books - even like this one - can paint a picture of leaving the old behind and stepping into God's 'new thing' that is rosy, clear-cut, and unrealistic.

The truth is that pioneering is difficult, messy, painful, and costly.

Jesus was clear that his followers should be realistic and informed before deciding to follow Him into the unknown:

"Suppose one of you wants to build a tower. Won't you first sit down and estimate the cost to see if you have enough money to complete it? For if you lay the foundation and are not able to finish it, everyone who sees it will ridicule you, saying, 'This person began to build and wasn't able to finish.'

... In the same way, those of you who do not give up everything you have cannot be my disciples." (Luke 14: 28-30; 33)

THE PRICE OF PIONEERING

In his book *Prophetic Pioneering*, Jeremiah Johnston issues the following warning:

493

"Pioneers, in order to deliver you from the praise of men, God will baptize you in their criticisms and attacks. It is painful. You will lose many friendships along the way, and the misunderstandings will be many. You will pay a price that most around you will never see or understand. You are speaking a language of reform and awakening that many in the body of Christ just don't have an eye or ear for yet. Do not grow discouraged, and most of all, do not be surprised when the attacks and criticisms come. Rather than rushing to defend or explain yourself, my advice would be to go before the Lord and ask Him, "What inside of me are You exposing through the accusations and attacks of others that needs to die?"

When you determine to unreservedly follow Jesus wherever He leads, there is a cost. There will be a price to pay.

It won't look the same for everyone.

However, a Christian life that costs nothing is probably not a life of obedience and faith.

Pioneering has a price. Because, by its very nature, pioneering involves doing something different.

You're going first.

Stepping into the unknown.

Forging new paths.

Questioning the norms.

Challenging the status quo.

Confronting outdated methods and traditions.

Defying the gatekeepers and powerbrokers.

Rethinking how things have always been done.

Coming up with fresh ways of expressing old truths.

Coloring outside the lines.

As I read that list, I immediately think of Jesus. It's no wonder he's described as *'the pioneer…of our faith'*. (Hebrews 12: 2)

He stepped into a religious system that was thousands of years old and completely redefined what it meant to have a relationship with Yahweh.

And confronting the established institution cost Him everything.

Even though He was never rude, obnoxious, or remotely arrogant, His presence and ideas were so offensive that the establishment had Him killed. His pioneering ways were too much of a threat to the existing order.

You probably won't get murdered for pioneer, but you may well face rejection, misunderstanding, and even persecution.

Some of the pain will come from the world. But most of your wounds will be inflicted by those within the church. They have a vested interest in keeping everything the same. Therefore, significant change will be opposed and resisted at every level.

The current religious ruling class may pay lip service to 'fresh expressions' and 'new ways of doing church', as long as these remain within the very narrow confines over which they have control. Mostly they just want to polish up and repackage the old thing.

Don't think I'm only talking about traditional churches or denominations here. I'm also referring to what we might call non-denominational or even 'apostolic churches' that were at the forefront of pioneering in the last 50 years.

History has shown that often the greatest resistance to any new move of the Holy Spirit comes from those who were on the cutting edge of the previous revival.

As I said yesterday, most people can only pioneer so far before too much change becomes more than they can handle. They reach a threshold and begin to resist the 'new thing' or even regress and return to the old ways they left behind. The children of Israel want to go back to Egypt.

As we emerged from 2020 and COVID, it was clear that there had been a seismic spiritual shift. Catalytic changes were surfacing in the Body of Christ. God was dismantling old structures and exposing the shallowness of our man-made kingdoms. He was bringing us back to something simpler and more authentic, but potent and presence-filled.

However, most of the 'big name' churches simply reverted right back to the old model that had worked for the previous decade. Even though it now looked and felt hollow, they had no other paradigm for how church could look and weren't willing to live in the tension of waiting for the new to emerge.

Pioneers will often be accused of being arrogant, prideful, and unwilling to submit to authority. In some cases, these criticisms are warranted. But mostly, we just can't toe the line and continue to prop up something that no longer has spiritual life. If the emperor is naked, we won't stay silent and pretend otherwise.

Ten years ago, I had more invitations to preach in churches across this island than I could handle. I've noticed that these have significantly reduced in recent years. And I don't think it's because my preaching has gotten worse! I just don't fit in most church contexts here any longer. I'm never intentionally rude or dishonoring. But I can't stick to the 22 minutes on the clock or avoid speaking about controversial subjects if that's where the Spirit leads me.

Pioneering is often a lonely journey. It's hard to find like-minded friends who are wrestling with the same issues as you and are willing to live without clear and defined answers. You will seem out of step with the rest of the church. While many people will share your concerns about the current system, very few are willing to risk the rejection or misunderstanding that comes from expressing them publicly. Some of you will stay in your current church structures while praying for change. Others will opt out in search of community with a small tribe of other pioneers, either in-person or online.

Pioneers refuse to compromise on the essential truths. We know in our bones that the old system is broken and becoming increasingly obsolete. And we long for a new, more authentic expression of church. However, we don't go down that hell-paved road of deconstructing the Christian faith or rejecting the Scriptures as the Spirit-inspired Word of God. Holiness, righteousness, and Godly living are our standard. We are devoted to prayer, fasting, purity, service, sacrifice, generosity, reaching the lost, and demonstrating the Kingdom in our words and actions.

The full price of pioneering in this new era is yet to be seen. We may lose friendships, titles, positions, status, finances, comfort, and reputation.

But, for those who persevere and press through, the rewards will always be greater. We have the promise of Jesus:

"Truly I tell you," Jesus said to them, "no one who has left home or wife or brothers or sisters or parents or children for the sake of the kingdom of God will fail to receive many times as much in this age, and in the age to come eternal life." (Luke 18: 29-30)

Let me encourage you to keep going with the words of Rick Pino from his song *Pioneer*:

Pioneer (Song by Rick Pino)

Pioneer, Pioneer
Keep pressing onwards beyond your fears
And only your Father goes before you to your own frontier
You're a Pioneer

Uncharted wilderness stretches before you
And you thrive on going where no one has gone
Still it gets lonely when darkness rears
So sing by the fire until the dawn

You travel light and you travel alone
And when you arrive nobody knows
But your Father in heaven, He is glad you can go
Cause those who come after you will need the road

And what you have done, others will do
Bigger and better and faster than you
But you can't look back, you gotta keep on pressing through
There's a wilderness pathway and it's calling you
Calling you, calling you
Keep pressing onwards, you can't stay here...
And only your Father goes before you to your own frontier
You're a Pioneer.

PROPHETIC ENCOURAGEMENT

THERE IS A GRACE FOR LASTING CHANGE

There is a grace, right now, to confront deep-rooted issues and long-standing hindrances.

The Father wants you to be totally free so you can be most effective and impactful for His Kingdom in these important days.

See what is coming to the surface.
What is He drawing your attention to?

As with the man beside the pool called Bethesda, Jesus is asking: *"Do you want to get well?"* (John 5:6)

Don't miss the opportunity to deal with the stuff that has been keeping you stuck.

Break the cycle.
Sever the cords.
Uproot the lies.
Leave behind the baggage.
Restore the foundations.
Rebuild the walls of protection.

498

It may take fasting, prayer, deliverance, counselling, transparency, accountability…but you can find true freedom and fulfillment.

You are not a passive or powerless victim.
You do not have to stay this way.
Strongholds can be broken.
No matter how long you've struggled.
No matter how often you've tried.
No matter how many times you've failed.
Your life can really change.

Things can shift. They no longer have to be the way they have been.
Even if you think it's been too long. It's not.
Or you've gone too far. You haven't.
Total transformation is available from the Holy Spirit.

Seize this *kairos* moment.
Take hold of His healing.
Receive His grace.
Embrace the change.

Confront anything that has brought containment.
You are no longer a slave.
Jesus has delivered you through His blood.
You are not defined by your past.
You are a new creation in Christ.
Step into your true identity.
There is freedom, wholeness, joy, and expansion waiting on the other side.

THERE IS A GRACE FOR LASTING CHANGE

DAY 47

WHY GOD REMOVES PEOPLE FROM YOUR LIFE

BIBLE READING

"I am the true vine, and my Father is the gardener. He cuts off every branch in me that bears no fruit, while every branch that does bear fruit he prunes so that it will be even more fruitful.

(John 15: 1-2)

Blessed is the one
who does not walk in step with the wicked
or stand in the way that sinners take
or sit in the company of mockers,
but whose delight is in the law of the LORD,
and who meditates on his law day and night.
That person is like a tree planted by streams of water,
which yields its fruit in season
and whose leaf does not wither -
whatever they do prospers.
Not so the wicked!
They are like chaff
that the wind blows away.

(Psalm 1: 1-4)

DEVOTIONAL

Many of us will have found that our circle of significant connections has grown smaller in the past five years. Some of that can be attributed to COVID and the pressure towards social distancing and isolation in that difficult season. Once the restrictions were lifted, we simply never reconnected with some people.

Other friends relocated to a different area. They moved house or changed jobs. We promised to keep in touch. But over time, the calls and texts became fewer and fewer.

Or perhaps colleagues were now working from home and so workplace relationships disintegrated. The occasional Zoom meeting replaced having coffee and lunch together each day.

And in other cases, when we did get together with old friends, we realized that something had changed. We didn't have the same commonalities or chemistry that had previously bonded us. We had little to talk about. Instead of energizing us, these interactions became awkward and draining.

It's natural and normal that relationships grow apart for many reasons. Other people change. And so do we. It's okay to acknowledge this and move on.

However, there are times when God removes people from our lives.

It can be confusing and disorientating. We may feel a sense of loneliness or rejection for a season. We wonder if we did something wrong. Did we push them away?

The reality may be that God was intentional and strategic in their removal. Their departure was for a greater good.

Today, I want to look at six reasons why God might remove people from your life.

1. YOU ARE NO LONGER IN ALIGNMENT.

We know that there is a season for everything in our lives (Ecclesiastes 3: 1). That includes relationships, alignments, and connections.

God often sends people into our lives for a reason and a season. They bring companionship and fun. They impart something into our lives or help us grow in some area. They provide assistance with our assignment. They open opportunities and facilitate significant contacts.

However, there often comes a point where that season has shifted. It doesn't have to be something negative or dramatic. You're just going in different directions. You have new priorities or a shift in focus. Your life situations have changed.

Maybe you've changed your views on some important aspects of life. You have different priorities and perspectives. You see the world differently than before. Or they have moved away from beliefs and values that brought you together. The things that initially bonded you are no longer there.

Whatever the reason, in this season there is a misalignment.

They have no desire to go where you're going. And you aren't going to change to become more congruent with them.

We see this with Abraham and his nephew Lot. When they set out on their journey in Genesis 12, they were in agreement. However, soon Lot's heart was drawn in a different direction. There was dissension between his herdsmen and Abraham's. It became clear that their futures were no longer aligned. We read:

"So Abram said to Lot, "Let's not have any quarreling between you and me, or between your herders and mine, for we are close relatives. Is not the whole land before you? Let's part company. If you go to the left, I'll go to the right; if you go to the right, I'll go to the left." (Genesis 13: 8-9)

This happens in friendships. But it also happens with churches and organizations. Sometimes it can be a change in theology and beliefs. At other times, it's simply about style and practice. Either way, your design and destiny increasingly look different from theirs. When there is no longer alignment, God will often remove people from your life.

2. THEY WILL KEEP YOU STUCK IN THE PAST.

Usually, we are friends with people because we like who they are and how they are when we first meet them. There's a compatibility or chemistry. We're on the same wavelength. We have similar attitudes to life. We are interested in the same things.

However, over time you may find that you have changed, grown, and developed in some important areas while they have stayed the same.

You have a passion to pursue more in life – to fulfil God's purpose and potential. On the other hand, they're very settled and content with where they are.

You want to be stretched and challenged so that you can live a fruitful and fulfilling life. They're happy to plod through life with few goals or ambitions.

Sometimes you're trying to break free from a habit or behavior that's become unhealthy or unhelpful. They don't see any problem with it.

Your growth may begin to make them uncomfortable. It can create tension in the relationship. They say things like: "You've changed." Or "What's happened to the old you?"

You still care about them. But increasingly, this relationship is hindering your growth. Like crabs in a bucket, any time you start climbing up, they try to pull you back down.

Maybe the problem is in how they perceive you. They have a fixed version of you in their minds – but it's five years out of date. You're not that person any longer. But they still relate to you according to who you were, not who you are. And when you're with them, you find yourself regressing into behaviors and conversations that don't reflect who you are today.

For example, when Jesus returned to his hometown of Nazareth, the people could only see him as the local lad who was a carpenter. Even though he had performed powerful miracles and healings in other places, his ability to ministry there was limited by their narrow and outdated perception of him. We read:

"Isn't this the carpenter? Isn't this Mary's son and the brother of James, Joseph, Judas and Simon? Aren't his sisters here with us?" And they took offense at him.

Jesus said to them, "A prophet is not without honor except in his own town, among his relatives and in his own home." He could not do any miracles there, except lay his hands on a few sick people and heal them. He was amazed at their lack of faith." (Mark 6: 3-6)

I find it incredible that Jesus' ability to do miracles in that place was limited in some way by how the people perceived him.

Sometimes your relationships can become a ceiling in your life. They bring control and containment. Remaining tethered to certain people is hindering your promotion and advancement. Therefore, to enable you to flourish and grow, God will remove people from your world.

3. THEY ARE SABOTAGING SOMETHING YOU CANNOT SEE.

Often, we wonder why things around us keep going wrong or falling apart. We are constantly surrounded by a swirl of drama or discontent.

Or no matter how hard we try, we can't seem to make any headway. It almost feels like there are invisible walls keeping us hemmed in and restricted. Instead of momentum, all we experience is tension and friction.

504

Of course, there can be many reasons for the above. But sometimes it's simply because we have the wrong people in our inner circle.

They may appear to be gifted and even Godly. But beneath the surface, they have hidden issues, toxic traits, destructive patterns, and unrepentant sin. They have given the enemy a foothold (or a stronghold) in their lives and his dark influence is spilling over into your sphere.

We see this in Joshua 7. God had promised the Israelites victory over their enemies in Canaan. Yet, they lose a battle against the men of Ai that should easily have been won. When Joshua goes before the Lord, the cause of their defeat becomes clear. Achan had stolen and hidden gold and silver that had been consecrated to pagan gods. His deception and sin had affected everyone around him.

Don't underestimate the damage destructive and deceptive people can have in your life. Of course, it's not always easy to initially discern good and evil, or the genuine from the fake. Like the wheat and the weeds in Matthew 13, they look almost indistinguishable. People with an agenda can be very clever and manipulative. However, if you depend on the Holy Spirit, He will help you discern those who have pure motives from those whose desires are selfish and sinful.

Often, the challenge is that people are a mixture of good and bad. They bring gifts, time, friendship, finances, commitment, and resources into your life. Yet, they also bring negativity, drama, discord, control, hurt, and selfishness.

We don't want to lose the good, so we tolerate the bad. Plus, we think we need them. They've possibly even created a sense of dependence upon them.

Often, that's when God steps in and removes them for us. He sees what we don't, and so He does what we won't.

Once they are gone, it's amazing how blessing, freedom, momentum, and a fresh sense of joy can fill your world again.

Pastor Alan Scott expresses this well:

"God has a way of removing people from your life to save you from their influence. When we think of deliverance, we think of the laying on of hands. It's true, sometimes deliverance comes in the form of God removing demons from you. But then sometimes God will remove a person, and by removing the person in your life, He's removing their demons too. He does that so we can walk in freedom. If you want to go where God has called you, you can't be friends with everybody and anybody."

4. THE RELATIONSHIP HAS BECOME DAMAGING OR UNHEALTHY.

Sometimes a relationship starts well. There is mutual respect, freedom, fun, and growth. However, over time, something shifts, normally with one party. It can happen suddenly or gradually. But the relationship becomes increasingly co-dependent, controlling, or even toxic or abusive in some way.

We see this in the Old Testament with the Hebrews in Egypt. Jacob and his family initially went to Egypt during a famine. There they found both food and favor. Because of Joseph's position and Pharoah's appreciation, they were given special treatment. However, over time something shifted in the relationship. Increasingly, the Hebrews were seen as a threat. The level of intolerance and mistreatment intensified to the point where Pharoah wanted to wipe out an entire generation of Jewish babies. That's when God raised up a deliverer to remove them from their oppressors.

We also see it with David and King Saul. Initially, David had a good relationship with Saul. He defeated Goliath and played the harp to soothe the king's manic episodes. However, soon things took a turn. Saul became jealous of David's popularity and sought to harm him. That's when David was removed into a new season elsewhere.

In our own lives, controlling or damaging relationships can initially be difficult to detect. The behavior can be subtle and seem like no big deal.

Someone going through a difficult season asks for more help from you.

506

Your church leader requests that you attend additional meetings.

A boyfriend goes into a mood when you meet up with your friends.

A friend texts you several times every day and expects an immediate response.

Everything is fine if you are compliant and meet their expectations.

However, the true nature of the relationship is seen only when you say *no* or fail them in some way. Or they become jealous or envious when you spend time with others or succeed in some area of life.

Many years ago, I led an older man to faith in Christ. We had been meeting every week for several months to discuss the Bible and I was overjoyed when he finally crossed the line and prayed to receive Jesus. I wanted to disciple him, and so we continued to meet for lunch every week.

However, around six months later, my responsibilities and workload increased significantly. While we kept in touch, I simply no longer had as much time as before for our lunches and long chats. Very soon, he became negative and critical, accusing me of putting everyone else before him. He gradually withdrew from church and developed a bitterness towards my ministry.

I realized a few things from this experience.

Firstly, I thought he was connected to Jesus when actually he was more attached to me. I had allowed an unhealthy co-dependency to develop.

Secondly, we both mistook a ministry for a friendship. They are two separate things. He saw me as a friend. I saw him primarily as someone I wanted to invest in. So, when I stepped back, he saw it as a rejection of his friendship. I saw it as a reprioritization of ministry.

Sometimes, God will remove people from your life because a co-dependent relationship has developed on one or both sides. The focus has moved from God to the other person. Or from God to a particular church. Our ultimate dependence must be on Him and Him alone.

In other cases, the relationship has become toxic or damaging. God will remove either them or you for your own safety and well-being.

5. GOD WANTS TO MAKE ROOM FOR NEW, SIGNIFICANT RELATIONSHIPS.

When too many devices are connected to a wi-fi router, it slows down the speed at which data can be transferred.

Similarly, when we have too many connections in our own lives, we aren't able to fully commit to those relationships that are most fruitful or fulfilling. We have lots of acquaintances but very few real friendships.

God wants us to have depth over breadth in our lives and relationships. He wants substance and strength over superficiality and shallowness. Therefore, He will sometimes remove people who are draining time, energy, and resources that could be better allocated to other people.

It's like the process of pruning that Jesus talks about in John 15. Not all of the branches that are pruned are bad. They're just not the best.

It's the same in our own lives. When God removes people, don't always assume that they're evil or have bad intentions. They could be perfectly decent people. But they're not those who He wants you to do life with.

Even Jesus said He had to leave the earth so the Holy Spirit could come:

"But very truly I tell you, it is for your good that I am going away. Unless I go away, the Advocate will not come to you; but if I go, I will send him to you." (John 16: 7)

When God removes, He replaces. Not always immediately, but eventually you'll look around you and be thankful for the pruning process that has taken place.

Before I met my wife, I had been dating another girl for almost two years. While the relationship was good, deep down I knew it wasn't moving towards marriage. A prophetic friend challenged me to let go of that relationship so that my hands would be open to receive God's best. It took a while, but eventually, we went our separate ways. Three months later I had my first date with Becky. Four months after that, we were engaged.

You only have so much capacity for relationships. When you try to cling to someone that God is trying to remove, you are separating yourself from an area of your future.

6.   THEY ARE HINDERING A WORK OF GOD.

In Mark 5, Jesus enters the home of an official named Jairus. Immediately he's met by a crowd who are loudly lamenting and mourning the loss of Jairus' twelve-year-old daughter. Look at how Jesus handles the situation:

"After he put them all out, he took the child's father and mother and the disciples who were with him, and went in where the child was."
(v. 40)

Jesus walks into this environment of noise, crying, despair, and death. And immediately, he clears the room. He says: "Everyone out!" He empties the space of almost everyone except the child's parents and three of his disciples. Then he performed the miracle and raised the little girl back to life.

Why was Jesus so intentional in removing everyone?

Jesus knew that to see God work powerfully in a situation, he needed to remove anyone who was draining faith and resisting what God wanted to do.

These people, well-meaning as they were, were taking up space, and filling that space with fear, death, defeat, and discouragement.

So, Jesus immediately takes authority over that space. He removes anything contrary to or resisting what He wants to do.

509

In our own lives, sometimes the miracle or transformation doesn't happen because something or someone is missing. Rather it's because too many people resisting the miracle are present.

During my twenty years in leadership, I have watched the atmosphere of churches change overnight when certain people moved on. Before that, it was as if there was a constant blockage in the ministry. We kept hitting a wall in our worship. There was tension and friction in relationships. We struggled to grow. People weren't released into the giftings and callings.

Then some people moved on, and suddenly everything shifted. There was freedom and life and growth and an increased sense of the presence of God.

While we don't want to become overly judgmental of others, neither should we underestimate just how much one or two people can quench the movement of the Holy Spirit. Sometimes God will remove people because their presence is hindering Him from working in a place.

In this time of continued shaking and upheaval, our relationships are changing. Don't be surprised if God removes some people from your life. It may be painful, but it is also purposeful. As pastor and author Dharius Daniels says:

"God has a way of taking people out of your life. The right relationships in your life will produce the kind of future that you envision. But the wrong relationships will divert you from your vision and from the plans God has for you."

PROPHETIC ENCOURAGEMENT

YOU ARE MOVING FROM CONTAINMENT TO RELEASE

You are moving from preparation and consecration into a season of permission and fulfilment.

From restriction into a time of release.

For some time, it has felt as if you have been in the wilderness - wandering and waiting.

There have been dead ends, delays, and detours. Nothing has been advancing.

Now God is giving you the green light.

The LORD has been working deeply in your heart, removing impurities and impediments to your future.

He has been refining your desires to be aligned with His.

He is now going to release you into the next stage of His good plans and purposes for you. But you will have to step into them.

Just as Nathan told David: "Do all that is in your heart, for God is with you" (1 Chronicles 17:2), so too, the Lord would say to you: "I am giving you permission to do that which is in your heart."

You have the freedom to innovate and create, to realign and reinvent, to express yourself and stop trying to impress others.

It's time to stand up and speak up.
To move out from obscurity into a place of visibility.
From limitation to enlargement.
From frustration to fulfilment.

YOU ARE MOVING FROM CONTAINMENT TO RELEASE

511

DAY 48

GOD, I FEEL LIKE AN IMPOSTER

BIBLE READING

And now the cry of the Israelites has reached me, and I have seen the way the Egyptians are oppressing them. So now, go. I am sending you to Pharaoh to bring my people the Israelites out of Egypt.'

But Moses said to God, 'Who am I that I should go to Pharaoh and bring the Israelites out of Egypt?'

God said, 'I will be with you.

… Moses said to the Lord, 'Pardon your servant, Lord. I have never been eloquent, neither in the past nor since you have spoken to your servant. I am slow of speech and tongue.'

The Lord said to him, 'Who gave human beings their mouths? Who makes them deaf or mute? Who gives them sight or makes them blind? Is it not I, the Lord? Now go; I will help you speak and will teach you what to say.'

But Moses said, 'Pardon your servant, Lord. Please send someone else.'

(Exodus 3: 9-12; 4: 10-13)

DEVOTIONAL

I felt it the first time I preached.

I also experienced it at college and when I stepped into my first professional job.

And in the next two jobs after that.

In 2003, when I started seminary, it went to a new level.

Then, in June 2006, on the day I was ordained into ministry, I was convinced everyone else could see it too.

Later, when I became a Senior Pastor, I was sure that it was only a matter of time before I was exposed.

In 2016, when I moved from preaching to 300 people to almost 2000 people each week, the feeling of it was intense.

In 2018, when I started Daily Prophetic, it was so very prevalent.

Then, in 2019, when I wrote my first book, *The Tension of Transition*, it was almost debilitating.

Last year, when I finally launched my *Prophetic Transitions* mentorship, it came back with full force.

I'm talking about **imposter syndrome** – that psychological experience of feeling like a fake, fraud, or phony despite any genuine success or accomplishments you have achieved.

You've probably felt it too. Most people have at some stage.

Do any of the following sound familiar:

- You doubt your own abilities, intellect, and skills.

- You feel unqualified or incompetent.

- You think that everyone else knows what they're doing except you.

- You don't feel like you belong in certain places and everyone else is thinking it too.

- Any success you achieve is merely down to 'luck' or exceptional circumstances. And any failure is 100% your fault.

- You work longer and harder than everyone else to compensate for your perceived deficiencies.

- You constantly downplay your ability or expertise in an area.

- You think that everyone else is better and more qualified than you.

- You fear that you won't be able to meet other's expectations of you.

- You self-sabotage, give up early, or avoid taking on new responsibilities so no one can see what an imposter you really are.

- The more you achieve or accomplish, the more you feel like a fraud.

- You don't believe you have what it takes to go to the next level.

- You stay small, remain silent, or hide to avoid drawing attention to your perceived incompetence.

- You overprepare or overcompensate in everything in an attempt to prove that you are worthy.

- You find it difficult to receive compliments from others.

- The smallest criticism sends you into a downward negative spiral.

- You're always worrying about the next task.

- You think you must have been invited to a social gathering or professional event by accident. You don't deserve to be there. Someone made a mistake and you'll soon be found out.

- You think you're the only one who feels this way. Everyone else is more secure, confident, and competent than you.

Please tell me that you could relate to some of the above. Or maybe I am the only one!

LIVING A LIE

Imposter syndrome is so debilitating because usually, it bears no semblance to reality. It is completely based on lies we have come to believe about ourselves, despite all evidence to the contrary.

Someone has described imposter syndrome as being like "professional anorexia".

What anorexia is to the body, imposter syndrome is to your competence.

An adult with anorexia could weigh just 80 or 90lbs, yet when they look in the mirror they see someone who is overweight. Everyone else can see how dangerously skinny they are. But the sufferer sadly has a warped view of reality.

Similarly, with imposter syndrome, someone who is competent, gifted, successful, and responsible stands in front of a mental mirror and sees a person who is incompetent, inadequate, underqualified, and a fraud.

When we experience imposter syndrome ourselves, it feels like truth. When we see it in others, we think: "How can you not know how great you are?"

515

Several years ago, I helped organize a large Christian conference. Somehow we managed to get a speaker for one of the evenings who is world-renowned for his communication skills, teaching gift, and ability to connect with a crowd. I happened to be in the hall with him during the hour before the event started. He was pacing around the room, anxious and nervous, riddled with self-doubt and insecurity. This is a man who has spoken to tens of thousands of people in stadiums all over the globe. Yet, even still, here at our conference with a few thousand people, he was almost debilitated by nerves and feelings of inadequacy.

Logically, imposter syndrome makes no sense. But that's because it's not logical. It's actually most common among high achievers and professionals. Their many successes and accomplishments do nothing to change their core false beliefs. If not confronted, imposter syndrome can lead to perfectionism, overworking, anxiety, burnout, and depression.

SEND SOMEONE ELSE

Many of the 'heroes' in the Bible experienced imposter syndrome.

We see it when God called Gideon:

"'Pardon me, my lord,' Gideon replied, 'but how can I save Israel? My clan is the weakest in Manasseh, and I am the least in my family.'" (Judges 6: 15)

The LORD has just addressed Gideon as a "mighty warrior", yet he sees himself as the complete opposite.

Imposter syndrome causes you to disagree with what God says about you. You depend on your abilities, accomplishments, and appearance as the foundation of your identity and worth.

Gideon also compared himself to others:

"I am the least in my family."

He saw himself as less capable and qualified to lead than everyone else.

516

Imposter syndrome will do that. **You always assume that others are more gifted, called, anointed, and capable than you.**

On the surface, this sounds like humility. But when it's based on a lie or contradicts what God says, it causes you to live below your potential. **If God wanted someone else for the assignment, He would have asked them and not you.**

Humility isn't thinking less of yourself or even thinking of yourself less. **It's having an accurate view of who you are and what gifts and talents you have.** And the only One who sees who you truly are is your Maker. He alone gets to define and assign you.

We see the same thing when God sends the prophet Samuel to anoint Saul as Israel's first king:

"Then he brought forward the tribe of Benjamin, clan by clan, and Matri's clan was taken. Finally Saul son of Kish was taken. But when they looked for him, he was not to be found. So they enquired further of the Lord, 'Has the man come here yet?'
And the Lord said, 'Yes, he has hidden himself among the baggage.'

They ran and brought him out, and as he stood among the people he was a head taller than any of the others. Samuel said to all the people, 'Do you see the man the Lord has chosen? There is no one like him among all the people.'

Then the people shouted, 'Long live the king!'" (1 Samuel 10: 21-24)

Saul was outwardly impressive - tall, wealthy, handsome, and a capable warrior. Yet, when called upon to lead his people, what does he do? He hides among the baggage! He obviously sees himself very differently from how everyone else perceives him.

Unfortunately, Saul was never able to let go of the 'baggage' of imposter syndrome and the deep insecurity that went with it. He was constantly trying to earn the right to rule, even though he already had it. Eventually, this caused him to self-sabotage his calling.

Imposter syndrome will cause you to hide. Of course, in a season of obscurity and development, sometimes God does lead you away from the crowd. However, when God calls you to step up and step into your calling, Satan will use intimidation and fear to send you into hiding. You don't ever feel ready. You don't think you have what it takes to succeed. You're more concerned with the opinions of others than with what God says. Imposter syndrome tells you: "If I can't be seen, I can't be exposed."

My own tendency is to veer towards hiding, probably because I'm more introverted and detest self-promotion. I prefer to 'fly below the radar' and avoid too much attention. However, I know God is increasingly calling me into greater visibility and influence. Therefore, I have to push through my reserved nature and act in obedience to Him, even when everything inside me wants to remain in obscurity.

CONFRONTING THE IMPOSTER

If you had an imposter in your home, you wouldn't tolerate their presence. You would evict them and keep them out.

Yet, we allow imposter syndrome to roam free in our lives and contain us. He seems harmless, even helpful. He's stopping us from being exposed as a fraud and a fake, after all.

Yet, imposter syndrome must be seen a work of the enemy to be confronted, not a personality trait to be accepted. Satan does not want you to fully express your gifts, talents, abilities, and skills. He doesn't want to have influence and make an impact for the Kingdom. He wants to keep you shrunken, small, and scared.

The devil is the "father of lies" (John 8: 44) and the "accuser of the brothers and sisters" (Revelation 12: 10). Whatever he says – the opposite is true. He only seeks to intimidate you because your potential intimidates him. He loves to elevate and amplify the ungodly and immoral voices in our culture while Christians remain silent and hidden because we feel insecure, inadequate, and inferior. As soon as we raise our heads above the parapet, he attempts to shoot us down, sometimes even using those in the church to "humble" us. And so, darkness engulfs the nations because of the absence of our light.

If you suffer from imposter syndrome, here are some ways to help you overcome it.

(i)   Get honest.

Make a realistic assessment of your strengths and weaknesses, your competencies and flaws, your successes and failures, your abilities and limitations.

Where have you been effective already?

What do other people compliment you for?

Where have you experienced blessing and favor?

Ask other people for their honest opinion.

Most of us are better at highlighting our deficiencies than our gifts.

You're not great at everything. Don't be like the contestant on American Idol who should have been told long ago that they can't sing.

But you are gifted and anointed for something. Don't hide your lamp under a bowl (Matthew 5: 15).

(ii)   Replace lies with truth.

Most imposter syndrome is simply not based on reality. The evidence tells a totally different story than your negative self-talk.

In no other area of your life would you accept constant lies and deception. So, don't passively believe the lies that the enemy feeds you to intimidate you into disqualifying yourself from the call of God.

In 2 Corinthians 10: 15, Paul says:

"We demolish arguments and every pretension that sets itself up against the knowledge of God, and we take captive every thought to make it obedient to Christ."

Identify and confront the lies you have been believing. They almost always sound something like:

"I could never _____"

"I'm not ____ enough."

"What would ____ think/say?"

"____ is more qualified/gifted/called/experienced than me."

Acknowledge the negative thought.

But then ask yourself: "Is this true? Why do I think this? Does the evidence support this belief? What does God say about this?"

Replace the lies of the enemy by continually speaking and declaring the truth over your life.

(iii)   Reframe imposter syndrome as a sign of growth.

Imposter syndrome shows up most often in significant seasons of transition. You're stepping into something new or different. There's bound to be some uncertainty and internal tension.

God loves to put us in situations beyond our current experience and abilities. It forces us to fully depend on Him. But it's also therefore completely normal to feel as if you don't belong or might not have what it takes to be successful.

Let me push this further. **If your calling doesn't bring up some form of imposter syndrome or insecurity, it's probably not from God.** You're thinking and living too small.

(iv)   Realize that you're not alone.

Often, we think we're the only one who experiences imposter syndrome. The truth is that everyone feels insecure, inadequate, and underqualified in some area. Some just hide it better than others.

Having honest conversations with close friends about how you feel can help. You'll quickly discover that you're not the only one who struggles with self-doubt.

(v)   Determine to obey God, even if you don't feel competent.

Moses had spent 80 years getting prepared by God to deliver the Hebrews from slavery, yet he still didn't feel competent or qualified. He made so many excuses hoping to persuade the Creator of the universe to select someone else for the task.

Finally, he realized that God wasn't going to change his mind. So, he reluctantly obeyed and was used powerfully to liberate his people.

God always blesses obedience. And even reluctant obedience is better than disobedience.

(vi)   Take your eyes off yourself.

The thing about imposter syndrome is that it's all about *my* ability and *my* competence and *my* feeling of confidence.

The reality is that God has only ever used imperfect, inadequate, unqualified people. That's all He has to work with!

My weakness doesn't disqualify me because when I am weak, He is strong (2 Corinthians 12: 10).

I'll never be fully ready for anything God asks me to do. That makes me depend on His ability, not my own.

Of course, I want to give His assignment 100%. And excellence is important. But ultimately, without Jesus' grace and strength, I am nothing and I can do nothing.

If God calls me, He will supply whatever I need. My job is to say "yes" and get moving.

Like I said at the start, I've experienced imposter syndrome at every stage of my faith journey. But I have determined not to allow it to control my destiny.

Only God gets to direct and determine my future. And if God is for me, who can be against me? Nothing and no one!

It's time to evict the imposter and step into the fullness of who you are in Christ.

PROPHETIC ENCOURAGEMENT

BE STILL AND KNOW...

"Be still, and know that I am God; I will be exalted among the nations, I will be exalted in the earth." (Psalm 46:10)

Be still, and know that... I see you today.
Be still, and know that... this too shall pass.
Be still, and know that... the tide is turning.
Be still, and know that... the darkness is lifting.
Be still, and know that... breakthrough is coming.

Be still, and know that... barrenness will be broken.
Be still, and know that... you're going to find freedom.
Be still, and know that... I have great plans for you.
Be still, and know that... I will vindicate you.
Be still, and know that... I will heal your pain.

Be still, and know that... I will carry you through this.
Be still, and know that... I will provide for all your needs.
Be still, and know that... My favor rests upon you.
Be still, and know that... I will never abandon you.
Be still, and know that... you're not finished.

Be still, and know that... I have heard every prayer.
Be still, and know that... I have seen every tear.
Be still, and know that... I will restore all you've lost.
Be still, and know that... My heart is for you.
Be still, and know that... you can trust Me.
Be still, and know that... I love you.

DAY 49

ALIGNMENT

BIBLE READING

The voice of one crying in the wilderness:
"Prepare the way of the LORD;
Make straight in the desert
A highway for our God.
Every valley shall be exalted
And every mountain and hill brought low;
The crooked places shall be made straight
And the rough places smooth;
The glory of the LORD shall be revealed,
And all flesh shall see *it* together;
For the mouth of the LORD has spoken."

(Isaiah 40: 3-5)

Trust in the LORD with all your heart
and lean not on your own understanding;
in all your ways submit to him,
and he will make your paths straight.

(Proverbs 3: 5-6)

Can two walk together, unless they are agreed?

(Amos 3: 3)

DEVOTIONAL

I got two new front tires fitted on my car today. A few days ago, I noticed that they were both very worn on the outside, but the inside was fine. That generally means only one thing – my wheels were out of alignment. Which was strange, because I had them aligned just a few months ago.

The thing is, I had been thinking about the subject of alignment in the days leading up to discovering that I needed new tires. I sensed some areas of my life and ministry were out of alignment. So, when I noticed my tires, I sensed the Holy Spirit speak to me: "You haven't made the necessary adjustments to come back into alignment."

The dictionary describes alignment as "the correct position or positioning of different components relative to one another so that they perform properly."

When things are aligned, they are in the right position and place.

When they are misaligned, something is out of place.

I did some research on the effects that wheel misalignment has on vehicles.

- You know when a vehicle is misaligned because the misalignment will cause the car to veer to the left or to the right when you are driving.

- If there is a misalignment, the tires might wear *unevenly* (and you might not even feel it).

- The tires might also wear out *prematurely*.

- Misalignment could also cause other parts of the vehicle to wear out due to *stress*.

- It can also lead to excess fuel consumption due to increased friction between the tires and the road. Your vehicle loses momentum more easily.

Misalignment can be very subtle. The wheels both look as if they are pointing in the same direction, but one or both of them is slightly 'off' causing the tires to almost fight each other as each tries to pull the other in

524

the direction it is going. The unnecessary friction is what leads to excessive wear and tear.

It also causes the car to sometimes veer to one side slightly when you think you're driving straight. You have to keep pulling the steering wheel back to the center.

I think that's a picture of what misalignment looks like in different parts of our lives.

- We feel subtly pulled in directions we don't want to go.

- There's more stress and friction than there needs to be.

- Greater levels of effort and input are required for straightforward tasks.

- There's unusual weariness and exhaustion when you haven't been doing anything especially difficult.

- Life just feels harder than it should be. You sense something is 'off' but there's nothing obvious that comes to mind.

- Something that should be easy requires more effort.

- Something that should be smooth is bumpy and uncomfortable.

- You feel unexplainable tension or anxiety when you're in certain environments or around particular people.

- You find it very difficult to connect with those who you should have lots in common with.

- You instantly find your energy and passion levels drop when you're doing certain things.

- You start well but lose momentum very quickly. It's hard to explain, but things just don't have an ease or a flow.

I can see you nodding your head as you picture certain places and people in your life.

It's very possible that there are areas of misalignment that require some adjustment.

Let's think about a few areas where alignment is important.

ALIGNMENT WITH GOD

We were made for a close relationship with God. When Adam and Eve sinned in the garden, they created a misalignment between us and our Creator. That's why they hid. Instinctively, they sensed that something wasn't right. God hadn't moved but they had positioned themselves spiritually in a place they shouldn't be. So, they felt shame.

When we receive Jesus Christ as Lord and Savior, we come back into alignment with God. We are restored to our rightful position as sons and daughters of our Heavenly Father.

However, even as believers, when we sin, we bring our lives out of alignment. We know it. We sense it. We're being pulled in different directions. Something isn't right. We feel conviction. Isaiah 30: 21 says:

"Whether you turn to the right or to the left, your ears will hear a voice behind you, saying, "This is the way; walk in it."

That voice is the Holy Spirit drawing us back into alignment.

The thing about vehicle wheels being out of alignment is that you can become used to compensating for the misalignment. After a while you hardly notice it. But the underlying tension is quietly damaging other parts of the vehicle and you're using more fuel than you need to.

The same happens in our own lives. When we ignore the conviction of the Holy Spirit and continue in sin and disobedience, our hearts become hard, and our consciences are less sensitive to our lives being pulled in the wrong direction. The misalignment is still hurting us, but often we don't see the full effects until it's too late. Eventually, things fall apart. Life stops working. The damage is done.

Repentance is the recalibration that brings us back into alignment with the Father. It restores us to our rightful place where there is no friction or hiding.

526

Life just goes better when we keep short accounts with God. It doesn't mean that everything is perfect. But there is a sense of freedom, confidence, and fulfillment that comes with being in right alignment with God. It's how we were meant to live. That's why Jesus said:

"If you remain in me and my words remain in you, ask whatever you wish, and it will be done for you." (John 15:7)

Jesus is talking about alignment in our relationship with him. When we're living in obedience and fellowship with Him, our prayers are more potent. We see His Kingdom come and His will be done in our lives and our world, as it is in Heaven.

Paul tells us to *"keep in step with the Spirit"* (Galatians 5: 25). That means we should pay attention to what the Holy Spirit is doing and align our lives with Him in a posture of submission and surrender.

ALIGNMENT WITH OTHER PEOPLE

We were created for connection. We were formed for friendship. But that doesn't mean we will naturally be aligned with everyone. Some people are a better 'fit' for us than others.

And those alignments can change over time.

You see, the wheels on my car didn't start out misaligned. A few months ago, they were perfectly straight. But something happened. I recall driving over a large pothole in the road. That probably knocked them out of alignment. Or maybe it just happened gradually. Either way, they're not as aligned as they used to be.

The same can happen in our relationships. There was once an ease, a fun, an ability to connect without any effort. Everything was smooth and simple. But something has changed. It could have been a single event. Like hitting a pothole. You had an argument, or you found out they'd said something about you.

Or perhaps it's been more subtle and gradual than that. You've just drifted apart. You're going in slightly different directions. They're maybe trying to pull you their way, but you're not going. And it's creating friction and tension. It's become less joy-filled and more exhausting.

Most of us are familiar with this verse:

"Do not be yoked together with unbelievers. For what do righteousness and wickedness have in common?" (2 Corinthians 6: 14)

Typically, we apply this to dating or marrying an unbeliever. And, of course, that is the context that Paul was writing about. However, when you understand the meaning of the verse, you can see that it applies to any close relationship.

In Bible times, two oxen were joined or bound together with a wooden yoke to keep them walking and working in sync. However, if the oxen didn't have the same core strengths it led to a problem. One would pull the other off course and they would walk in circles.

It didn't make either of the oxen bad. There were just certain things they couldn't do together until the weaker one became stronger.

Just because you like someone doesn't mean your life is aligned with them. They could be a great person. But you're going in different directions. And if you keep them too close, you may find that you're frustrated as you spend your life walking in circles but not getting anywhere. As Amos 3: 3 says:

"Can two walk together, unless they are agreed?"

I know I've said this before, but don't underestimate the importance of your alignments in this significant season. There has been so much dismantling and stripping back in many areas, including your relationships.

In the in-between stage, you can feel lonely and isolated. But trust that God has new friendships and connections coming that will be more aligned with who you are and where you're going.

SPIRITUAL ALIGNMENTS

I know many people get nervous when there's any talk about spiritual 'covering'. There has been much misuse and abuse of the term and how it's been practiced.

However, I am still fully convinced that it is vital that we align our lives with anointed men and women who carry genuine spiritual authority and who walk in holiness and integrity.

528

Any time I get a message or email from someone who seems to go from crisis to crisis, I ask them what their pastor has told them. Nine times out of ten, I receive the same response: "I'm not going to church right now."

Listen, I understand that it can be very difficult to find a spiritual home where you fit. And there has been so much hurt caused by the church. Sometimes I don't want to go back to church – and I'm the pastor! I get it.

However, we all need proper spiritual alignment in our lives. Psalm 133 tells us that the oil runs from the head down to the rest of the body. I really do believe that when we come under anointed leadership, what is on them drips onto us.

I see spiritual covering as being like an umbrella. It doesn't stop it raining over your head, but it does provide some shelter from the torrent.

Be careful who you align yourself with spiritually. Alignment with Jonah led a ship into a storm; alignment with the Apostle Paul saved a ship from the storm.

If you remain in a church where there is ungodly and carnal leadership, their behavior will soon begin to affect the entire congregation. It may be subtle at the start, but things just begin to go wrong. There will be friction and tension. Relationships fracture. Unexplained sickness and other ailments spread. The presence of God lifts. The blessing of God is removed.

Sometimes an alignment was intended by God to get you to a certain stage or place in your walk with Him. But then, it becomes limiting and containing.

Loyalty is important. But never allow misplaced loyalty to keep you stuck somewhere when God is calling you to move on.

Things will grow and flourish much better when they are planted in some environments than in others.

WORKPLACE ALIGNMENTS

When you have alignment in your job or career, again there's an ease, a grace, and a flow. It's not to say that there aren't challenges and difficult days. But overall, it energizes you. You feel fulfilled. You may come home tired, but it's a 'good' tired.

When there is misalignment, every day is a challenge. You don't want to get out of bed. You're counting the minutes until your shift finishes. It's not physically demanding work but it's exhausting. Nothing seems to run smoothly and efficiently.

You feel like David when he tried to wear Saul's armor. It just doesn't fit you. Nothing about it comes naturally to you. Everything is an effort.

While there are seasons when we need to stay in a place or position simply to earn money, you don't have to stay stuck there. But it's up to you to do something about it.

No one will do it for you. Not even God.

You must be the one who takes responsibility and begins to make some adjustments to bring your life back into alignment. You are the steward of your life. Don't live like a victim of your circumstances. Start to make decisions today that begin to move you in a better direction.

GOD WANTS YOU TO BE ALIGNED

When you are properly aligned with God, in the right place, with the right people, doing the right things, there is a flow, there is flourishing, and there is fruitfulness. The pieces fit together. There's synchronicity and momentum.

Yes, there will still be ups and downs. But everything is moving in the same direction reducing friction and fatigue. The oil is flowing.

Today, you may want to examine the different areas of your life and ask God:

- *Where am I out of alignment?*

- *What do I need to do to recalibrate my life?*

- *Are there people and places I should disconnect from?*

- *And are there some others that I should seek to be more closely aligned with?*

PROPHETIC ENCOURAGEMENT

THE LORD IS DISMANTLING AND DEMOLISHING STRONGHOLDS THAT HAVE BEEN BUILT UP IN OUR LIVES AND IN HIS CHURCH.

He is tearing down false altars and restoring true worship.

He is dealing with idolatry and immorality.

For too long His people have been enamoured by all the wrong things - the surface, the superficial, even the sinful.

God wants our hearts back.

He is longing for a people who are wholly holy and who belong fully to Him.

Pure devotion and a demonstration of His power go hand in hand.

He is cleansing and washing His bride to make her radiant again.

His light is exposing our nakedness and uncovering our wounds.

His desire is not to hurt us but to heal us; not to ruin us but to restore us.

A broken and frightened world needs a bold and fearless Church.

He will come with power once again.

There will be fresh wind and fresh fire.

Repent and return to Him.

Submit your heart and will to His Lordship.

Give Him your worship.

Surrender your pursuits and passions on the altar.

Let Him burn what isn't from Him so that only the holy may remain.

DAY 50

GET READY TO CROSS OVER

BIBLE READING

After the death of Moses the servant of the LORD, the LORD said to Joshua son of Nun, Moses' aide: "Moses my servant is dead. Now then, you and all these people, get ready to cross the Jordan River into the land I am about to give to them - to the Israelites. I will give you every place where you set your foot, as I promised Moses. Your territory will extend from the desert to Lebanon, and from the great river, the Euphrates - all the Hittite country - to the Mediterranean Sea in the west. No one will be able to stand against you all the days of your life. As I was with Moses, so I will be with you; I will never leave you nor forsake you. Be strong and courageous, because you will lead these people to inherit the land I swore to their ancestors to give them.

"Be strong and very courageous. Be careful to obey all the law my servant Moses gave you; do not turn from it to the right or to the left, that you may be successful wherever you go. Keep this Book of the Law always on your lips; meditate on it day and night, so that you may be careful to do everything written in it. Then you will be prosperous and successful. Have I not commanded you? Be strong and courageous. Do not be afraid; do not be discouraged, for the LORD your God will be with you wherever you go."

So Joshua ordered the officers of the people: "Go through the camp and tell the people, 'Get your provisions ready. Three days from now you will cross the Jordan here to go in and take possession of the land the LORD your God is giving you for your own.'"

(Joshua 1: 1-11)

DEVOTIONAL

Recently, out of the blue, I received a phone call, from a church enquiring if I would consider becoming their pastor. While I have no intention of leaving HOPE right now, I was reminded of different moments in my past when one such call or conversation has completely altered the trajectory of my life.

You will have experienced this too. You're just getting on with things. Your days are generally routine and predictable, even mundane. You aren't expecting change.

And then – seemingly from nowhere - something happens, and your life begins to go in a totally new direction.

You are presented with an unexpected opportunity or open door.

You're offered a role or position that will bring greater responsibility.

You meet someone who will become a very significant part of your future.

A person who you thought would be around forever suddenly exits your life.

You have a conversation that brings major upheaval and change into your world.

We all have these pivotal moments that shape our lives and our destinies.

We may not see them coming, but afterward, things are never the same again.

They are the demarcation lines. The thresholds.

And once we cross them, we enter into a new land.

Today, as we finish up this journey, I want to bring everything together by looking at one such threshold moment in the Bible.

It's a familiar one, in the book of Joshua.

I want us to look at five shifts that happen in a season of significant transition.

534

1. NEW SHAKING.

"After the death of Moses the servant of the LORD, the LORD said to Joshua son of Nun, Moses' aide: "Moses my servant is dead." (vv. 1-2)

It's difficult to overestimate the magnitude of this moment in the life of God's people. This was Moses, the only leader they had ever known. The one who delivered them from oppression and slavery in Egypt and led them through forty years in the wilderness. The one who mediated between the people and God. The one whom they depended upon for everything.

And now he's gone.

Their whole world is shaken.

It appears that they had no preparation for Moses' departure. His health didn't slowly deteriorate. We're told:

"Moses was a hundred and twenty years old when he died, yet his eyes were not weak nor his strength gone." (Deuteronomy 34: 7)

Moses was a fit and healthy 120-year-old!

But the LORD decided that it was time for a shift. And that required the departure of Moses.

We're told that the people mourned for 30 days. The normal period allotted for mourning in Israel was seven days. But such was the impact of this loss, that they needed much more time to even begin to process their grief.

This was an unprecedented moment in the life of the nation. A turning point. Things would never be the same.

Most major transitions in our own lives begin with some sort of significant shaking or disruption.

Something or someone enters our settled world and disturbs it.

It might be good or bad.

535

But suddenly we find ourselves thrust into having to make decisions, interact with different people, and make adjustments that stretch and pull us in new directions.

It can be deeply unsettling and disorientating.

But it can also be exciting and full of possibilities.

The death of Moses was all of the above. The loss of their leader was devastating and deeply disruptive. However, it also brought with it new opportunities and potential. Because now, they could finally cross over into the land of promise:

"Moses my servant is dead. Now then, you and all these people, get ready to cross the Jordan River into the land I am about to give to them - to the Israelites." (v. 2)

Don't miss what God is saying here. Moses' death means that the people can now cross the Jordan and enter Canaan.

Years before this, Moses had sinned and God told him that he would never enter the Promised Land:

"But the LORD said to Moses and Aaron, "Because you did not trust in me enough to honor me as holy in the sight of the Israelites, you will not bring this community into the land I give them." (Numbers 20: 12)

As wonderful as Moses was, while he was still alive, the people were confined to the wilderness.

They could have Moses or the Promised Land – but they couldn't have both.

Every major shaking in our own lives usually brings loss and pain.

Something is stripped away.

Our world becomes unsettled.

There are challenges and obstacles.

We face opposition or conflict.

Relationships break down.

There's agitation or anxiety.

We have to say goodbye to people and places we love.

There's grief and confusion.

On a global scale, the events of 2020 brought a major shaking into the world, the reverberations of which are still being felt today. I believe it initiated a huge transitional shift into a new era. We might think we're back to 'normal'. But the truth is that the old 'normal' we had become used to is gone forever. The 'new normal' is still being established.

Truthfully, I believe it will take until at least 2030 before things will begin to settle and we feel some sense of stability. That's why I have called the 2020s "a decade of disruption". The shaking isn't stopping.

We are living through a pivotal point in history. And while it is unnerving and unpredictable, it is also pregnant with opportunity and possibility. The LORD is at work and He is inviting His people to cross over into a new dimension of His presence, provision, and power.

He's saying: *"Moses is dead. Now get ready..."*

2. NEW RELATIONSHIPS.

"Just as we fully obeyed Moses, so we will obey you." (v. 17)

The people had only ever related to Moses as their leader. Now that he is gone, their loyalty is transferred to Joshua. He's very different to his predecessor. But he's the person who God has appointed to be the voice in their lives for this season.

Significant transitional moments often bring changes in our relationships, alignments, connections, and alliances.

Some people exit our lives, others enter.

This can happen for many reasons.

Some friendships may unexpectedly fall apart. I know this happened to me at a major turning point. Seemingly out of nowhere, close relationships began to fracture. These were people I thought I would do life with forever. But overnight, something changed. Things were said that couldn't be unsaid. I forgave them (eventually), but I could no longer have them in my life.

Honestly, it was heartbreaking. But I can see God's hand in the dismantling of those relationships. They were aligned with where I was but not with where I was going. The relational shifts reinforced what God had already been telling us. It was time to move on.

You may experience something like this. It could come through a breakup of a long-term romantic relationship or even a divorce. It can be deeply painful, even traumatic. But it can also be purposeful.

Other relational shifts don't have to be so dramatic. Perhaps a close friend moves away. Or your kids go off to college. Or you simply decide to relocate to another place.

At transitional moments, sometimes God also sends people into your life who you might not normally have associated with. We see this with an unusual connection in the next chapter:

"So they went and entered the house of a prostitute named Rahab and stayed there." (v. 1)

Not only was Rahab a Canaanite. She was also a woman of disrepute. Yet, the men who were spying out the Promised Land found favor with her. She helped them and hid them in return for protection when they conquered the land.

Sometimes God will signal a major shift in your life by giving you unusual favor in unexpected places among surprising people. You are divinely connected into relationships with people that you would not naturally be drawn to or have much commonality with. And yet in those alignments, you will find favor and resources for the future.

In 2015, I was invited to preach and prophesy at a large church in a local city. While I had visited this congregation in the past, I had never ministered there. That night, a young man called Ryan was leading worship. The following day, he contacted me on social media to say how the message had spoken to him personally. We connected and soon Ryan and his wife Erin became close friends with Becky and me. Over these

538

past nine years, Ryan has not only become a good friend. He has also been a great blessing and resource in my ministry.

I thought I was going to that church to preach. But God used that evening as a Divine appointment to connect me with a new friendship for the next season.

Our resources are in our relationships. When God wants to get something to you, it almost always comes through people.

In this season, take notice of the people who the Father is sending into your life. Recognize them as a gift and value them as such.

3. NEW RESPONSIBILITY.

"Be strong and courageous, because you will lead these people to inherit the land I swore to their ancestors to give them." (v. 6)

Joshua had been Moses' deputy, his number two. While he had some responsibility, the weight of major decisions was carried by Moses. Joshua played a supporting role.

Now, overnight, he is thrust into a new level of leadership with significantly greater responsibility. Moses is gone. The buck now stops with him.

There is a huge difference between function and responsibility. A number two in an organization may be highly gifted and able to perform everything the number one does. But they don't carry the weight or burden of responsibility.

This was illustrated to me several years ago when I was asked to help carry a coffin at a funeral. There were six of us evenly positioned around the casket. One of the men took a fit of coughing and had to step away for a moment. However, the weight the rest of us were carrying didn't change at all. In that moment, I realized that not everyone who is touching the weight is carrying the burden. Not everyone in proximity to the work feels the same pressure.

If you are the CEO of a company, you have sleepless nights while your employees don't even think about work until the next morning.

If you are a senior pastor, you feel the weight of pastoral care and spiritual warfare, as well as taking the brunt of criticism from disgruntled church members.

Everyone loves a number two because they don't make decisions that upset anyone! But when the number two gets promoted, suddenly everything changes. They now carry the weight. They shoulder the responsibility. And they face the attacks.

Your transition may not be to be a pastor or CEO of a business. But every significant transition brings new responsibilities and pressures. As God moves you, elevates you, or promotes you, be prepared to carry more weight.

Ten years ago, I was leading a church. Outside of my family, that was my sole responsibility.

Currently, I am still leading a growing church. But I am also writing this book, mentoring hundreds of people from around the world online, meeting with leaders who are struggling, responding to requests for podcasts and interviews, speaking prophetically into some difficult situations, and preparing for a building project.

I'm not complaining. I wouldn't have it any other way. Greater responsibility brings greater rewards.

But there is a pressure and a burden that comes with the new level of influence God has given me. I don't think I've taken a full day off in six months. I never sleep past 6 am. And I work at least 12 hours most days. (Don't worry, I am taking a sabbatical soon!)

People see the fruit, but they don't see the labor.

They see the blessing, but not the burden.

Joshua wasn't being given a title. He was being passed a mantle. And with that came great responsibility.

When God is transitioning you, don't be surprised if you begin to feel more pressure or if you start to get asked to carry more responsibility. Your willingness to step up and carry weight will determine how far God can take you.

4. NEW COURAGE.

"Be strong and courageous, because you will lead these people to inherit the land I swore to their ancestors to give them.

"Be strong and very courageous. Be careful to obey all the law my servant Moses gave you; do not turn from it to the right or to the left, that you may be successful wherever you go.

...Have I not commanded you? Be strong and courageous." (vv. 5-7; 9)

Three times God says the same thing to Joshua: *"Be strong and courageous."*

That would indicate that Joshua was perhaps somewhat nervous and apprehensive about stepping into this new position.

When God transitions you into something new, different, or bigger, it will almost always bring psychological discomfort and emotional stress. Not because it's wrong or bad. Just because you haven't done it before.

You will be stretched.

You will feel insecure and inadequate.

You will have imposter syndrome.

Your surroundings may be unfamiliar.

You may feel alone, isolated, or vulnerable.

At times, you won't have a clue what you're doing.

You will want to retreat back to the safety and comfort of the old and familiar.

All of that is natural and normal.

The only people who avoid this internal tension are those who never change, grow, move, or try anything new.

But that's not you. You're called, anointed, and appointed for such a time as this. And so, you will have to step into places, positions, roles, and relationships that will be outside of your comfort zone.

You will be asked to take new territory and enlarge your current boundaries.

You will have opportunities presented that appear to be far beyond your education, experience, and abilities.

You will find yourself in rooms that you don't feel qualified to be in.

You will be invited to speak into situations that you think you know little about.

As you look around at everyone else, you will feel inferior and inadequate.

That's why you need strength and courage.

Everyone feels fear and anxiety. But only a few press through it because they realize that all of the best things God has for them are on the other side.

Fear is a mile wide and an inch deep. It looks daunting, but when you step into it, you see that it really isn't that intimidating after all.

And God promises to be with you as you confront your fears:

"Do not be afraid; do not be discouraged, for the LORD your God will be with you wherever you go." (v. 9)

This isn't some vague promise or shallow sentiment. As you step into this next season, Yahweh promises you His presence, power, provision, protection, blessing, favor, direction, abundance, and anointing.

Take it! Receive it!

And, when the pressure comes and the critics get louder and the challenges seem never-ending, take a moment and remind yourself: "God called me to this, and He is with me. Therefore, I can do this."

This new era requires new courage from the people of God.

5. NEW CONSECRATION.

"Joshua told the people, "Consecrate yourselves, for tomorrow the LORD will do amazing things among you." (3: 5)

Over the past five years, there has been a level of sifting and exposure in the church, unlike anything I have ever witnessed. It has been deeply painful and the fallout has been devastating for many.

Yet, we must also step back and ask - *why?*

Why is God cleaning His house?

I believe it's because He is bringing His people into a level of His presence, power, and harvest beyond anything we have ever experienced.

I really do.

I sense that we are on the edge of a mighty move of God in the nations.

Like the Israelites with the Promised Land, we have heard the prophecies and promises, and we have even tasted samples of them. But now we are going to cross over and fully enter into everything that God has prepared for us.

The church as it was had many good qualities. But it had lost its way. In attempting to be culturally relevant and reach the unchurched, it had traded encounter for entertainment.

It served up formulaic songs rather than Spirit-filled worship.

It gave motivational messages rather than proclaiming the truth of God's Word.

It took the hard edges off the Gospel to make it more palatable to the masses.

It became a corporation measuring success by the metrics of buildings and budgets rather than an authentic community of devoted disciples with Christ at the heart, known by our love, generosity, integrity, and spiritual authority.

A purging has taken place. And it is still continuing.

God is restoring holiness, reverence, true worship, prayer, and a fear of the LORD back to His people.

As a pastor, it's beautiful to watch and experience.

But personally, it also brings a requirement for greater personal holiness and ongoing sanctification.

I'm far from perfect. But I want to keep short accounts with God. The only sin that won't be exposed is that which is under the blood of Jesus. So, I keep coming back to the cross in confession and repentance.

Purity and power go together.

So do holiness and harvest.

I know you don't want to miss out on what God is doing through compromise and carnality.

So, humble yourself under God's mighty hand and ask Him to remove anything in you that might be a hindrance to His power working in and through you.

The church is being called to a higher level of consecration because the Father is positioning us for revival and awakening.

Don't hold back. Don't sit on the sidelines. Don't disqualify yourself.

This is our moment in history.

The fields are white for harvest.

The land is waiting to be taken.

Get ready to cross over.

PROPHETIC ENCOURAGEMENT

THE LORD IS REBUILDING YOU.

He is bringing you back to yourself.

So much has been stripped away in this past season that you have almost lost the core and essence of your identity. At times, you're not even sure who you are any longer.

Yes, some things needed to be removed.
They were hindering you. They were keeping you stuck.
But other things were robbed from you by the enemy.

Some of you lost your joy and passion.
Some have lost your laughter and sense of fun.
Some became too isolated and insulated from life-giving relationships.
Some lost your zeal for ministry.
Some of you were robbed of your confidence.

In these days, the Lord would say:
I am restoring and bringing recompense for things that have been lost and stolen.

You will have new important relational alignments. There won't be many, but they will be strong and deep.
I am rebuilding you.
I am reforming your heart.
I am breathing fresh life into your desires.
I am re-envisioning you for the future.

Just as after 40 years of wandering, the people cross over into the Promised Land in three days, so there will be a Divine acceleration on your advancement and progress.

I am going ahead of you.
I am your defender.
I am your shield.
I am your protector.
I am your vindicator.

You will have everything you need.
And anything that you lack is not required for the next season.

As you consecrate your heart before Me, I will move you into the right place, with the right people, doing the right things.

I am promoting those who have sought after Me in the secret place
I am exalting those who care more about my presence than their platform.
Those who have walked through the barren wilderness, the hidden ones - they will be rewarded. They will inherit the promise.

I am restoring your joy.
I am renewing your call.
I am replenishing your passion.
I am remantling you.
I am reclothing you.
I am realigning you.

I AM REBUILDING YOU.